Last Moments

Sentenced to Death in Canada

Last Moments

Sentenced to Death in Canada

Dale Brawn

QUAGMIRE
PRESS

The Publisher: Quagmire Press Ltd.
Website: www.quagmirepress.com

Library and Archives Canada Cataloguing in Publication

Brawn, Dale, 1948–
    Last moments : sentenced to death in Canada / Dale Brawn.

ISBN 978-1-926695-15-0

    1. Capital punishment—Prairie Provinces—History. 2. Crime—Prairie Provinces—History. I. Title.

HV8699.C2B73 2011   364.6609712   C2011-900197-7

Project Director: Hank Boer
Project Editor: Kathy van Denderen
Cover Image: © Sergey Nezhinkiy | Dreamstime.com
Back Cover Image: © Photos.com
Photo Credits: All photos by Dale Brawn, except for p. 287 (Archives of Manitoba)

We acknowledge the support of the Alberta Foundation for the Arts for our publishing program.

PC: 1

Contents

INTRODUCTION 8

CHAPTER 1:   SOME DEATH ROW REALITIES 13

CHAPTER 2:   HOW DID IT COME TO THIS?
             MOTIVE FOR MURDER 36

CHAPTER 3:   GETTING RELIGION 75

CHAPTER 4:   RITUALS 100

CHAPTER 5:   LAST WORDS 141

CHAPTER 6:   WITNESS TO AN EXECUTION 187

CHAPTER 7:   ON THE SCAFFOLD 213

CHAPTER 8:   MISTAKES HAPPEN 239

CHAPTER 9:   PLEASE HELP ME KILL MY HUSBAND 273

CHAPTER 10: WHAT COMES AFTER? BODIES AND BURIALS . . . 293

CHAPTER 11: THE UNUSUAL 316

CHAPTER 12: THE DANCE OF DEATH 337

NOTES ON SOURCES 363

Dedication

This book is dedicated to Gloria Rochelle Dallas.

Acknowledgements

A number of people in one way or another assisted in the writing of this book. Prominent among them are Hank Boer, the publisher, and Kathy van Denderen, the editor. Both believed in the project, and it was very much because of their efforts that this book became a reality. Two other people were exceptionally helpful—Marilyn Spocci, for her professionalism and dedication as a researcher, and Pauline Begin, who gave so freely of her time and computer expertise.

Two other individuals who indirectly influenced this work are professors Jeffrey Pfiefer and Kenneth Leyton-Brown of the University of Regina. Their book *Death By Rope, Volume One: 1867–1923: An Anthology of Canadian Executions* was published in 2007, and like Dr. Leyton-Brown's more recent *The Practice of Execution in Canada*, is a must read for anyone interested in learning more about Canada's experience with capital punishment.

Introduction

~

For a number of years I wrote a weekly column for a western Manitoba newspaper, and while working on a series of articles, I came across stories of women and men who were sentenced to death in Canada. Over time, I noticed commonalities in the circumstances of these people and came to realize that little has been written about the execution process.

In short order I was drawn to studies of capital punishment and soon discovered an important body of material prepared by the National Archives of Canada. *Persons Sentenced to Death in Canada, 1867–1976* lists the salient details of the more than 700 men and women hanged since Confederation. It provided me with the names, dates and locations necessary to study the execution process further.

In time I learned two things. The first is that we will never know how many people were actually hanged in this country. Data collection in the late 19th and early 20th centuries was haphazard, and people who were not executed are listed on government records as having been put to death, while the execution of others was reported in newspapers but not recorded officially.

The second thing I learned was that the actual number doesn't matter. Occasionally, numbers are important, but not always. The greater lesson to be learned about what killers did to earn a cell on death row and what happened to them when they got there comes from looking at the bigger picture. That is what this book is about. Even informed readers might come across information that would not have been discovered had the focus of the work been on individuals, rather than on the similarities shared by those who took the life of others.

My research into the last moments of Canadian killers was revealing in several ways. I discovered, for example, that hanging was not always about condemned prisoners plummeting to their death through a scaffold floor. For a time, the lives of these individuals ended when they were jerked up, not dropped down. And when people were hanged, the gallows was not necessarily the kind depicted on television and in movies. It wasn't unusual for killers to be executed in jail corridors and unused bathrooms. A couple of other interesting revelations are that dozens of murderers went to their death on bended knee, and that when it came to hanging people, speed was of the essence. By the 1930s, it was a rare killer who was still conscious 60 seconds after leaving his or her cell.

Academics have long argued that if we are to die a violent death, it will almost certainly be at the hands of someone we know, and I found that to be true. Murder is an intimate act, and victims usually know their killers. My stories are about spouses killing spouses, of children slaughtering parents, of fathers murdering their families and of arguments with neighbours, landlords and drinking companions that ended in the tragic loss of life. It goes without saying that in civilized societies, murder never makes sense, but it is deeply disturbing that so much violence is inflicted without reason.

Religion played a critical role in both the execution process and in the last moments of the women and men sentenced to death. The central figures in many of the stories are jail chaplains. Their daily visits distracted condemned prisoners from thoughts of the horror to come, ensuring that death rows were, if not peaceful, at least devoid of mayhem. Few prisoners were prepared to jeopardize the possibility of going to a better place by causing trouble in the one they were about to leave.

Part way through my study of Canadian executions, I began wondering why it was almost unheard of for a prisoner to go to the gallows unwillingly. By the time my work was complete, I had the answer—scaffold fights were uncommon because the men and women put to death in Canada were usually drugged, and, occasionally, drunk.

It might come as a surprise to many readers that during the 95 years that killers were executed in this country, there was a line-up of people wanting a ticket to watch them die. Executions were community events, and as such attracted their share of eccentrics. Examples abound, such as the Barrie, Ontario, hanging that was interrupted when rowdies broke into the shed where a bound and noosed man stood waiting to hang. Incredibly, the group included the doomed prisoner's son.

Rowdy crowds often attended Canadian executions, and the rowdiness sometimes made its way to the gallows floor. On more than one occasion, the platform of a scaffold was filled with so many people, executioners were forced to elbow their way to the trapdoor, doing what they could to avoid fights and the jockeying for a position closest to the drop.

Examinations of capital punishment necessarily include a discussion of botched executions. Executioners sometimes had to grab the rope by which a victim was hanged and haul the prisoner off the ground to ensure that the unfortunate individual strangled to death before regaining consciousness. And, of course, there are the several instances where someone literally lost her or his head. It seems ironic that with the exception of these last mistakes, the bodies of hanging victims rarely displayed any suffering.

Probably because I have been around the practice of law for a long time, I was not surprised to find so many unusual stories associated with the administration of our criminal justice system. Still, I didn't know about the man who murdered and ate all nine members of his family, or about the two killers who refused to tell authorities which victim they killed first, thereby kicking off an estate battle among the heirs of their murder victims. And I certainly did not realize we used to hang people while they were strapped into an armchair, nor did I know about the cat that refused to leave a Montréal man, even as his body hung suspended below a gallows.

On the other hand, I was not surprised to discover that when a man and a woman committed murder together, the punishment meted out varied according to their gender.

My study of Canadian executions has allowed me to reach several conclusions about capital punishment. Among the most surprising is the speed of our justice system. Most of those sentenced to death were executed less than six months after committing their crimes. I also concluded that a great many of the men and women put to death in Canada murdered more than once before they were finally caught.

In this book I share what I know about the last moments of Canadian killers sentenced to death. Some of my observations may surprise readers, but I hope they all entertain.

Chapter One

Some Death Row Realities

~

The hangman wasted neither time nor effort. As soon as he stepped on the gallows, he approached the prisoner and put his hand on the man's shoulder, directing him toward the trapdoor. Two chalk marks indicated where the killer was to stand. The condemned man stood with his arms strapped together behind his back, fighting to maintain self-control. For just a moment the executioner looked into the man's eyes, trying to gauge whether there was going to be a problem. Occasionally a prisoner would collapse before the trap could be released. That meant guards were forced to hold the unconscious man upright while the hangman tied the person's feet, pulled a hood over his head and tightened the noose around his neck.

But there would be no problem this time. The morphine administered before the prisoner left his cell was working, and the condemned man stood in a daze. Still, some sense of anxiety must have remained, since he was drawing short, deep gasps of air, like an animal being led to slaughter. The hangman could sense rather than see that his every movement was being watched. He finished buckling the leather straps around the man's ankles, and more quickly than normal, pulled the black cotton hood over the distraught killer's face,

The executioner took no time to reflect on it just then, but later he wondered what it felt like; standing completely helpless, anticipating the opening of the trapdoor and the fall that would snap your head back, allowing the rope around your neck to tighten and close off the blood to your brain. With luck, his victim's neck would break when his body reached the end of the drop, but even if he strangled to death, he would be unconscious before his body started closing down.

Anticipation made the process difficult. As long as the prisoner was distracted, there was no problem. It's almost as if in moments of crisis our brain can focus on only one thing at a time. That was a trick he picked up early in his career— distraction. Just before pulling the hood down, the hangman looked to one side, as if waiting for a signal. Whoever was standing on the trap invariably looked to see what was going on. As soon as he did, the hood and noose were positioned, and the trapdoors opened, leaving no time for last-minute tears or fuss.

Everyone knew that when the prison chaplain started the Lord's Prayer it was just about over. A few seconds later, the hangman received a signal from the sheriff that the trapdoor could be opened. Just before he did, the executioner knocked his foot against the lever. It never failed to attract the attention of his victim. As soon as he saw the man's head turn toward the sound, the hangman dropped him.

In seconds, everyone present knew whether he'd done his job properly. Done right, the rope should hang straight down, barely moving. Done wrong, it would start swinging in large, jerky circles. In a worst-case scenario, the rope might snap back as blood started cascading from where the condemned man's head was once attached to his torso.

Tonight, everything went well. With one hand on the rope and the other still holding the lever, the hangman leaned over and glanced into the pit. He was almost overcome, not by what he saw, but by what he smelled. The abruptness of the killer's death caused his bladder and bowels to empty, and beneath the suspended corpse the executioner could see a widening pool of waste.

As usual, the guards posted below the scaffold took one look at the unconscious form that appeared as if from nowhere and turned away. The local coroner did not have that luxury. As the hangman looked down, he saw the doctor briefly hold a stethoscope to the chest of the hanging man, then shake his head—not dead yet. Although the process was repeated again and again, it was obvious from the start that however long it took this killer to die, he was as good as gone from the moment he dropped.

Death was declared after eight minutes. With two guards holding the killer's body so it would not drop, the hangman cut the rope. Some members of the coroner's jury were already in the pit and could see for themselves that the man was dead.

Still, the law was the law, and they would have to agree unanimously that the sentence imposed four months earlier was carried out. Only then could family members reclaim their loved one.

Usually the person they got back looked little different from the man they'd spoken with just a few hours earlier. Sure, the rope left a red mark around his neck, but that was about it. While you could not say the killer looked happy, he at least appeared calm. There was no indication that he died in terror or that he suffered. That was what everyone wanted to know—is hanging painful? The executioner's answer was always the same: "No, it isn't. All the same, I wouldn't hang my favourite dog."

More than 700 people were hanged in Canadian jails between 1867 and 1962, and during that time, officials followed an unofficial protocol for their housing and execution. For one thing, the living dead were always kept sequestered. It was not good for other prisoners or the public to be reminded that the State was about to take a life. Nor was it appropriate that killers be made into victims. Newspaper accounts of their emotional suffering and struggle to be strong until the end made killers into heroes, at the expense of innocent victims. That was why access to death row inmates was kept to a minimum.

It was also thought necessary that those sentenced to death be kept in a cell located as close as possible to the place where they would be executed. The longer the walk, the greater the chance a distraught prisoner would be overcome by emotion and have to be dragged or carried to the gallows.

Interior of the death chamber in Headingley Jail. After an executed prisoner was declared dead, a guard pulled the rope by which the person was suspended toward the hangman, who cut it so the body could be lowered to the ground.

Any kind of drama automatically became a news item and served to remind jail staff that they were participating in a murder, albeit a legal one.

To avoid stories that humanized killers, or sensationalized accounts of their hanging, only a few spectators were permitted to witness executions. Most sheriffs tried to exclude reporters from attending a hanging, thereby limiting what the public learned about the event.

The principle object of curiosity at executions, apart from the person about to die, was the executioner. Before Confederation, these individuals were often recruited from among the condemned. They were given two options—kill or be killed. Between 1867 and the 1930s, however, Canadian executioners were public and well-recognizable figures. Their comings and goings were routinely reported in newspapers, even when an appearance had nothing to do with a hanging. To most newspaper readers, a hangman was the only person with a licence to kill.

However, during the mid-20th century, executioners were robbed of their celebrity status because executions were carried out with such speed and news reports were prohibited. Apart from what they wore and perhaps the mistakes they made, little was said about hangmen. No one was certain how many worked for the government, who they were or where they lived.

Executioners were encouraged to say as little as possible. Therefore, their conversations with prisoners sentenced to death and with jail staff were almost always remembered and eventually reported. It was in everyone's best interest for a hangman to maintain a distance from other participants in the execution process. Any breach of that rule almost certainly resulted in the loss of future employment. An executioner was a key actor in a highly ritualized performance, and under no circumstance was he to interact with his audience.

Jail officials tried hard to depersonalize the relationship death row prisoners had with prison staff. Certainly, late-night conversations between members of a death watch and a sleepless killer couldn't be prevented, but guards were not to initiate such interactions. For much the same reason, prisoners were not permitted to wear colourful clothes of their own choosing, or to personalize their surroundings or their relationship with those who monitored their every move.

The only people residents of death row were encouraged to talk to were spiritual advisers. Trained in death talk, these individuals worked tirelessly to help convicted killers come to grips with their impending demise. Their job was to minimize the horror associated with an execution by shifting the focus of a prisoner's thinking to what comes after. While the women and men hanged in Canada were not forced to accept the services of a prison chaplain, doing so was a welcome distraction from hours spent alone in a cell. The State, too, benefited from such relationships, since a prisoner properly prepared would die without a fuss.

Canadian jailers tried to keep the time between a condemned prisoner's departure from a death cell to his or her execution as short as possible. In some provinces, the distance between cell and scaffold was fewer than 10 steps and could be covered in seconds. The pinioning straps and hoods used by executioners were designed in such a way that they could applied quickly, ensuring that killers were dropped before they realized what was happening.

But speed was not always of the essence. In the late 19th and early 20th centuries, executions were not hurried affairs. Because newspapers reported every detail of a hanging, from the construction of a gallows to the arrival of the executioner, murderers became public figures. People wanted to know what happened to them and especially how they died.

Even when hangings were carried out in the yards of provincial jails, it was not unusual for 50 or more people to be there to watch. Occasionally, those about to hang even acknowledged the presence of a friend or acquaintance, a practice that continued into the 1950s. And for a time, executions were carried out by inexperienced hangmen unfamiliar with the proper methods of pinioning and noosing. As a consequence, death struggles were common. These events were chronicled along with the efforts of compliant prisoners wanting to help their executioner complete his task, often by better positioning the noose or moving to the centre of the trapdoor.

Beginning in the 1920s, prisoners were increasingly denied the chance to make a last statement from the gallows. In their cells, they could talk as long as they wanted, but on the scaffold, speed was considered essential. Anything that prolonged the process was discouraged.

In addition, allowing those sentenced to death to say something just before hanging reaffirmed their personhood and encouraged others to think of them as a victim rather than a killer. Executioners played a significant role in ensuring that last words were as few as possible. By adopting an abrupt, business-like approach, from pinioning a prisoner in a death cell to preparing him or her on the gallows, a good hangman intimidated even the most talkative killer.

Officials also sought to conceal the bodies of hanging victims from witnesses and jail staff. When the trapdoor opened, the person simply disappeared, leaving spectators with only a brief sense of what was. The actual dying part of a hanging occurred below the floor of the scaffold, away from curious eyes. Executions were done so quickly because the faster everything happened, the less likelihood the event would be remembered.

Drop 'em Down Gallows

All of the women and men executed in Canada died on a gallows. That is not to say, however, that they were executed on similar structures. No law or regulation mandated precisely what a scaffold should look like, and as a result, its appearance varied considerably. By the closing years of the 19th century, most gallows were built from a common design. Because they were similarly constructed under the supervision of the executioners who used them, mechanical failures were rare. When executions were moved indoors and centralized, the design became even more universal.

Most outdoor gallows were a closed-bank affair, in which the lower portion of the scaffold was boarded in, so spectators could not actually see the body of the executed prisoner.

The height of the scaffold floor varied, occasionally requiring a prisoner to ascend for some distance to reach the gallows platform. The notion that a gallows was reached by walking up 13 steps is a myth; the number of steps was always dependent on the height of the scaffold.

To prevent anyone from accidently falling off the scaffold, a railing usually surrounded the structure. A thick beam ran overtop a trapdoor built in the centre of the floor, and the rope by which the prisoner was to be suspended was wound tightly several times around it and then tied to another part of the gallows. To make sure a killer dropped far enough to break her or his neck, a pit was usually dug directly below the trap.

After 1868, Canadian executions were by law private affairs, and to ensure they were, hangings were moved behind jail walls. For many years, however, the law was ignored. Scaffold platforms were often either level with the top of prison walls or could easily be seen by spectators perched on trees or the roofs of adjacent buildings.

Occasionally, an outdoor gallows was covered to prevent the execution from being seen from afar. The scaffold on which Marion "Peg-Leg" Brown died in 1921 was one such structure. It was entirely enclosed so that even spectators standing in the yard of the jail saw nothing but a plain board fence about five metres high and four metres long. At one end of the scaffold, a flight of steps led to a platform three metres above the ground.

Over it was a beam, and above the beam a roof of boards. A two-metre-deep pit was dug below.

For many prisoners, their last moments were made infinitely worse when the gallows was built right outside their cell. For example, the only anxious hours Omar Roberts spent on a Yarmouth, Nova Scotia, death row were those during which the carpenter built his gallows. Some Nova Scotians thought the agony of his last days ought to have been made much worse.

In 1922, the 68-year-old employed a teenage girl to keep up his Kemptville home. The relationship between the two seemed normal until late in August, when the young woman spurned Roberts' overture of love. The enraged man tied her up, soaked her in gasoline and set her on fire. Roberts watched the object of his love burn nearly to death before rousing his neighbours to ask for help putting out the fire he said was consuming his house. Miraculously, his housekeeper was discovered alive. Although she died within hours, Roberts' fate was sealed. Less than three months later, he joined her in death.

Some jail wardens were sufficiently sensitive of the feelings of prisoners on death row to move them to a different cell while their gallows was built. In 1894 that was an offer Albert Stroebel may well have accepted, but the British Columbia officials presiding over his execution did one better—they had the scaffold built in pieces elsewhere. Hours before the young American was to hang, the various parts were brought from a local joinery and swiftly fitted together.

JERK 'EM UP GALLOWS

For many of the executions carried out in eastern Canada in the 1880s and 1890s, convicted killers were not dropped to their deaths, but instead were jerked upward. An advocate of this unusual method of hanging was one of Canada's first hangmen. He said he much preferred jerking someone up than dropping them down. "In the old-style scaffold, the condemned man must climb steps almost as high as the top of my scaffold. That is terribly trying; and their knees get very weak before they get to the top. With this style they just have to walk out on the grass and stand on a certain spot."

A "jerk 'em up" gallows consisted of three long pieces of lumber. Two of the pieces were about 5 to 5.5 metres long and were erected upright, two metres apart. The third piece sat atop the upright sections, extending just over 1.5 metres beyond one end. This crosspiece was approximately four metres above the ground. The hanging rope ran up through a hole in the crossbeam and over a pulley fastened midway between the two uprights. The rope then ran along the top of the crossbeam out onto the extension and down through a hole to a 158-kilogram weight.

Prior to an execution, the weight was hoisted to within a metre of the extension by means of a block and tackle. It was secured in place by a chain. When an executioner pulled the pin and the weight dropped, the person being executed was jerked two metres into the air. The body received a second jolt when it came down. Theoretically at least, between the two jerks, the neck of the prisoner would be broken.

The jerk 'em up gallows fell out of use relatively quickly because there was no effective way of shielding spectators from the sight of gagging and convulsing bodies swinging wildly above them in the air. Even when a victim died without struggling, the waste dripping from the body repulsed onlookers. In a conventional gallows, such scenes occurred below the scaffold, out of sight.

REPRIEVES AND COMMUTATIONS

Regardless whether people sentenced to death were to die by being jerked up or dropped down, the reality is there was a 50–50 chance that a condemned prisoner would not die at all.

The one thought that kept condemned prisoners as calm as their circumstances permitted was the hope that their sentence might be commuted. The authority of the federal government to reduce a prisoner's death sentence served several purposes. Occasionally it ensured that a questionable verdict did not result in the death of an innocent person. In that sense, it softened a sometimes harsh and unyielding law. But commutations also reinforced the authority of the State and the majesty of Canada's system of justice.

The power to commute death sentences was once described as the brightest jewel in the British crown.

Historically, petitions for mercy followed a set pattern. Most were desperate pleas from people who had run out of options and hope. An example is the mercy plea of 30 men occupying British death cells in 1826:

May it please your Most gracious Majesty:

We the undersigned most unfortunate wretches and unhappy Subjects under Sentence of Death in your Majesty's gaol of Newgate, do most Humbly implore your Majesty's Clemency and Mercy to rescue us from the Dreadful and most awful fate which awaits us.

Sire, We are fully sensible of the great Crimes we have committed against the Laws of our Country yet do most fervently hope that your Most Gracious Majesty will be pleased to spare our lives and not thus cut us off without giving us an opportunity of amending our lives and repenting of our former Transgressions.

And may it please your Most Gracious Majesty as the Almighty Desireth not the Death of a Sinner, but rather that he may turn from his evil ways, and live, so do we most humbly trust in your Royal Majesty's well known Mercy and Humanity, may be extended towards us in our hour of Danger.

O Sire, consider the lives of your Majesty's unhappy Subjects and do not cut us off from the face of the Earth amidst the lamentations of our Fond wives and unhappy offspring without one cheering hope of Atonement for the great offences which we have committed against the Laws of God and our Fellow Creatures.

And may it please your Most Gracious Majesty, what ever Situation your Majesty may be pleased to place us in, we will with true humility endeavour to atone for the past and to show that Clemency has not been misapplied.

O Sire, take our petition under your Merciful Consideration and for a long Continuance of your Majesty's prosperous and Happy Reign we your Most Humble petitioners As in duty bound will ever pray.

In 1931, William Wilkinson killed a young restauranteur during a hold-up. Before mounting a Montréal gallows, he sought a stay of execution from the province's chief justice. It was worded quite differently from the petition of the Newgate prisoners just described:

That your petitioner was condemned on November 19th, 1931, to be hanged, and the said hanging is to take place on February 19, 1932.

That there was during the trial of the said case, grave irregularities and more particularly the charge of the Honorable Justice Loranger to the Jury is illegal, irregular and caused a severe prejudice in the minds of the Jury against the accused.

That the accused petitioner desires to have a respite to the execution and a stay of execution for at least three months in order to permit him to apply for the necessary remedies including a new trial.

That your petitioner was unable to present this petition before the date because his mother who is his only relative, was sick and practically out of her mind, and consequently could not give the necessary instructions for these proceedings.

That your petitioner is entitled to obtain a respite and a stay of execution in order to permit him to apply for the proper remedies of the judgement.

Wherefore your petitioner prays that this court doth grant a respite and a stay of execution; that your Lordship order the

Governor of the Montréal Jail, the Honorable N. Séguin, as
well as Omer Lapierre, the Sheriff of the District of Montréal,
not to proceed with said execution and hanging fixed for Febru-
ary 19, 1932, and that instead of that date, that the date of the
hanging shall be three months hence, namely May 30, 1932.

Chief Justice Greenshields was impressed with neither the content of the petition nor the individual on whose behalf it was presented. In dismissing the application, he noted that it was his personal opinion that society was well rid of such individuals as Wilkinson.

While most prisoners sentenced to death wanted to have their sentence commuted, occasionally that was not the case. In 1941, Arthur Simoneau murdered his wife, and on the surface he seemed just as deserving of a second chance as Wilkinson. Yet he did not want one. His apparent indifference was a stumbling block to efforts made on his behalf to secure a commutation.

Mr. Justice Wilfrid Lazure presided over Simoneau's trial, and the quiet, scholarly judge remained interested in the case. When he heard that Simoneau refused to ask for clemency, he visited Montréal's Bordeaux Jail to persuade Simoneau to change his mind. Simoneau refused to see him. Without a petition for clemency, the federal cabinet had nothing to consider, and the killer was hanged.

Not everyone was in favour of giving convicted killers a second chance, however. Rarely did an entire community rise up in opposition to a petition for clemency. A case where that did happen involved Valentine Shortis. His brutal 1895 murder of two local men during a failed robbery attempt of a cotton mill in Salaberry-de-Valleyfield, Québec, inflamed a large portion of the community, and many made their feelings known.

Their sentiments were shared by the editors of Montréal's *La Presse.* They suggested that when the federal government commuted Shortis' sentence, it provided others with an incentive to commit similar crimes and was deplored by all honest people. "That a murderer who after having received as fair trial as any man ever received, should have that sentence reprieved and the minor punishment of imprisonment substituted is more than the public of this town can understand."

Sometimes, an application for clemency was supported by an unexpected source. The widow of Montréal constable Daniel O'Connell was one such individual. Her husband was murdered in 1910 when he arrested Timothy Candy for trying to sell a bag of stolen boots to a city storekeeper. Candy was almost at the police station when he drew a revolver from his pocket, and in the ensuing fight, O'Connell was shot.

Though Candy was eventually executed, the constable's widow wrote a letter to Governor General Earl Grey asking that he spare the life of the man who killed her husband:

> *I hate the thought of a hanging being associated with my life and darkening that of my children. The evil that has been done to us should be pardoned and forgiven and it is because of this that I, wife of the victim, pardon this poor unfortunate in the name of my three children. I have read the touching letters of his*

poor wife and my heart is broken to think that her children will
be made orphans under such terrible circumstances.

REPRIEVES AS A DISTRACTION

There is little doubt that the reason federal officials took so long to advise prisoners on death row whether their sentences were commuted was to distract them from thoughts of their execution. Until final word was received, it was a rare prisoner who did anything to lessen his or her chances of being reprieved. Many prisoners took their last-minute bad news in stride.

Just hours before his 1931 execution in Prince Albert, Saskatchewan, Peter Knudsen, who murdered his partner, was told that his plea for clemency was denied. The trapper appeared indifferent to the news. He just nodded his head and went back to reading the book he had put down when the sheriff entered his cell.

In the hours preceding their scheduled execution, most prisoners clung to the hope that their sentence would be commuted. In 1940, 41-year-old Joseph Dlugos was sentenced to die for murdering his landlady during a quarrel over a barrel of homemade wine. No one could convince the doomed man that he might actually be hanged, and even as he entered the death chamber at Toronto's Don Jail, he expected his sentence to be commuted.

Eighteen-year-old Wallace Ramesbottom felt the same way, and suffered the same fate, though he had more reason to expect a commutation than did Dlugos. In January 1932, the teenager killed a London, Ontario, store owner during an attempted holdup. Because of his youth, Wallace was convinced the government would reduce his sentence to life imprisonment. When told he must hang, Wallace was literally left speechless. Ironically, the terrifying image of what it would be like to hang, painted by his lawyer during his trial, became a reality.

Whether out of a sense of bravado or because they were genuinely prepared to die, some killers received the news that they were denied a reprieve with equanimity. Shortly before his 1929 execution, Saskatchewan killer Mike Hack wrote a note asking his spiritual adviser if there was any news about his application for clemency. The minister took a pencil and a pad of paper and replied, "You have lost." The deaf murderer read the note then turned and walked back to his cell.

Nine years later, another Saskatchewan murderer was equally nonplussed by his bad news. In 1938, Harry Heipel robbed and murdered a farmer who'd stopped to give him a ride. Twelve hours before he was executed, Heipel was told all hope was lost. His reaction: "Well, I guess it's got to be, that's all."

More often than not, however, prisoners sentenced to death reacted with considerable emotion when informed that their petition for a reprieve was not successful. Roy Hotrum killed the owner of a Toronto pharmacy in early 1921, and the day before he was to hang, he was told that the federal government turned down his application for clemency. When he heard the news, the young killer broke down and cried.

Henry Wagner, the British Columbia killer who claimed to have ridden with Butch Cassidy and the Sundance Kid, reacted the same way in 1913. When advised that he was going to hang, Wagner, referred to as "The Flying Dutchman," began weeping like a child.

PLACES OF EXECUTION

Until executions were carried out in dedicated death chambers, scaffolds were constructed in prison yards wherever space permitted. Occasionally that was in a coal bin or wood shed. Because these places were often not high enough to accommodate a gallows of normal height, the pits were dug deeper. When James Allison was hanged in a stone shed in Kitchener's Waterloo County Jail in 1898 for killing the wife of his employer, the ceiling was so low there was barely enough room for him to stand upright.

Even if space in an outbuilding was available, it was not uncommon for hangings to take place on makeshift gallows somewhere inside the jail itself. In 1880, one such improvised gallows was used in the Brantford Jail. It was constructed in a short, narrow, second-floor corridor. With its low, arched ceiling, the gallows was dramatically different than that envisioned by most Canadians. From the ground floor a staircase led up to the place of execution. An improvised trapdoor was built over the well hole created by the stairs. It consisted of two iron doors supported by a bolt. When the bolt was drawn, the shutter-like doors opened, dropping the person being executed.

The execution of Emerson Shelley took place on an ad hoc gallows, though his was in a prison cell rather than in a corridor. The 21-year-old committed his first murder when he was a teenager. Probably because of his age, Shelley was given the benefit of the doubt and acquitted. Six years later, he murdered another neighbour. This time he was not so lucky, and in 1915, he found himself on a Simcoe, Ontario, gallows.

Shortly after breakfast, the killer was led to a second-storey cell in the floor of which a hole was cut. The cavity was covered by a trapdoor, and that's where the youthful killer was placed. But the hanging nearly went awry. The force of the drop stretched Shelley's neck so much that his body came to a rest almost on its tiptoes.

In 1946, George Norman Bilton was in love with a married mother of six. After much persuasion, the woman finally agreed to run away with him, but she insisted on bringing along her four-year-old daughter. When his lover would not yield on the point, Bilton picked up a 20-kilogram rock and beat both the mother and child to death. He then wrote a detailed confession, and for three days wandered around Whitby, Ontario, waiting for the police to arrest him. On at least one occasion he returned to the scene of the murder to stare at the bodies of his victims.

It took a jury less than an hour to find Bilton guilty of murder, but it was only by chance he was alive to hear the verdict. While his trial was in progress, the accused killer made a rope of strips cut from a blanket and tried to hang himself. The rope broke, and he was discovered before he could make another attempt.

The second time Bilton hanged, the rope did not break. His gallows was built in the office of the governor of the Ontario county jail. A hole was cut in the floor of the room, and the killer was dropped through an improvised trapdoor.

When Frederick Bussey was hanged in Owen Sound in 1948, the city's sheriff took no chances. He built a gallows using three unused rooms, two of which were situated directly beneath the room where the child murderer would plummet to his death. By cutting a hole in the floors and ceilings of lower rooms, the sheriff produced a drop of just over nine metres.

As jails across Canada aged, they were replaced by more modern structures that contained space set aside for executions. One such was Manitoba's Headingley Jail. When the facility opened in 1930, it contained the province's first and only death chamber. To get to it, witnesses passed through two barred doors and along a corridor separated from a row of cells by a common area where prisoners sat or played cards. A steel door at the end of the hallway opened into a room not much larger or higher than a living room.

A one-metre walkway was built along each wall, separated from a raised platform by a wooden railing. Opposite the door through which witnesses entered the room was another door. When it opened, everything happened very quickly. Directly behind this second entrance was a death cell.

The death chamber was dominated by a thick, laminated beam that ran over the raised platform, supported at either end by a square, 16-centimetre post. A set of double doors was built into the floor, directly under the middle of the beam, and large hinges supported each section of the trap. Above the trapdoor a rope dangled, wrapped several times around the beam. The distance between the head of someone standing on the doors and the overhead beam could be measured in centimetres. Below the death chamber was a room of similar dimensions, where a coroner's jury gathered to declare the prisoner dead.

Other Canadian death chambers varied in size and construction. In the case of British Columbia, hangings took place at the Oakalla prison farm. The facility opened in 1912, and its first execution took place seven years later. A gallows was built in a low-ceilinged room on an upper level of the main prison building. A little over a decade after the jail came into use, officials commandeered a dumb waiter that once carried meals to upper floors. The shaft of the elevator became the hanging pit.

Regardless where and when they were executed, most Canadian killers shared a common characteristic—their crimes were not well thought out. The next chapter discusses some of the motives behind those crimes.

Chapter Two

How Did It Come to This? Motive for Murder

~

Murders are typically committed by men and women who have little self-control and whose acts are seldom the result of forethought. Nonetheless, most killers have a motive for their actions, though they gain little, in terms of money, and some murderers just resort to outright brutality.

The first murder examined is typical of so many in Canada, in that it was the result of an escalating series of family disagreements, ending with the killing of a spouse. That story is followed by two involving the deaths of children, both at the hand of a parent. Next come two stories dealing with the murder of parents then a bizarre tale of the slaughter of four siblings in 1897 Québec and the murder of an entire family.

People rarely kill strangers. The most common targets are family members, and prominent in that group are in-laws and girlfriends. Disagreements between neighbours and landlords illustrate how quickly a small dispute can escalate.

How Did It Come to This?
Motive for Murder

37

Killing a Spouse

The Zybhleys came to Canada from Austria at the turn of the 20th century to take up a homestead near Mundare, Alberta. After becoming naturalized citizens, they sold their holdings to their son and moved to the United States. Two years later, they returned, both to the province and to the bickering that defined the couple's married life. Eventually, their relationship deteriorated so much that in September 1909, Herycko Zbyhley's wife, Anna, moved in with her son and his wife. Herycko soon followed, insisting she return home with him. She refused, and Herycko returned home.

Three days later, he was back, this time demanding the $70 he alleged Anna stole from him. She denied taking the money and demanded that he leave. Herycko was starting to scare her. In an effort to avoid a physical confrontation, Anna left the house and started toward the barn, followed closely by her husband. A minute later, the couple's daughter-in-law heard a scream, and when she ran from the house she found Zbyhley smashing his wife's head with an axe.

Zbyhley went to trial a month later and was sentenced to hang four days before Christmas in 1909. His gallows was erected in the carpentry shop at the barracks of the Royal North West Mounted Police in Fort Saskatchewan, and if his life was eventful, the same could not be said of his death. Mounting the scaffold with neither protest nor fanfare, he was dispatched by a Winnipeg hangman who used the same rope, death hood and black flag he had used in an execution a few months earlier.

When Herycko Zbyhley murdered his wife, he was responding to marital stress in a way typical of a handful of Canadian husbands. As was the case for the Zbyhleys, money and living apart were the driving forces in the disintegration of the marriage of Luke Phipps, and eventually, the motive for the murder of his wife.

By mid-August 1883, the Phipps had been living apart for months, in large measure because of Luke's temper and refusal to support his family. Mrs. Phipps had just taken her seat on the ferry *Hope*, which plied the waters between Detroit and Windsor, when she saw her husband rush on board. In a fruitless attempt to escape, she ran to the upper deck, but he quickly followed, firing three shots at her as he neared. By the time the ferry arrived in Windsor, Mrs. Phipps was dead.

The execution of Luke Phipps was a huge community event in Windsor, attracting people from both sides of the border. City officials issued 200 tickets to the hanging, but that was nowhere near enough. Hundreds more camped outside the jail, or the more adventuresome of the lot climbed onto the roofs of nearby buildings. Still, the streets around the courthouse and jail were blocked for hours with people waiting for the execution to get underway. When it did, Phipps appeared anxious to play his part in a centuries-old pageant.

How Did It Come to This?
Motive for Murder

39

On the scaffold, he looked out on the huge crowd assembled to watch him die, and, before stepping onto the trap, thanked those who had been good to him during his detention. He then stood patiently while his short, young and well-dressed hangman bound his legs, pulled a cloth covering over his face and adjusted the noose. Phipps dropped a little over two metres, never moving a muscle.

Murdering a Child

As tragic as the killing of a spouse may be, even greater sadness is associated with a parent murdering a child. It is a social reality that some parents are ill prepared for the appearance in their lives of an infant. Occasionally, to solve their dilemma, they resort to murder. At least that was the case of Toronto resident Alexander Martin. He and his wife were on a day trip to the country with their baby son when they decided to rent a rowboat and for one afternoon put their cares behind them. It did not work. Depressed by his circumstances, which included lack of both a job and money, and tired of constantly bickering with his wife, Martin, on an impulse, threw his son overboard.

His action did not go unnoticed, and within days, he and his wife were jointly charged with killing their son. At trial, Martin was found guilty, but the jury did not believe that a mother would willingly participate in the murder of a seven-month-old child, even though the judge did not entirely agree. Nevertheless, when Martin ascended the gallows in March 1905, he did so alone. Shortly before he left his cell for the last time, he admitted to his spiritual adviser that he drowned his son but said he was outraged at the suggestion made during his trial that he had beaten the baby first.

In a letter to his lawyer, Martin explained his motivation. "I had a quarrel with my wife, I had no sign of work, and our money was low. We tried to get the baby into several homes, but could not. I was near mad, and did not know what I was doing when I threw the child in the water."

Comforted by his confession, Martin went to the gallows with a determined step and a resigned air, his hands cuffed behind his back. As he walked, he glanced with disdain at the 25 spectators assembled to watch him hang, swearing as he made his way to the scaffold. In one way he was luckier than his son—he at least died instantly.

Although it is relatively rare for a Canadian parent to kill an adult child, such events do occur. Only once, however, was a father hanged for the rape and murder of his daughter.

Alexandre Lavallée was 73 and separated from his wife, and he and his married daughter Rose Anne lived in a village near Trois-Rivières, Québec. One evening, they sat down for supper, and a few hours later, Lavallée rushed to the home of a neighbour, exclaiming that on his return from Trois-Rivières, he found his daughter lying on her bed in a pool of blood. It turned out that as well as being stabbed 15 times, her skull and jaw were fractured.

How Did It Come to This?
Motive for Murder

41

Clearly evident under her fingernails were pieces of hair. The hair matched that of her father, and because he was unable to explain the fresh scratches on his face, Lavallée's fate was sealed. He was immediately held as a material witness and charged with murder. Seven months later, a jury spent little time finding Lavallée guilty. They did not recommend mercy.

Lavallée was hanged on August 12, 1927, a year and two days after he murdered his daughter. That morning, he was calm, and after Mass and a cup of coffee, walked with obvious determination to the gallows. As he stood on the scaffold, Lavallée repeated the prayers offered by his priest, and he was still praying when the trapdoor sprang open. Seventeen minutes later, Lavallée's lawyer claimed his body.

TAKING THE LIFE OF A PARENT

Children murder their parents more often than parents kill their children. Usually such tragedies follow a bout of drinking. In early February 1899, that is precisely what occurred in the Hamilton, Ontario, home of Benjamin Parrott and his mother, Bridget. Parrott started drinking in the morning, and the two quarrelled all day. Late in the afternoon, the infuriated and drunk deliveryman, incensed at being locked out of the family home, grabbed an axe and chased his mother into the street, where he battered her to death.

A little over four months elapsed between Bridget's murder and her son's execution. The evening before he was hanged,

Parrott spent a half hour with his spiritual advisers before trying to get some sleep. He tossed and turned until about 5:00 AM then gave up, and for another hour simply lay on his bed thinking. Jail officials offered him a special breakfast, but all he wanted was ham and eggs. He ate little.

Perhaps influenced by his spiritual advisers, he agreed to apologize publicly for his crime. "I am very sorry for what I have done to my mother. I hope that any of my companions who have not given their hearts to God will do so, and that young people will be warned by my example not to lead a life of drink and bad companions."

Parrott grew increasingly anxious and angry as the minutes ticked by. When he finished smoking a cigar, he put on a tweed suit and a black cotton shirt, all the while cursing the policeman who arrested him. As he was walking to the scaffold, the focus of his anger changed, and Parrott began swearing at his hangman.

Parrott appeared pale when he stepped into the jail yard, perhaps startled by the huge gallows looming in front of him. Spared the suffering inflicted on his mother, for him death came quickly. According to the jail surgeon, the killer was dead 18 seconds after the trapdoor opened.

As horrified as we are at the thought of a father raping his daughter or a son murdering his mother, we are equally appalled at how little a child seeks to derive from the murder of a parent. Edward Kolesar's 1941 axe murder of his father is an

How Did It Come to This?
Motive for Murder

43

example. The 20-year-old Ontario farmer's motive was the $30 pinned to his father's shirt, saved to pay for the old man's funeral. But Kolesar was after money, a common reason to murder. The motive behind the horrific slaughter carried out by Thomas Nulty was simply bizarre.

Slaughtering Siblings

Thomas Nulty lived with his parents, three sisters and a brother on a farm in Québec. To suggest that the family was poor is a gross understatement, and the thought that they could afford the addition of another mouth around the kitchen table ridiculous.

That was a problem for Tom, the oldest of the Nulty children. He badly wanted to marry, and the only thing stopping him from asking for the hand of his girlfriend was lack of a place to live. His solution: kill his siblings. While his parents were away one day, Tom slaughtered them all then calmly left for the home of his girlfriend, no doubt to talk about the couple's future. Like his sisters and brother, he had none.

Nulty murdered his siblings in early November 1897, went to trial a little over two months later and to the scaffold four months after that. During his last hours, he was restless. He tossed and turned all evening then gave up on sleeping and got up to chat with the Sisters of Providence. They kept a vigil over him throughout the night and remained until shortly before he was led to the gallows.

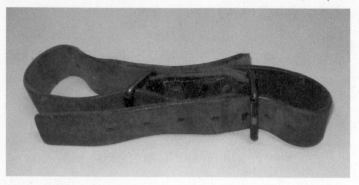

Leather pinioning straps used to bind a prisoner's arms behind his or her back

•◆•

Before his last walk, however, Nulty had one final thing to say:

> *Before I die, I wish to publicly declare that I am guilty of the crime for which I have been sentenced. I ask pardon for it with all of my heart. I ask pardon of my family, whom I have plunged in mourning and affliction. I ask pardon also of society, which I have greatly scandalized. I wanted to get married at all costs, and in order to have room in my father's house for my wife and myself, I did not shrink from the murder of four innocent persons, whom I loved, although I sacrificed them to my passion. More than once I meditated my monstrous act, before performing it.*

An hour prior to the execution, Canada's symbol of death was raised atop the jail's flagstaff, but even before that, a crowd gathered in front of the jail demanding admission. Without a ticket, however, no one was allowed in. That did little to deter several hundred of the ticketless. Ladders were propped against

Leather straps used to bind the ankles of a prisoner once he or she was placed on the trapdoor of a gallows

exterior walls, allowing dozens to literally drop in to the hanging. Others simply sat on top of the wall and watched the event. In the end, nearly 400 people saw Nulty hang.

Just before 9:00 AM on May 20, 1898, Canada's official executioner fastened Nulty's arms, and his march to the scaffold began. When the procession emerged from the jail, a hush fell on the assembled crowd, and in a heartbeat, the laughing and joking stopped.

Nulty quickly climbed the 15 steps to the gallows platform. With a single sweeping glance, he took in the crowd below then stared at the rope dangling in front of him. Not hesitating even a moment, he walked to it and took up position on the trapdoor. The hangman moved up behind Nulty, stooped to bind his legs just above the ankles, then raised his right hand. Nulty's priest nodded, and with that the executioner whipped out of his pocket a black hood, yanked it over the killer's head and adjusted the noose under his victim's left ear. All spectators saw next was the blur of a body dropping then they heard the trap banging against the scaffold, a loud crack from the cross-beam and a dull thud.

In 13 minutes, his life was pronounced officially over, and Nulty was on the way home.

KILLING FAMILY

Among Canadians executed between 1867 and 1962, there are a handful of men who killed their entire families. William Harvey is one of those men, with a slight qualification. He killed his wife and two daughters, who lived at home, but he was arrested before he got close enough to make his adult son victim number four.

The events that led to the murder of the Harveys started on March 25, 1889, the night before the three were killed. William for some time had been employed by the World Publishing Company as a bookkeeper, but unbeknownst to his family, was arrested for embezzling $400. Within hours of the theft, however, Harvey was bailed out by a friend. When he got home, Harvey said nothing of his arrest and release, keeping to himself the news that his first court appearance was scheduled for the following afternoon.

The next morning Harvey bought a revolver. When the city's chief of police got word of the purchase, he asked the

How Did It Come to This?
Motive for Murder

47

bookkeeper to turn it in. Harvey agreed to give up the gun, but insisted on returning it for a refund. Instead, he made his way home. His 12-year-old daughter was at school and her older sister was across the street on an errand. He found his wife in a little room off the kitchen, and he shot her in the back of the head. When his 21-year-old daughter returned home, Harvey followed her upstairs and shot her in the head as well. He then went to the private school where his youngest was a student and took her out of class. Minutes later she was also dead.

Harvey did not show up in court that afternoon, and the city's police chief was sufficiently alarmed by his absence to rush to the man's residence. With the doors locked and no one answering his knock, he was forced to climb through a rear window to get to what he was convinced was likely a crime scene. He was right.

Meanwhile, Harvey was on his way to Toronto, determined to murder his son. He registered at a hotel, made his way to the Canadian Pacific Railway dispatch office and hired a messenger to take a note to his son's boarding house. It said:

MY DEAR BOY. – I am in town for the night. Will you come down and stay all night with me? Walk down the west side of Yonge and north side of King to Palmer house. I may come up to meet you. YOUR FATHER.

Before the message arrived, however, Harvey's son received a telephone call from Guelph, advising him of the murder of his mother and two sisters, and promptly left for home.

A police detective was still at the son's boarding house when the note from Harvey arrived. The officer at once set out for the rendezvous. He arrested the fugitive as he neared the corner of King and Yonge, walking with his hands in his coat pockets, apparently on the lookout for his son.

William Harvey was hanged in the Guelph county jail on November 29, 1889.

QUARRELLING WITH IN-LAWS

Most murders committed in Canada seem to be spontaneous acts, but many are actually the result of years of quarrelling. That was certainly what caused Théophile Bélanger to shoot his brother-in-law early in 1903.

Antoine Séguin lived with his sister and her husband near St. Eustache, Québec, and for years caused the couple nothing but grief. Fed up, Bélanger bought a shotgun. After one fight too many, he confronted Séguin between two barns on the family farm and shot the troublemaker squarely in the face. Bélanger hid the body in a sheep barn until nightfall then moved it to a hay shed belonging to his victim, about a kilometre away.

When Séguin was reported missing, his killer was part of the search party that found the body. Bélanger may well have gotten away with the murder had he not been discovered hauling a sleigh load of bloody ice and snow away from the murder scene. Confronted by the police, he broke down and made a complete confession.

How Did It Come to This?
Motive for Murder

49

The night before he was hanged, Bélanger went to bed at 10:00 PM and slept until morning. After a breakfast that included wine, he put on a fashionable black Prince Albert coat, black vest and trousers then for a time knelt in prayer with his priest. Ready at last, he calmly waited for the arrival of his executioner, sipping thoughtfully on coffee and brandy.

Following tradition, Bélanger's arms were pinioned by his side before he left his cell. Fortified by all the alcohol he'd consumed, and determined to get the morning's events over with, the killer walked to the scaffold with the calmness of one who has accepted his fate. On the gallows platform, Bélanger stood in silence as his legs were strapped, a covering was draped over his head and the noose was adjusted around his neck. A second or two later, with a tap of his foot, the hangman dropped his victim. To the 50 spectators watching, Bélanger's death was instantaneous.

THE REVENGE OF THE JILTED

It is no doubt a fact of life that some relationships end badly. Occasionally, a rejected suitor punishes his paramour not directly, but by killing those nearest and dearest to the former lover. In May 1931, that was the motive that drove Winnipegger John Strieb.

He shot the young man first. The 18-year-old victim had been laid off the day before, and for the first time in years was sleeping in. His mother had left for work an hour earlier.

Lillian Walters was the sole provider for the family of five, which included a 16-year-old daughter institutionalized in Portage la Prairie. When her two youngest girls got home from school, they immediately headed upstairs to the bathroom. The nine-year-old came out first. Strieb led her by the arm into her bedroom, leaned her over the bed and calmly shot her three times in the head with a .22 pistol. Seconds later, the 12-year-old girl opened the door, and he repeated the process, this time with a .38-calibre revolver.

Ironically, the previous few days had been good to Lillian. The kitchen worker was finally able to get a few more hours a week at work, and the extra money was helping her deal with some of the pressure she was feeling since her son told her that he was about to be laid off. And she finally summoned the strength to tell her boarder, who was jobless, that he had to go. He was good with the kids, but his romantic overtures were making her feel uncomfortable.

Walters was proud of her two-storey home and enjoyed walking through the flower garden that filled her front yard. She was puzzled, then a little alarmed, when no one greeted her at the door. The first thing she noticed when she stepped into the kitchen was that the stove was unlit. Concerned, she went upstairs.

In her daughters' room she saw two forms lying under a sheet. Her first reaction was to laugh at their crude attempt at hiding. "I thought they were playing a prank on me. I turned over the sheet and looked at them. It was horrible." All she could see was blood.

How Did It Come to This?
Motive for Murder

51

As soon as she collected herself, Walters raced to her son's room. She found him lying on his bed, face down, head turned to one side as if he were asleep. She sat with her arms around him for a moment before realizing he was cold. Looking at her son more closely, she noticed a little blood on the back of his head.

Across the room, her boarder lay on a cot, his throat bloody. Beneath him she saw a razor.

The terrified woman ran out of the house, screaming that her children were dead. Two blocks away she rushed into the home of her pastor, almost incoherent with grief. As soon as he realized what she was saying, he phoned the police and then tried to calm his distraught parishioner. After her hysteria subsided into tears, he walked Walters to his door, and the two, holding each other, started back to her house.

They arrived a minute or two before the police and just stood on the sidewalk, not sure what to do. Their uncertainty did not last long. A squad of police officers soon arrived, followed immediately by the coroner.

The first thing they noticed in the girls' bedroom was that both victims were fully dressed, except that the shoes of one of them lay on the floor, and that both had been shot and their throats cut. Their brother's room was also full of blood, but most of it came from the boarder. Instinctively, they realized he was likely the killer. Any doubt they had was dispelled when the 45-year-old regained consciousness in the hospital and confessed to the murders.

Nine-year-old Doris was the second of the three Walters children murdered by John Strieb in May 1931. All of the victims are buried in Winnipeg's Elmwood Cemetery.

Exactly a month later, Strieb went to trial, charged only with the murder of his oldest victim. The Crown decided to proceed cautiously with separate trials for each killing, so if the accused was acquitted of the first murder, he could be tried for the other two. But it never came to that.

In his confession, the boarder said he could not remember much of the days before the killings, so devastated was he after being told that he had to find another place to live. "I don't know what happened to me, and I don't care."

He did recall, though, that on the morning of the slaughter, he waited for Walters to leave for work then returned to the

How Did It Come to This?
Motive for Murder

53

room he shared with her son. A pistol in each hand, he walked over to his victim, put the larger revolver to his head and pulled the trigger. A second shot glanced off his skull.

The boarder then waited three hours. He was upstairs when the sisters came home. The older girl walked out of the bathroom just as he'd finished shooting her younger sibling. He immediately took her in his arms. Because he had always been good to the girls, "She thought I was going to play with her." Instead, he shot her twice.

"Then I decided to go and give myself up to the police. I threw both of the revolvers in the river and decided to return home." He thought the girls might still be alive and, "so they wouldn't suffer," he cut their throats before using the razor on himself.

The killer's trial was marked by a couple of postscripts. For one thing, it is among the shortest murder trials in Manitoba history. It started exactly a month after the killings, lasted parts of three days, and the summations of the lawyers, the judge's charge and the deliberation of the jury collectively took less than an hour. The other postscript occurred two months after the trial ended, when John Strieb became the first person hanged in Headingley Jail's new indoor execution chamber.

George Walters and his sisters, Irene and Doris, were murdered on May 20, 1931. Their killer was executed three months and one week later.

MURDEROUS NEIGHBOURS

When Canadians kill, most often it is family members who are victims of their violence. Right after them in the high-risk category are friends and neighbours.

For some time prior to the late-August day in 1878 that ended in murder, Michael Farrell had been arguing with his neighbour. A railway line ran through Farrell's property near Québec City, and he had built a fence across the track to prevent cattle from eating his crops. Farrell accused his neighbour of taking the fence down. Their argument continued to escalate until, angry beyond self-control, Farrell brought an end to it with a gunshot. He immediately contacted the police, firmly believing he acted in self-defence. This killing, however, was one too many. Fifteen years earlier, he was charged with another murder, and that time, too, he said he was acting in self-defence. It had worked then; this time it did not.

The morning before he was to hang, Farrell was sitting down to tea when his wife and children arrived for their last visit. The sight of the prisoner's wife, arms clenched around her husband's neck while the couple's children wailed in anguish nearby, was heart-wrenching to the death watch. Farrell bore it all until his family was led away, leaving him to die alone. It was then he broke down and cried.

The next day, Farrell woke, resigned to his fate. Had he known the horrific agony he was about to suffer, he may not have been so sanguine. By the time the black flag was raised over

Québec City's jail, signalling that an execution was about to take place, 2000 people had surrounded the building. Two hundred had tickets to watch the execution, up front and personal.

Shortly before eight o'clock on the morning of January 10, 1879, the hangman appeared. He was a short, slender man, and his identity was disguised behind a black mask and gown. His attempt to pinion Farrell in front of the man's cell was a foretaste of what was to come. The executioner was so nervous it took him several tries before he succeeded in tying Farrell's arms. The calmest person present was Farrell. He stood motionless throughout the whole process, never moving a muscle. In the end, only his elbows, rather than wrists and elbows, were tied, and they were tied in front, instead of behind him.

Once Farrell was prepared, the death march began. When it reached the gallows, he stepped onto the scaffold and, for the last time, looked around. He then knelt and was joined in silent prayer by his priest. As soon as the convicted killer stood up, the hangman approached. After binding Farrell's legs, the executioner tried several times to adjust the noose around his victim's neck. When he was done, the long loop dangled in front of Farrell's left shoulder, instead of behind it.

The delay in getting his execution over with finally seemed to affect Farrell. He cast an anxious glance to his left, his face coloured and his fingers began to twitch. Then things began to go south. Hooded, Farrell bid his priest farewell and was supposed to drop. He did not. When the trap opened, he instinctively reached up with his left hand and grabbed the loop of rope left hanging in front of him. With all the strength he could muster, he held himself suspended over the open space where the trapdoor used to be, moaning over and over, "Oh, my God."

After what seemed to spectators an eternity, the hangman finally lunged forward. He grabbed Farrell's hand and pulled it off the rope, causing the struggling man to drop to his death. After the body was cut down, a messenger arrived bearing a request from the sister of the dead man. She wanted the silver crucifix he wore around his neck. Her request was granted.

LANDLORD AND TENANT DISPUTE ENDS IN MURDER

Michael McConnell was a short man, considerably less than five feet tall, but what he lacked in stature he made up in temper. A butcher by trade, he worked hard but occasionally fell behind in paying the rent on his Hamilton, Ontario, home. In late 1876, his excuse was that he would not pay until certain repairs were made. Fed up, his long-suffering landlord finally obtained a court order seizing McConnell's furniture. When McConnell's wife arrived at his shop with the news, the furious meat-cutter sharpened one of his largest knives and headed off.

Shortly after reaching his landlord's home, McConnell noticed his antagonist approaching. The two met on the street, and without any hesitation, McConnell stabbed the unsuspecting man in the head. Bleeding profusely, the landlord tried to run, but within seconds fell to the ground. McConnell immediately

How Did It Come to This?
Motive for Murder

57

rushed to him, stabbing his victim several more times. The land-lord staggered to his feet and tried to flee a second time, making it almost to his front door when he again fell. One more time, McConnell pounced. This time one of his stabs ripped open his victim's stomach, dooming both men.

Before a month passed, McConnell was tried and sentenced to hang. His date with destiny arrived a month and a half later, and his execution was attended by nearly 4000 people, about 100 admitted to the jail itself. The first thing they saw was the scaffold, a huge black structure built on one side of the yard, and rows of barred cell windows visible behind. In one of the cells was the man about to be put to death.

A half hour before McConnell was to hang, his executioner made his way through the crowd camped out in front of the jail and was promptly taken to a room where he donned a mask of black crepe and a small hat that held the mask in place. Fifteen minutes later, reporters were escorted to the death cell, where McConnell was praying with his spiritual adviser. He came out of his cell to greet the reporters, shaking hands and conversing without obvious nervousness.

To many, McConnell appeared to think of himself as victim rather than killer. "I am going to be the victim of something I never planned; I am not a man who worked for this." Speaking to no one in particular, he smiled and said, "Isn't it a good thing to be blessed with presence of mind in a case like this?"

When McConnell saw the masked executioner approaching, carrying a small rope, he seemed for the first time to realize that his fate was truly sealed. After a second or two, he regained his composure and stood with his hands behind his back, waiting for the hangman. While his hands were being tied, McConnell looked over his shoulder and spoke to the executioner. "I don't know you, poor man, but I forgive you, yes I forgive you." Looking up, he saw the bailiff who served the distress warrant on his wife. "A little moderation on your part," he said, "would have saved both of us."

After the pinioning was complete, the death walk started. The sheriff of the city of Hamilton went first, followed by jail officials. McConnell, the executioner and several spiritual advisers came last. As the solemn procession marched through the jail to the scaffold, the doomed man repeated over and over, "Poor McConnell! Poor McConnell!"

When the procession reached the jail yard, its members walked for a few metres between two lines of spectators then the entire group, including reporters, climbed to the top of the scaffold. Once everyone was in place, the sheriff read the official warrant of execution, adding that it was his hope no one present would again witness so painful a scene. Turning, he asked McConnell if he had anything to say before he was hanged. The killer did not hesitate. Walking to the front of the platform, he said:

> It was not my intention to have said a single word, but, as
> I see so many people here, I think it shall be justified on this
> solemn occasion in expressing a few of my sentiments. A little

How Did It Come to This?
Motive for Murder

59

moderation of Mr. Mills' part would have saved both our lives.
I only owed him $14, and I had been his tenant long enough for
him to know that I was worth more than that. If he had given
me a week, or told me he was going to put on a bill of distress, it
would have saved all the trouble, but he put the sheriff on me to
drag me to pieces. I lost my temper, and I hope from my soul out
that it will be a warning to the men of Hamilton to deal with
a little moderation in all their transactions.

Finished, McConnell stepped onto the trapdoor. As the hangman moved into position to strap his legs and pull the black hood over his face, the obviously distraught killer said a final goodbye to everyone then in a voice infused with emotion, began to pray. When he could feel the rope being placed around his neck, he stopped and started to moan, "Poor McConnell, poor McConnell, you deserved a better fate," stopping several times to ask the hangman to pull the noose tighter.

McConnell's spiritual adviser was just finishing the Lord's Prayer when the trapdoor opened and the hot-tempered butcher fell three metres to what spectators reported was instant death. A few minutes later, the jail doctor pronounced the man's life extinct. Before the morning was out, Michael McConnell was buried just a few metres from where he died.

An Excuse for Murder

Perhaps because most Canadians find the idea of killing someone unimaginable, they are not surprised that convicted murderers feel compelled to offer an excuse for their behaviour.

Often what they have to say is incredible. In 1947, Harry Medos said he felt badly about killing patrolman Charles Boyes, but he blamed his life of crime on cheap detective magazines. Forty-three years earlier, Ottawa-area farmhand Clément Goyette said he murdered his employer because the farmer criticized the way he fed the cattle. The motive of neither, however, could match that advanced by Clark Brown's doctors at his 1879 trial.

By the time his son killed him, Robert Brown was nearly 70 and one of the most respected farmers in the Ottawa area. He got along with everyone, including his 21-year-old son. On the day of his murder, Robert was working the family farm alone. Clark was confined to his room by the combined effect of depression and an acute headache.

Almost immediately after coming in from the field, Robert went to bed. He and his wife were no sooner asleep than they heard someone banging on their back door. Robert got up to investigate, and in the kitchen met his 12-year-old daughter, who was also woken by the pounding. Within minutes, Robert's wife heard the sounds of struggle. Rushing downstairs, she found the bodies of her husband and daughter lying in a pool of blood, and her son standing over them.

During the 18 hours it took the police to arrive, virtually everyone in the area showed up, one after another tiptoeing through the crime scene to get a good look at the two corpses. When pressed to explain what happened, Clark said he, his father and his sister were attacked by a stocky, axe-wielding

How Did It Come to This?
Motive for Murder

61

intruder. While trying to protect them, his gun jammed, and the attacker fled. No one believed him.

At the inquest that began two days after the murders, Clark's uncle offered a motive for the crime. A day before Robert was killed, he told Clark that his father had been secretly mortgaging the farm, jeopardizing the future of everyone in the family, including that of Clark's new bride.

Clark went to trial three weeks after the murders. Several doctors testified that when he killed his father and sister, he was temporarily insane. They differed, however, about what made him that way. The experts hired by Clark's lawyer said he was driven crazy by his compulsion to masturbate. While the Brown family doctor said that may have been a contributing cause, in his opinion, his patient was driven insane by an insatiable desire to engage in sexual intercourse.

The jury did not buy either excuse. After deliberating just 17 minutes, it returned a verdict of guilty. To many in the courtroom, however, the real killer was never held to account. Brown's mother, nearly 25 years younger than her husband, had for months been pushing her spouse to turn over half the farm to her. Many felt that when she heard he had been mortgaging it, she snapped.

Regardless of who actually committed the murders, the end for Clark Brown was not long in coming. He was sentenced to hang on the last day of October, a month after his trial ended.

On the morning Clark was to die, 60 people were waiting in the Cornwall jail yard for his appearance, and several hundred more stood outside the walls. Those waiting for a bit of drama were bitterly disappointed. When a pale-faced Brown stepped out of the jail, he walked with a firm step and an apparent sense of resignation to the gallows. He quickly ascended, stepped onto the trapdoor then waited a few seconds while he was made ready. The moment the noose was tightened, he dropped, mercifully, to a quick death.

SEX CRIMES

It is unfortunately a statistical reality that sexual offences often result in murder, usually because a victim or an offender panics. While we are disturbed by all such assaults, few upset us as much as those involving a child.

Before Gerald Edward Eaton went to the gallows in 1957, he confessed that, like everyone else in British Columbia, he, too, was disturbed by what he had done to the eight-year-old girl he raped and murdered. Throughout his two trials and much of the time he awaited execution, he continued to protest his innocence. In the long hours spent by himself on Oakalla's death row, however, he began keeping a diary, and to it he told the truth.

The 51-year-old said he assaulted his victim in his home then mutilated her body before dumping it in a walnut grove. He knew he'd committed the crime but had no idea why. "I keep asking myself that over and over, Why? Why? I don't know.

How Did It Come to This?
Motive for Murder

63

It was an urge, and once I started beating her, I could not stop. It seems to me now as a dream that happened in the long ago. I must have been in a haze of some sort."

When Eaton went to the gallows, he was determined to die with more courage than he had exhibited in the past. Refusing any kind of sedation, he walked to the scaffold unaided and without hesitation. Watching with cold, unforgiving eyes was the father of the youngster Eaton murdered.

Asked by reporters why he wanted to see Eaton hang, the distraught father said he had two choices. "One was to continue through life with the mental picture of this man beating my daughter to death with a tire iron. The other was to see him hang. I have chosen the latter. Only that can obliterate from my memory the former picture."

The execution was carried out with the speed and efficiency that characterized almost all Canadian hangings. The warden of the Oakalla prison farm was the first to enter the death chamber, followed quickly by a procession of guards and assorted other officials. As witnesses began lining up behind the wooden railing that separated the execution platform from the rest of the room, six guards took up position around the trapdoor.

Once everyone was in place, the door leading into the gallows room opened, and with slow, measured steps, Eaton entered. Wearing prison pants and a brown shirt, he was followed by his spiritual adviser, whose soft words to the child killer could barely be heard by those standing in silence around the scaffold.

While everyone's attention was focused on Eaton, the hangman suddenly appeared, as if from nowhere. He guided the condemned man onto the trap, facing away from the spectators. Eaton was looking down when, in what seemed a single motion, the executioner yanked a cloth covering over his face, tightened the noose then reached behind him and pulled the lever. In an instant, Eaton was gone.

For a time, the father of Eaton's victim stared at the barely moving rope, then slowly he started down a series of steps leading to the area below the scaffold. Eaton's body already lay on a stretcher, his face visible above a white sheet. As soon as the six members of the coroner's jury were satisfied Eaton was dead, a guard called out, "All right, gentlemen," and the group was ushered into an adjacent anteroom to await the formal inquest. The vote was unanimous—Gerald Edward Eaton was dead, the result of a broken neck.

MURDER TO CONCEAL ANOTHER CRIME

Murders carefully planned and carried out with neither passion nor impulse are extremely rare. They fascinate us probably because they are so unusual. For the women and men who commit them, however, the result is often two deaths, not one.

Although June 20, 1902, was an unusually cold morning in Brandon, Manitoba, the main topic of conversation in the city was not the weather. Uppermost was the execution of the man convicted of killing two area farmers a couple of years

How Did It Come to This?
Motive for Murder

65

earlier. Walter Gordon was only 21 when he arrived in the province from Whitby, Ontario, and just a year older when he met his first victim.

After working for a year as a farm labourer, Gordon entered into an agreement to purchase the Boissevain farm of Charles Daw. When the money to complete the transaction was not forthcoming, Daw confronted Gordon, and the discussion quickly became heated. It was brought to an abrupt end, however, when Gordon suddenly drew his revolver and shot Daw. A few days later, a friend of the murdered farmer showed up to inquire about Daw's whereabouts. When it became obvious that Gordon's explanations were not convincing, the friend became the murderer's second victim, and his body joined that of Daw at the bottom of a well.

Friends of the missing men eventually contacted the authorities. When the police arrived, a neighbour told them that Daw's dog had been acting strangely about the time of the farmer's disappearance, particularly around an abandoned well.

News of the murders quickly spread, and wanted posters were distributed throughout Canada and the United States. When Gordon was recognized in South Dakota, he promptly returned to Canada, where he joined a regiment on its way to fight in the Boer War. He was arrested in Halifax just hours before his unit was to board a ship for South Africa.

The morning Gordon was to hang dawned cold and overcast. The wife of the governor of the Brandon jail delivered the young killer his last meal, but Gordon politely declined the food. Two hours later, the 150 spectators who managed to obtain tickets to the execution saw the jail door open and the condemned man approach the scaffold. After Gordon stepped onto the trapdoor, he was asked if he had any last words. When he shook his head, a black hood was pulled over his face. Eighteen minutes after the trap was sprung, he was declared dead.

The young killer's body was released to his father and buried in an unmarked grave in what at the time was a Roman Catholic cemetery. Two years later, his mother arranged to have a modest grave marker erected, bearing only the initials "W.G."

Walter Gordon died on a gallows because of greed, but in his case, risk and reward were each considerable. The same could not be said of Frederick Thain. The Belleville-area man owned a farm adjacent to that of two friends, both of whom were nearly 80 years old. For some reason never explained, Thain stole $14 of grain from the couple. Instead of acknowledging what he had done and making arrangements to return an amount equal to what he had taken, he began to obsess about what would happen when they found out. His solution was to kill them.

The events that followed that decision began to unfold in a barn belonging to the victims. In a brutally chilling confession made shortly after committing the murders, Thain said his male victim was milking a cow and had his back to Thain when he entered the barn. "I saw Mr. Wellman milking a cow. Walking up behind him I hollered and let him have both barrels. I then

How Did It Come to This?
Motive for Murder

67

went outside and cried." Thain then entered the dead man's house, looking for Mrs. Wellman. He found her lying in bed, where she had been for some time recovering from a heart attack. He shot her in the head.

A postman discovered the dead couple, and less than 30 hours later, their killer was apprehended. Thain's three-day trial ended on the last day of October 1940, and the 49-year-old went to the gallows a month and a half later. Any concern he might have had about his fate was not obvious to jail officials, who said he spent his time on death row seemingly content, putting on weight. In a sad postscript to the murder, Thain's two victims were buried on what would have been their 55th wedding anniversary.

Murder for Mother

There are perhaps as many motives for murder as there are murderers, but few excuses for killing can match that advanced during a 1936 murder trial held in Dorchester, New Brunswick.

The Bannisters were extremely poor. The family of six lived in an isolated shack in conditions best described as desolate. The matriarch of the clan was a plump 41-year-old who kept her family of four in what little food they had by spending time with, and extorting money from, Moncton-area men. Her *modus operandi* was simplicity itself—sleep with a man, then nine months later demand that he support his illegitimate child.

No one knows for sure how many times the scheme worked, but by the end of 1935, events were not unfolding as planned in May Bannister's efforts to extort money from two separate men, both of whom demanded to see their children before paying up. She first tried to satisfy their curiosity by removing the noise-making mechanism from a doll, wrapping it in a blanket and offering each a quick glimpse of his "baby." The men were not convinced.

Desperate to come up with a newborn she could produce as her own, May began to focus on a baby born four months earlier to a family of squatters who lived nearby in conditions as primitive as those of the Bannisters. Five days into the new year, May sent her two sons, one a teenager and the other just 20, to the home of her target.

The young men were accompanied by their 15-year-old sister, Frances. She later testified that when she and her brothers arrived at their destination, Arthur, the younger of the two men, went into the shack. He returned with the baby, then re-entered the building. Seconds later, Frances said she heard a rifle shot. When Arthur came out, the three siblings started for home, seemingly oblivious to the fire that was quickly consuming what had once been home to four people.

The next day, a passerby noticed that the home of his neighbour was now a smouldering wreck. He moved closer to investigate and noticed the body of woman lying in the snow, her head badly beaten. Beside her was the frozen corpse of

How Did It Come to This?
Motive for Murder

69

a young child. Only later did authorities locate the skeletal remains of the owner of the home.

It did not take long for police to arrest the Bannister brothers, nor a jury two months later to sentence them to hang. The men's execution was delayed for six and a half months, however, when the appeal of the older brother succeeded, and he stood trial a second time. On September 23, even his luck ran out.

Arthur and Daniel Bannister began their walk to the gallows at 2:00 AM, and in the death chamber each was led to his own trap. Six minutes after leaving their cells, they dropped to their deaths. The two bodies were viewed by a coroner's jury, placed in a single, cloth-covered pine coffin and interred behind the jail.

In a postscript to the saga, Frances was convicted by a juvenile court judge of abduction, and her mother spent 42 months in prison for harbouring the baby her sons kidnapped.

Explaining Away Murder

A surprisingly large number of Canadian murderers actually moved into the residence of the person killed, telling the victim's friends that the missing homeowner had sold out and left for parts unknown. Statistics suggest that as often as not, no one believed it.

For two days in February 1906, Nova Scotian George Stanley was a busy man. Early on a Friday evening, he borrowed a jackknife from a friend of Freeman Harvey, the man with whom Stanley was staying. The next morning, he returned it, informing the knife's owner that he had just purchased the Harvey farm, and that Harvey was off to see a lawyer about transferring the title. Then, as if the idea had just come to him, Stanley asked the man if he and his son would like to work for him, father as a full-time hired hand and son for $1.50 a day.

A few hours later, with the help of his new employees, Stanley began selling Harvey's furniture and stock. By the next day, word spread about the sale, and friends and neighbours began turning up, demanding to know what was going on. No one, however, was permitted to go into the cellar. Nothing could have raised a red flag faster, and early Monday morning, two of Harvey's acquaintances returned to the farm and insisted that the hired man let them into the house.

He would, he said, but he did not have a key because Stanley had taken it. The more the three men thought about Harvey's disappearance, the more convinced they became that something was not right. They found an axe and soon forced open the door. In plain sight, at the bottom of stairs to the cellar, was a pair of feet. The rest of the body was buried in a pile of potatoes. Missing was the head.

A further search located the head under a pail. From the condition of the face, and the disarray in the kitchen, it appeared the elderly Harvey was attacked as he sat in his dining area then his corpse was dragged to the cellar, where his head was removed.

How Did It Come to This?
Motive for Murder

71

The discovery of the headless body of the missing farmer solved one mystery, but another remained unsolved—where was Stanley? Before the day was out, it, too, was solved. Stanley was located, arrested and charged with murder. Six months later, he was hanged in Windsor, Nova Scotia.

Was It Worth It?

It goes without saying that the crimes that led more than 700 Canadians to the gallows were not worth their consequence. In 1948, for example, the value of the life of northern Ontarian John Gagné was pegged at just $28, the amount on the pension cheque Gagné stole from his murder victim.

For Arthur Bruce Cunningham, the pay-off for murder was less than $50 and a bitter killer. When the slight, 65-year-old labourer shot a Prince Rupert, British Columbia, farmer in 1951, his take was $40. Asked during his trial if he committed the murder, the greying Scotsman said sure he did, "and I'd do it again for your pay cheque." No one doubted him. Ten years earlier, he was acquitted on another murder charge, and during the trial that set the stage for his execution, he bragged that in addition to that victim, he had killed three or four other men, though he was not exactly sure of the number.

The murder that resulted in the execution of three Fort Frances, Ontario, men in 1945 netted them even less than the amount Cunningham stole, but it did earn the trio the reputation as arguably the most sadistic killers in this nation's history.

The ringleader of the group was 28-year-old William Schmidt. Some years before the killing, he dated the daughter of Viola Jamieson, and during that time came to know his future victim well. So well, in fact, that he heard about the $1200 Viola kept secreted in a fruit jar in her root cellar. When he told the two Skrypnyk brothers about the stash, he had the accomplices he wanted, and the three took the money.

By June 1944, Schmidt convinced himself that Jamieson had more money hidden away, and he persuaded his friends that the time was right for a return engagement at the Jamieson residence. When Viola stepped into her home one evening, the three were waiting. They threw a blanket over her head and demanded that she tell them where her money was hidden. When she refused, they held her arms over burning newspapers. She still would not talk, so the men turned things up a notch. They lit the elements of the woman's stove and made her sit on top. The grandmother remained silent.

Schmidt and George and Anthony Skrypnyk finally gave up and left their victim to her fate. In a sad irony to the tragedy, Schmidt's mother took flowers to her friend during the three weeks the woman lay dying in hospital.

The killers were quickly caught, and after a brief trial, sentenced to death. No one had been hanged in Fort Francis before, at least legally, and so jail officials built the gallows outside, six metres high, which presented a problem. The jail was in the heart of the town's residential district, and the longer area residents watched the construction, the more upset they became. Local authorities responded to the protest by abandoning plans to hang the three killers outside and instead cut a hole in the floor on the second storey of the jail and covered it with a trapdoor made in Toronto.

It took carpenters a couple of days to complete the improvised gallows, their hammering clearly heard by Schmidt's parents, who lived next door. They spent most of the two days on their knees, praying for both William and his victim.

By the time their death walk started, Schmidt and the Skrypnyks were in a state of near collapse. The two brothers requested that they die together. The authorities agreed and hanged them back to back. As soon as they were pronounced dead, it was Schmidt's turn. It took a total of 20 minutes for the law to run its course. At the Schmidt home, the thud of the trap being sprung resonated like a clap of thunder.

A small group of onlookers started to disperse when they saw the black flag going up. They stopped to watch, however, when three pine caskets were carried out of the compound, and behind a 1.8-metre board fence, lowered into graves dug three months earlier, when the killers were originally sentenced to hang.

Gagné, Cunningham and the three men who killed Viola Jamieson murdered for money. While financial gain was often the driving force behind a murder, on occasion it was secondary to a more important motive. In the case of William Hammond, the objective was getting rid of a troublesome wife.

In March 1896, Hammond was a law student, married to a woman he no longer loved. His way out was poison, his reward the $5000 insurance policy he took out on the life of his wife. When she collapsed on the way home after visiting his parents, the doctor who rushed to her aid detected the odour of prussic acid on her lips, and a post-mortem revealed it elsewhere in her body. Hammond's arrest soon followed

At his first trial, a jury could not agree on a verdict. During his second, a deposition he made during the inquest into his wife's death was admitted as evidence. According to the Ontario Court of Appeal, it should not have been. Before his third trial got underway, the Crown agreed to stay the murder charge if Hammond pled guilty to manslaughter. He refused, convinced he would be found not guilty. The risk, he felt, was worth it. Only he knows if that was true. What is known for sure, however, is that William James Hammond was hanged in Bracebridge, Ontario, on September 15, 1898.

Chapter Three

Getting Religion

~

New York State executioner Robert Elliot hanged or electrocuted almost 400 men and women over his lengthy career. He observed that the vast majority of them went to their deaths remarkably composed. In many cases, the sense of calmness Elliot reported was the result of a new-found belief in religion.

It should be no surprise. In Canada, as elsewhere, the expectation was that those sentenced to hang would pass the time between their sentence and execution seeking atonement for their sins. Most killers tried to live up to this expectation, regardless of the dissolute life they lived prior to their incarceration. In the face of certain death, all but a few sought comfort in a spiritual place previously unknown. On the other hand, some likely embraced religion in the hope a forgiving federal cabinet would commute their sentences.

The involvement of religious advisers in the execution process served two purposes. Men of the cloth truly did help guide the spiritually ignorant toward the path of salvation, but their presence was also a much-needed distraction and helped shift the focus of condemned prisoners away from the terror to come. A second result of clerical involvement in executions was that Canadian hangmen were seldom confronted by combative, or even reluctant, prisoners.

The clergy who ministered to the needs of our nation's murderers embraced their role with determination, if not enthusiasm. They realized that the public regarded a prisoner's "good death" as a demonstration of God's forgiving power, and that the church played a pivotal role in bringing even the worst sinner to Christ. And while spiritual advisers did not control the execution process, their presence did much to dampen criticism of the State's involvement in killing its own citizens.

The efforts of death-row clergy often produced dramatic results, as the case of a teenage killer illustrates.

By the summer of 1945, many of the residents of Burstall, Saskatchewan, were tired of the carrying on by 20-year-old Jack Loran, which included harassing women and making a drunken nuisance of himself at community gatherings. A neighbour was particularly irritated by Loran's antics, and to get even, advised the police that his neighbour was selling illegal liquor. In revenge, Loran shot and killed the complainant, then stole his car and wallet. At trial, the accused murderer pleaded insanity, and his lawyer offered in support evidence that his client regularly had sex with animals. Jurors may have been disgusted, but they were not sympathetic; Loran was sentenced to hang.

A local priest shared Loran's last moments. He was amazed at the change religion brought to the life of the young killer:

> There was a radical change in the young man's attitude, a spiritual change. Loran had such a wonderful death. If you can call a hanging a wonderful death. I said Mass for him in his cell, and the guards seemed to be impatient to get on with it, and tried to rush us. I told them to stay away until I had finished. Together, the lad and I walked down the long corridor to the execution chamber, and up the steps to the gallows. He went willingly; they didn't have to shackle him and tie him and drag him along. We had a spiritual talk along the way, and I have no doubt I was walking with a very holy man. He was, at the moment of his death, a blessed, holy man.

RELIGION AS DISTRACTION

For most prisoners sentenced to death, visits from a spiritual adviser provided emotional comfort and a welcome distraction from long hours alone in a tiny cell. Although confinement was a physical reality, through religion, convicts could escape to a more beautiful and better place. Every day was truly a new beginning, and apart from their circumstances, nothing bound them to the past. What was important was preparing for the next life.

Some killers embraced religion with a sense of devotion bordering on fanaticism. Joseph Truskey was of that group. He was living on his Windsor, Ontario-area farm in 1894 when a local constable arrested him for beating a horse to death.

After he was tried and fined, he swore to get even with his accuser and, a few months later, announced to neighbours the time was now. Truskey was drinking in a village tavern when the constable appeared, and the two had words. When the police officer left, Truskey followed. Moments later, three shots rang out, and the constable was mortally wounded.

During his time on death row, Truskey sought comfort in religion, and in the last days of his life did so with such enthusiasm that jailers questioned his sanity. While having his face shaved in anticipation of his execution, the farmer seemed to realize for the first time that his life was about to end. Gazing at the remains of his supper, he appeared on the verge of collapse. Then his spiritual adviser arrived. The Church of England rector was allowed to minister to Truskey in the jail corridor, and the two prayed together before Truskey said he wanted to sing.

After Truskey tired of singing, he told his death watch that he was at last ready to die and that they should take a lesson from his awful fate. Between midnight and his morning date with the hangman, Truskey felt lonely, but when it counted most, his faith held firm.

Although Truskey embraced religion with an enthusiasm that concerned his keepers, he was at least reluctant to die. The same could not be said for George Merle, who seemed determined to speed up his execution at Montréal's Bordeaux Jail in 1927.

Two hours before Merle was to hang, for shooting an acquaintance in a Montréal residence, journalists began arriving at the jail, followed by a succession of police officers, guards and court officials. The hangman hired for the occasion made his first appearance a day earlier, when he tested the scaffold's trapdoor and obtained the height and weight of the condemned prisoner.

Throughout the night, the jail chaplain stayed with Merle, and by morning, the killer said he was finally prepared to even the score, to atone with his life for the life he took. His fellow prisoners certainly wanted to witness that death, and they crowded around the windows that overlooked the yard. Those who could not see the scaffold from their cells attached mirrors to sticks and waited for the spectacle to get underway. Some prayed as they looked out, while others laughed and jeered.

Shortly before Merle made his appearance, a black flag was hoisted to the top of the jail mast, and a chapel bell began tolling. Spectators then heard the voice of Merle's spiritual adviser, and in response, that of the killer. While the death procession made its way to the gallows, the hangman once more tested the trap and quickly left the scaffold to examine the structure's underpinnings.

When Merle appeared in the doorway leading onto the gallows, he seemed calm, almost serene. He stepped forward without urging and stood on the trap. Although his hands were fastened behind his back, his legs were free, and the executioner quickly tied them with a leather strap.

Merle's religious counsellor prepared him well for the end, and as Merle stepped onto the trap, he immediately thrust his head into the noose. But the executioner was not yet ready. The cooperative prisoner politely obeyed instructions to step back and withdrew his head to permit the hangman to adjust the black cap. Only then was the noose slipped into place. As Merle dropped into the scaffold well, spectators hear a muffled "Seigneur, je crois," then a thud. Twelve minutes later, his corpse was removed by two prisoners whose sentences were about to expire. Their job completed, the pair was released from jail.

Merle's body was left in the jail basement, where a coroner's jury viewed it and returned the customary verdict of "death by strangulation." Within minutes, the finding was posted on the door of the jail.

NEEDING TO CONFESS

Confession has been part of Christian faith for millennia. To many Christians, forgiveness requires not only belief in divine mercy but also a public acknowledgement of past wrongdoing. At law, such acts of contrition are important affirmations of the authority of the legal system. But unlike churchgoers, who typically survive their act of confession, the condemned were put to death, and their confession was not merely a powerful lesson to other sinners, it was proof of guilt.

Jail guards often grew close to death row prisoners and were significantly effected when someone about to die refused to confess. Even hangmen were relieved when a prisoner admitted guilt. A famous 20th-century English executioner recalled that on one occasion, just as he finished binding a killer's legs, the man shouted for his attention. But he had already pulled the lever, and before the trap opened, all the prisoner had time to shout was "guilty, executioner, guilty, guilty." According to the hangman, with those words, an enormous sense of relief immediately washed over everyone present.

In Canada, confessions were always considered a good thing, both for the condemned person and for the judge and jury who tried him or her. Obtaining a confession was a prison chaplain's duty. In the case of Albert Stroebel, that duty was performed to perfection.

In mid-September 1893, Stroebel was 21, unemployed and, for some reason, determined to rob and kill an elderly resident of Sumas Prairie, British Columbia. The Vancouver Island youth loved to talk and, before the killing, told a friend of his plans. Despite this, no direct evidence connected Stroebel to the crime, and not everyone on the first jury that heard his case was convinced of his guilt. A second group of jurors had no doubt, particularly because Stroebel could not account for his whereabouts on the night of the murder.

The young killer was on death row for two months. He spent his first days drawing up one escape plan after another, but when it became clear to him that leaving jail alive was not an option, Stroebel turned to religion. In short order, bravado gave way to resignation. As part of his desire to die truly repentant, he confessed his guilt to his girlfriend. "I did it, Mary, I'm guilty all right. I pulled out my revolver and fired; he fell, and when he was down I put another bullet in his head. I didn't plead guilty before, because I thought they'd never prove it against me."

While his confession may have been good for Stroebel's soul, it did little for his emotions. The killer's last night alive did not pass smoothly. Unable to sleep, he spent the early part of the evening copying passages from the Bible, and the second tossing and turning in his bed. Finally, sometime after midnight, he fell asleep. He was to hang early the next morning, and no doubt coached by his spiritual adviser, agreed to prepare a statement acknowledging his guilt and apologizing for his three earlier, false confessions.

Stroebel was to be executed in the smaller of the court-yards behind the Victoria jail. When his time arrived, he walked unsupported to the gallows. For a few moments, he gazed at the sky and the ocean and finally at the spectators assembled below him. Prompted by his priest, he delivered his last statement:

> I can only say this much, I am very thankful to everybody for the kindness they have shown me. No one need have no fear but that you're hanging a guilty man. I don't hold no grudge against nobody. I hope to meet you all in the better land. I wish you all good bye. That's all I have to say. The reason I say this is to free the jurymen's consciences in thinking they've done anything wrong. The jury done their duty all through and everybody else has.

After hanging for 10 minutes, the body of Albert Stroebel was cut down. When everyone on the coroner's jury agreed he was dead, Stroebel was buried in the yard of the Victoria jail.

Usually the responsibility for obtaining a confession from someone about to hang fell to a jail chaplain or a member of the local clergy. But that was not always the case. Occasionally, obtaining a last-minute confession was a job passed on to the local sheriff. That was probably appropriate, since according to law, he was the person responsible for carrying out an execution. The hanging of Ned Elfors in 1908 is an example. While waiting patiently to be noosed, the native of Finland was suddenly confronted by the Yukon sheriff.

> *Elfors, I want to have a few words with you. You are about to pass over the Great Divide, and this is the last opportunity you will have to enlighten the public and clear the public mind of who is the guilty party that killed that poor man on the 8th of June last. You have been accused and been tried and found guilty, but you have not yet confessed. If you are an honourable man, you want to do your duty before you face your maker, you have a duty to perform, a duty that you owe to yourself, to the jury, to the Judge, to everyone connected with your trial. Who killed Dave Bergman?*

The sheriff's harangue had its effect. Elfors confessed.

Thankfully, not many of the men who ministered to the needs of Canadian killers achieved the level of cruelty of an English prison chaplain in 1849. For two minutes the man held a condemned woman's hand over a candle flame, to give her a fore-taste of what awaited. Other British ministers may have been less cruel, but most were just as determined to extract a confession from their charges.

Canada, too, has its own history of gallows confessions. Few involved more pressure than that applied by a Dawson sheriff in 1901, when nearly 40 stood crammed together on the scaffold where George O'Brien was to atone for the murder of three prospectors. The problem for many witnesses, including the sheriff, was that O'Brien denied he committed the murders.

The condemned man and his hangman were forced to elbow their way through spectators to reach the trap. As soon as O'Brien was ready to drop, the sheriff approached him. "Now, O'Brien, you are standing on the threshold of eternity and in a few brief moments you must meet your God. For the last time, I ask you, are you man enough to tell the truth about the murder of Clayson, Relfe and Oleson on that fatal Christmas day."

O'Brien was in no mood to confess. Not in the least deterred, the sheriff again put the question to the prisoner and got the same response. Finally giving up, the sheriff signalled the masked executioner to begin. Less than a minute later, all appeared ready, and the sheriff snapped his fingers. In a flash, the trap fell away, and O'Brien disappeared.

Sometimes, obtaining an admission of guilt from someone charged with murder was not enough for a jail chaplain. On one occasion, what was done with the confession had a fatal consequence, at least for the person being asked to confess.

That was what happened in 1880, when a Brantford, Ontario, man was charged with murdering his wife.

Benjamin Carrier was the father of five and a hard worker, but he was in love with a woman to whom he was not married. While gathering wood, an argument between the Carriers erupted. Mrs. Carrier began scolding her husband about his wandering ways, and the more she talked about what he had done, the angrier she became.

Carrier later said his wife became violent and threatened to hit him with a stick. Although his first response was to laugh, in time he, too, became angry. When the couple came to a creek, Mrs. Carrier crossed first. Then it happened. "Something seemed to strike my heart. I was shaking. I drew my axe and struck her in the head. She fell into the creek and was still breathing. I struck her agin."

That confession put Carrier squarely on the gallows, a place he would not have been had he not confided in a local minister. Although the police quickly arrested Carrier after finding his wife's body, they actually had no evidence linking him to the crime. And even if they could prove he killed his spouse, there was no reason to think he would not be convicted of manslaughter rather than murder, since the woman's death appeared to have occurred in the heat of passion. The possibility of going to jail rather than the gallows, however, was an option denied Carrier after the Reverend Cameron visited him.

Cameron realized that Carrier felt guilty about what happened, and well before the man's trial, extracted the truth from him. The minister promptly shared what he learned with the police. His comment that Carrier confessed to striking his wife more than once left the Crown with no option but to proceed with a murder charge, sealing the man's fate.

The Canadian public expected killers like Carrier to confess, no doubt believing that no one should meet her or his maker without acknowledging past bad deeds.

The puzzle to those who followed the exploits of the country's various executioners over the years was not that many murderers confessed, but that so many refused to do so. John Tryon is an example.

In 1873, Tryon and his son entered into an agreement to trade in furs in the Georgian Bay region of Ontario with a German immigrant, who financed the venture. Before long, Tryon's son announced that he and the German were going to head out on their own. Upset over the German's interference in the affairs of his family, the elder Tryon resorted to murder.

A month and a week after his trial, Tryon Sr. died on a Barrie gallows. Shortly before going to his death, he was asked if he felt remorse for his crime. His response was chilling. "I did not feel any compunction in killing the man. My heart was as hard as a stone. I felt no more than if I was killing a mad dog."

Someone then inquired about why he did not confess. Tryon admitted he probably should have, but he said he was reluctant to do so as long as he thought his sentence might be commuted. But hang he did.

CONFESSION, A PATH TO THE GALLOWS

Even if Saint Augustine is right, and the confession of evil is the beginning of good works, confessions often lead to very different results than those intended by the confessor. In the case of two Manitoba men, it was the first step on a walk to the gallows.

Shoal Lake, Manitoba, farmer John Kooting seemed to get along with his neighbour Dymtro Czayka, and when Czayka left his job at the local creamery, it did not appear out of place that he boarded for a time with the Kooting family. What did seem unusual was that in the first week of November 1921, Czayka returned to his native Austria without telling anyone of his plans.

Two months after the creamery worker was last seen, police questioned Kooting. Kooting's suggestion that his lodger was staying with a friend was a lie, and the farmer was arrested and charged with murdering the missing man. After a short preliminary hearing, he was committed to stand trial. When a local grand jury heard his case in early 1923, its members were convinced he was likely guilty and brought in a true bill.

The problem for the Crown was that there was no real evidence that Czayka had been murdered. Instead of prosecuting the Shoal Lake farmer, the grand jury stayed his charge and allowed him to return home.

For the next two years, everything returned to normal for the Kootings. Then in the spring of 1925, Kooting became bedridden. Guilt-ridden and convinced he was going to die, he contacted the nearest RCMP detachment and asked if a couple of officers might come by his home. He had, he said, something to tell them about the disappearance of Czayka.

In a written statement, Kooting said he killed Czayka because he needed the man's money to feed his family. After hitting Czayka over the head with an axe and taking his cash, Kooting buried the dead man under a manure pile. Some months later, he built a pigpen over the grave.

Although all that remained of Czayka were bones, a 10-centimetre hole in his skull corroborated Kooting's statement. At trial, Kooting's son offered further corroboration, testifying that on the night of the murder, he was sitting on the stairs of his parents' home when his father came in and told his mother that he had just killed their neighbour. The young man also testified he later found blood-soaked clothing hanging in a shed and bloodstains on the hay rack his father used on the evening of the murder.

The only real issue was whether Kooting's confession should be admitted into evidence. A Shoal Lake doctor testified that although Kooting was sick when he confessed to murdering Czayka, the accused was physically and mentally fit to make "an intelligent statement." The jury was convinced. In less than an hour, it returned a guilty verdict.

Shortly before 8:00 AM on the third Friday in February 1926, Kooting was led from his death cell in the provincial jail at Portage la Prairie, Manitoba, to a gallows erected in the yard. The trap was sprung moments after he reached the top of the scaffold. Although witnesses later said that the execution was carried out without a hitch, the coroner presiding over the inquest noted that Kooting died from strangulation, rather than a broken neck, caused by the 2.5-metre drop.

Another murder that resulted in the death of a "confessor" bore striking similarities to the crime committed by Kooting, though this time, suspicion was immediately aroused when the victim left behind a suicide note, despite being illiterate.

By 1935, John Pawluk had farmed in the Gonor district north of Winnipeg for several years. His relationship with his wife had not been good during that time, and on at least two occasions Julia disappeared for days before returning to her husband and three young children. Therefore, local authorities were neither surprised nor alarmed when Pawluk reported his wife missing.

Genio Bulega lived near the Pawluks. Four months after Julia Pawluk went missing, a neighbour arrived at the Bulega farmhouse to ask for help loading hay. He found the yard strangely quiet. Concerned, he entered the residence, where he found Genio sitting in a chair, the top of his head blown off. A shotgun lay beside his body. One end of a piece of binder twine was tied to its trigger, and the other end was wrapped around one of the feet of the dead man.

On a table across the room, police discovered a bloodstained letter, held in place by a long carving knife. Investigators became suspicious when they read the suicide note. It was dated more than a month before its author allegedly shot himself, and it urged police not to suspect Pawluk of killing his missing wife.

> *Please dont bother anybody about* [Julia Pawluk] *she was at my place on Monday…she want me to go away with her and I told her I couldnt go with her she had been bothering me all summer I couldnt go with her and I cant stand her now wherever she went…dont bother him* [John Pawluk] *any because he is not to blame for anything this all I have to say goodby everybody please dont bother about his wife.*

Any doubt investigators had that Bulega was a murder rather than a suicide was dispelled when they noticed blood on the inside of the note. Not only was it impossible for Bulega to have shot himself and then fold the note, but it was also unlikely he could have handled the shotgun without leaving evidence that he had done so. The gun had been wiped completely clean of fingerprints.

Notwithstanding evidence pointing to his involvement in the death of Bulega, and possibly that of Julia as well, Pawluk may have avoided the gallows had he not on two separate occasions confessed to killing his wife.

The first time he unburdened himself occurred before Bulega died. A neighbour dropped by for a visit following Julia's disappearance and, without prompting, Pawluk told his startled guest that he no longer had a wife. Asked what happened, he said he shot her with a .22-calibre rifle and buried her body under a manure pile.

Pawluk's second confession came after Bulega's body was found, while the accused was being held in jail awaiting trial for killing his wife. A friend serving a six-month sentence for obtaining goods by false pretences was sharing a cell with Pawluk when, again without prompting, Pawluk confessed to killing his wife and burying her body. "I hope, now that they have me, they will hang me right away. I don't want to be continually pulled around in the courts."

Pawluk need not have worried. His jury took less than an hour to return a verdict of guilty. Pawluk did not react when he was sentenced to hang, and after his judge left the courtroom, calmly relit a half-burned cigarette and walked back to his cell with a smile on his face. There were no smiles two months later when the 49-year-old farmer was led to the gallows.

The *Winnipeg Free Press* summed up the feeling of those who witnessed the hanging. "Had he been less talkative it might have been difficult to connect him definitely with the killing." John Pawluk was hanged on August 21, 1936.

SETTING THE RECORD STRAIGHT

John Yuzik was unique among Canadians hanged for murder, and, at the same, ordinary. He was unique in that just 15 days after he murdered an elderly farm woman near Wakaw, Saskatchewan, he was tried and sentenced to hang. His trial lasted about six hours, and his jury returned its verdict in 40 minutes. By the time the 19-year-old was executed in July 1914, he was determined to die with a clean conscience. And like so many killers before and after him, he gave a statement to the authorities absolving others implicated in his crime.

Shortly before career criminal Joseph Gordon was hanged in British Columbia in April 1957 for killing a police officer after a botched break-in, he informed officials from the federal department of justice that he committed a crime for which another man was sentenced to six years in jail. Gordon told authorities that he had carried out the drugstore holdup for which the innocent man was tried and convicted.

In like manner, before cop-killer Leonard Jackson was put to death in 1952, he told officials of Toronto's Don Jail that Anthony Brunet, already serving a 15-year term of imprisonment for taking part in a Toronto bank holdup, was innocent of the crime that put Brunet in jail. Jackson swore that Brunet and Louis Stavoff, also sentenced in the same case, were not with him when he robbed the bank.

The thoughtfulness of condemned prisoners did not always focus on others. Sometimes, in their last moments, killers acted just as they would have were they not about to be executed. Tom Hutchings was 22, married and a member of Britain's Royal Air Force when he raped and beat to death a woman in Blacks Harbour, New Brunswick. As he left his death cell in late 1942, his training was not forgotten. He and two guards no sooner began their short walk to the gallows at St. Andrews when Hutchings suddenly stopped and re-entered his cell. He'd left a light on when summoned and wanted to turn it off. He then rejoined the small death procession.

As he approached the gallows, Hutchings looked neither right nor left and never for a moment hesitated as he walked up the scaffold steps. Once he took his place on the trap, he stood motionless, his only movement a slight tilting of his head so the hangman could pull a hood over his face. Seconds later he was dead.

DIRECTOR IN A PAGEANT

It should come as no surprise that in the hours preceding an execution, the mood in death cells was usually depressed, notwithstanding the best efforts of a spiritual adviser. Before the execution of the last two men hanged in Canada, the chaplain of the Don Jail begged his charges to tell him what to do. "Do you want me to pray? Read from the Bible? Poetry? Do you want me to sing?"

The real importance of spiritual advisers, however, was not in lightening the atmosphere. They shared control of the scaffolds with hangmen. Men of the cloth were responsible more than any jail official for ensuring that killers died with decorum.

Occasionally, maintaining order required spiritual advisers to play a more active role than would normally seem appropriate. In April 1884, brothers George and John Stevenson were scheduled to hang for the murder of a farmer near the community now known as Qu'Appelle, Saskatchewan. The two priests who attended to the spiritual needs of the Métis brothers were on the scaffold praying when the brothers demanded that their hangman leave them alone. They wanted to be executed by the priests. The Stevensons insisted that the fathers and they alone place the nooses around their necks and pull over their heads the black death hoods. George's last words were of encouragement. He told his priest to have no fear and to just make sure he put it on tight.

Ministering to the spiritual needs of prisoners was no doubt for most churchmen a labour of love. But despite the emotional distress they suffered in witnessing the execution of women and men with whom they had become close, jail chaplains were not without their critics. In 1923, a Member of Parliament said he was incensed that spiritual advisers recited the Lord's Prayer seconds before their charges dropped to their deaths. The Lord's Prayer was being used to assist legalized murder, the Montréaler argued, "and I cannot understand how any pastor can dare to use this prayer on such an unchristian occasion."

REMORSE, RESIGNATION AND ACCEPTANCE

The certainty of their impending death took many prisoners sentenced to death on an emotional roller coaster. On good days, they agreed that they deserved to die, but at other times they wallowed in self-pity, filled with hatred toward those responsible for putting them on death row.

Sometimes it was curiosity rather than anger that characterized the last days of a prisoner. When Canadians were hanged outdoors, newspapers were filled with stories of killers spending hours watching the construction of their gallows and the digging of their graves. Only one Canadian, however, demanded the right to rehearse his execution. In 1917, the soldier was to be hanged in a British prison, and as his end approached, he grew increasingly obsessed with thoughts of what was to come. His fear, he told his death watch, was that something would go wrong. Over and over, he worried that a mistake would be made, insisting in vain that he be given the right to rehearse his own demise.

For many prisoners, acceptance of their fate came late, after all alternatives to their execution were spent. For Carlo Battista, hope for a reprieve or commutation disappeared a day prior to his December 1912 execution. The Italian immigrant was a member of the Black Hand, precursor to our modern Mafia. In the days before his execution, he began telling authorities of his involvement in a number of crimes, including the murder of a New York police detective.

When these disclosures did not gain him a commutation, he turned to the comfort of religion. That surprised Montréal prison officials, who were making arrangements to have him hanged while strapped in a chair, to avoid a possible scaffold confrontation with his executioner. After a lengthy talk with a Montréal archbishop, Battista finally resigned himself to the fact he was going to die. His demeanour underwent a dramatic change, and in the end he was hanged without protest.

DOUBTS ABOUT CONVERSIONS

Anecdotal evidence suggests that many prisoners on death row accepted the ministrations offered by jail chaplains to impress prison authorities and hopefully earn them a pardon. Veteran newspaper reporters, like experienced police officers, could not help but notice that seldom did a religious conversion persist after a prisoner's sentence was commuted. For many denied a second chance at life, however, religion was the only comfort that remained.

Early in the 20th century, an astute Canadian observer of capital punishment said that after years of observing hardened criminals, he was offended when he heard it said that a murderer died confident his sins were forgiven, and that all was well. Such last-minute conversions were made all the more unbelievable, he suggested, when one recalls that these people were career criminals who earned a cell on death row by dealing in drugs and the death of innocents.

Even to the most forgiving observer, the sincerity of the religious conversion of hardened criminals like Joseph Mauro was indeed hard to believe.

In late July 1925, Mauro entered a Montréal nightclub, drew a gun and ordered a waiter to relieve everyone of money and valuables. As he was backing out of the club, a man threw a chair at him. Mauro's first shot hit the man, wounding him, but a second went wide, killing a member of the house band. Mauro escaped to Vancouver, where he was caught and returned to Montréal.

A few who knew Mauro watched him during his pre-execution Mass and gave credit to the prison chaplain for bringing about a remarkable change in the character of the killer. Others were sceptical. One reporter said he could not forget that the man who stood on the gallows talking of God and forgiveness was the same person who told a detective after his arrest that he was sorry he had wounded and not killed the guy who threw the chair at him.

In 1870, Daniel Mann was hanged for killing a penitentiary guard during an escape attempt. The man beside whom he was executed was convicted of poisoning his wife. Mann and James Deacon became close friends while on death row and each said that in his last hours he forged a new and wonderful relationship with God. Witnesses at their execution believed one of the killers but doubted the credibility of the other.

Mann and Deacon stood on a trap two metres long. Each had his own hangman, both wearing black gauze bags over their heads and floor-length frocks.

While the official party made its way to the gallows, reporters were conducted to a spot in a corridor at the foot of the drop, where they could watch the bodies fall through the platform above. Standing nearby was a group of doctors and medical students.

Deacon died more quickly than Mann. Other than a single twitch of his shoulders, Deacon made no movement. Mann's body convulsed for 20 seconds, and his groans sent shudders through the crowd of horrified spectators. Then he was dead. The bodies remained suspended for an hour before they were lowered to the ground and examined by the prison surgeon.

Shortly before the prisoners were executed, reporters had the opportunity to talk to the two men. Asked if he was ready to die, Deacon replied with confidence that he was, and that he knew his sins were forgiven. Until a week earlier, he said, he was tormented by uncertainty and agonized over what was to come. Then he somehow experienced a change of heart. "I got down on the floor and prayed all night, and before the morning it pleased God to give peace to my soul."

Those who talked with Deacon listened to his sighs and groans with doubt. They felt he was acting a part, trying to persuade himself that all was well, when in truth he knew it was not.

Of Mann's beliefs the reporters had no doubt. Although he, too, said he was saved and was certain that God forgave him his sins, he only spoke of his feelings when asked. He was not trying to impress anyone and spoke as if the matter of his salvation was decided, and nothing more need be said.

Chapter Four

Rituals

~

Executions in 19th- and 20th-century Canada were elaborate and highly ritualized pageants. This was in part because prisoners on death row took comfort in knowing what was to come. Those about to pay the ultimate price for their sins were actors in a drama they would not survive, but everyone was determined to play their roles well. No one wanted a surprise or a mistake. Executions were also visible manifestations of the majesty and power of law. As such, they were as much about ritual as were trials. This chapter is about some of those rituals.

DEATH CELL

Regardless what the condemned did in the last moments of their lives, they did it in living quarters as primitive as any space created to house human beings. Death cells were just that—places designed to accommodate the living dead. Occupants were never alone. A detachment of prison officials known collectively as the death watch sat close by and watched their charges eat, sleep, pray, cry or engage in any of the activities someone might engage in during the days and weeks spent alone in an area little larger than a closet.

While conditions improved slightly in the latter years of Canada's experiment with capital punishment, death cells were never comfortable. The one that housed prisoners in Goderich, Ontario, in 1869 was typical of most late 19th-century cells.

Death cell in the Headingley Jail. The cell is located three or four steps from the trapdoor on which the condemned prisoner was placed.

The surroundings were Spartan at best. The death cell in that jail was 1.8 metres wide, two metres long and 2.4 metres high. Its bed was a five-centimetre-thick wooden platform. The walls were made of hand-hewn timbers 30 centimetres thick, and the cell door was constructed of two layers of oak bolted from the outside. Opposite the door, just below the ceiling, was a tiny window. Through it a prisoner could barely manage to look into the exercise yard, and in the last days, watch the construction of the gallows.

Condemned prisoners housed in such cells during the dark days of fall and winter lived in a cold so penetrating it sapped the body and spirit. These lairs were as clammy and ugly as any on earth. In the late 1890s, only lanterns lit the cells, and by the end of a night, the gloom and the stench from a latrine pail were overwhelming. Days were better, and a prisoner could make use of a knocked-together privy in the corner of the exercise yard. Sleep was impossible, even if the doomed man or woman wanted it. There was constant noise: the never-ending slamming of cell doors, prisoners cursing, the incessant buzzing of flies during summer, and almost always, the primal screeching of the mentally disturbed. And in a scene straight from Dante's *Inferno*, children were occasionally imprisoned with their parents, because without the support of an adult, they were regarded as vagrants.

In Goderich, the cell was in a dark nook off a jail corridor. When it was occupied, members of a death watch sat nearby at a table, writing down whatever small thing a prisoner did or said. Every day such reports were given to the jail warden.

Regardless where condemned prisoners spent their last months, until the 1930s, most death row cells looked into the yard where a gallows would be built. The noise of its construction was the last straw for many, who embraced either madness or suicide in an attempt to avoid its fatal grip.

The death cell where Thomas Collins resided in Hopewell Cape, New Brunswick, for almost all of 1907 wasn't much better. The prison was a two-storey structure, built in 1845. The centre cell of the building had a low vaulted ceiling of rough stone, and prisoners and guards alike referred to it as the dungeon. It typically served as a drunk tank, or when needed, a solitary confinement cell.

A heavy ringbolt was fixed permanently in the centre of the concrete floor and was used to secure stubborn or rebellious inmates. Like cell doors in most prisons, this one had a 20-centimetre square opening fitted with a sliding panel, where meals and heating fuel were supplied to occupants. This particular cell had a single window set high into one of the room's half-metre-thick stone walls. Instead of a plank bed attached to the wall, Collins slept on a straw pallet thrown on the floor, and he survived the cold with the help of a small wood stove.

When he was not housed in the dungeon, Collins resided in a smaller, slightly more comfortable cell beside it, which was designed to hold people awaiting trial. It had a wooden bed, plank floor and a plaster ceiling.

The Toronto death cell of William McFadden was typical of death cells built in the 1920s. It had an ordinary jail bed welded to the bars at one end of the room, a toilet and washstand, and a single chair and table. Such cells were invariably located a few metres from the gallows, and it was a rare prisoner who was conscious more than two minutes after leaving the cell.

LAST REQUESTS

Of all the rituals associated with capital punishment, accommodating a prisoner's last request was arguably one of the most difficult. Very often it was a simple thing. In 1883, for example, double murderer Michael O'Rourke wanted only to have his photograph taken, and 17 years later, when George Pearson of Hamilton, Ontario, was hanged, a similar request was granted.

On some occasions, a last request seemed perfectly appropriate because of the background of the person being executed. Frank Spencer was a cowboy in every sense of the word. In the mid-1880s, he worked on a cattle ranch near Kamloops, British Columbia. He loved the work and the lifestyle that came with it. In late May 1887, his circumstances changed. On his way into town, a fellow ranch hand gave Spencer some money and asked him to buy four bottles of cheap whiskey. Spencer did, but on the way home he consumed the contents of one of the bottles. The cowboy who gave Spencer the money was irritated at getting less than he'd paid for and a fight ensued.

When Spencer pulled a knife, his opponent exercised considerable discretion and ran off.

Spencer was a little drunk and a lot angry, and when he saw the ranch hand walking toward the bunkhouse, he grabbed a rifle and shot him. For the next two years Spencer roamed the American west, working wherever he could. In 1889, he returned to Canada. When the fugitive sat down in a New Westminster saloon for a drink, a police officer recognized him, and a little over two months later, the killer was lodged in a Kamloops death cell.

As he prepared to leave his cell for the gallows, Spencer made a last request. In a symbolic gesture to the wild and woolly west of his past, he asked for a pair of slippers. He told his guards that above all else, he didn't want to die with his boots on. His request was immediately granted.

Some last requests were not so well received, either in Canada or its neighbour to the south. On the day of his execution, American outlaw Scotsman Jock Donald was led to a grove of trees and told that by tradition he could select the limb from which he was about to be suspended. Donald chose a small sapling. When the sheriff told him it was far too small, Donald replied that it was okay, he was in no hurry, "I'll just wait 'til it grows."

In 1897, New Brunswick resident John Sullivan wanted his execution to be carried out in private, away from newspaper reporters. He feared their presence would make him anxious. His request was denied. The last request of William Robinson also was denied. The man who strangled his wife in 1904 before cutting up her body and burning it in the couple's home in Burlington, Nova Scotia, asked for a public execution. He said he wanted his death to be a statement. It took some time before the local sheriff persuaded him that he would be much better off hanged in private, away from the gaze of a crowd possessed of absolutely no sympathy for him.

Early in November 1936, three British Columbia men were hanged, two for murdering police officers and the third for killing a bank teller. The last meal of each was bacon, scrambled eggs and coffee. Only Charles Russell, the bank robber, made a last request. He wanted a cigar.

Occasionally, last requests were made on the scaffold. Because of their timing, few were granted. If made early enough, the demands of the condemned were likely accommodated.

Benjamin Parrott and his mother were heavy drinkers, and their Hamilton, Ontario, neighbours often heard them quarrelling about one thing or another. In early February 1899, a disagreement got out of hand, and Benjamin killed her.

The killer was most likely mentally ill. According to his sisters, he suffered from convulsions throughout his life, and family members felt he could not be blamed for his actions. Local reporters were less sympathetic, referring to Parrott as a young man of low instincts and foul tongue. Before leaving his cell for the gallows, Parrott made two requests. One was for a glass of brandy, which was given him. Then he demanded a chew of tobacco from one of the witnesses who showed up to watch him hang. That too he got.

Hooded and standing on the trap waiting for the door to open, Parrott said his one regret in life was not killing the police officer who had arrested him. Apparently thinking about that for a moment, he added a second regret. He said he'd also like to get at his executioner.

Twenty-four years after Parrott was executed, Fred Huss robbed a poolroom in the small Saskatchewan town of Dollard, killing a man in the process. While on Regina's death row, Huss wanted nothing, spurning even the last rites of the Catholic Church. All he wanted were his cigarettes, and the night before he was to hang, he smoked them one after another.

Standing on the scaffold, seconds from being hanged, Huss changed his mind. He did want something special. He told his hangman that he had been promised a drink of whiskey, and he wanted it now. He did not seem particularly surprised, however, when it was not forthcoming.

The Last Hours

No two prisoners spent their last moments in exactly the same way, although generally, many did similar things. A member of the 1890 death watch of Thomas Kane kept a record of everything the killer did the night before he was hanged. His notes offer a unique insight into how condemned prisoners spent the hours immediately preceding their death.

I went on duty alone at 8 PM when Wright [member of death watch] left. Little was said by Kane, only that he had said farewell to his friends in the afternoon. Fathers Cassidy, Cruise and McPhillips came about this time. Father Cassidy cried, and so did the prisoner. Kane remarked, "My relatives took a parting farewell this afternoon." I left the cell until 11 o'clock, when Fathers Cruise and McPhillips, who remained after Father Cassidy's departure, came out and took chairs by the fire in the main office and remained there until 5 AM. When they left the cell I returned. Kane began to talk about Rev. Mr. Caswell. He wanted him [Kane] to answer too many questions. That is, he pressed him not to go to the gallows with a lie on his lips, and that he ought to confess to the murder, of which the prisoner still professed to be innocent.

He got up for a while after I returned, but went to bed at 12.15. He did not undress, save that he had his coat off. He lay on the top of the bed clothes. At 1.15 he sighed heavily and turned and put the bed quilt over him and I believe went for sleep. He awoke at 1.10 and asked me what time it was. I told him. He turned on the bed and went to sleep as I thought. He did not sleep soundly but sighed and moaned constantly. He turned on his side and moaned loudly all the time he lay on the bed. The two clergymen returned to the cell at 5 AM and I left.

At 6.15 the Governor sent some toast and coffee to the cell and Kane ate a little. The two priests aroused Kane when they entered. He did not appear nervous, but seemed resigned to his awful fate. He made no allusion to the crime, and the spiritual advisers made none either. Mass was said in the cell, and Kane partook of the communion. He wanted to say something on the scaffold, but the priests advised him not to, and he agreed that he would not.

He smoked a good deal almost up to the end. During the time the priests were with him last night, he talked much about Ireland. At 8.05 the sheriff, governor, hangman and the guards entered the cell, and the hangman pinioned the arms of the condemned man securely behind. At 10 minutes past eight the procession passed out of the condemned man's cell directly into the yard.

A few destined to die on a Canadian gallows seemed to have spent their time on death row in a fantasy world, one presumably in which they had a future. Reginald Birchall was among that number. The young, Oxford-educated British immigrant came from a well-respected and financially secure family, but he went through money quickly and was devoted more to gambling than his studies. After spending considerable time in Canada in 1888, he returned to England to plan an elaborate scheme to gain wealth.

Birchall placed advertisements in prestigious British newspapers, offering for sale nonexistent Canadian estates. In time he attracted the attention of two potential buyers, and both accompanied him to Canada. One man he killed while ostensibly showing him around a southern Ontario farm. The second was less gullible, and when he heard of the death of his travelling companion, immediately assumed Birchall was somehow involved. So did the authorities, and in late September 1890 the young Brit was tried for murder.

The con man was given just under two months to prepare for his death. Instead of being dejected, Birchall did everything except think of the great beyond. In fact, to some of those who spent time with him, he seemed to have worked himself up to a state not far removed from insane merriment. He joked about the gallows, smoked cigars left him by admirers and even sold both his story and his clothes. The latter upset his hangman considerably, who, in anticipation of the execution, agreed to sell Birchall's clothes to Madame Tussaud's Wax Museum in London, England.

Birchall took a particular interest in the construction of the scaffold on which he was to die. He could hear it being built but could not see the structure from his cell window. He asked one of his guards to draw him a picture and to explain how it worked. Birchall stared at the picture for some time, concluding, "My, but it's crude." Still, he soon convinced himself that his death would be quick and painless. "I will never know what struck me."

Birchall spent much of his last day alive cleaning his cell and readying his effects for pick up by one of the executors of his will. He should not have bothered with the cleaning. The sheriff of Woodstock, Ontario, became concerned with Birchall's cavalier attitude toward his pending execution. He moved the condemned man to another cell, out of the misguided fear that Birchall had somehow managed to hide a quantity of poison, which he would take just before the end.

COMPANY OF FRIENDS AND RELATIVES

Most prisoners on death row approached dying with considerably more solemnity than Birchall did. In their last moments, many wanted contact with someone who cared about them, someone who would give them strength in a time of great turmoil. Even hardened criminals welcomed the chance to spend time with a friend or relative.

In the early 1920s, Sidney Murrell was a member of a gang that reminded residents of Toronto and southern Ontario of American gangsters, who, like Murrell, often sped away from the scene of their crime in a hail of bullets. In April 1921, Murrell's gang robbed a bank in Melborne, Ontario, and in the process killed an innocent bystander. In the first of his two trials, the 26-year-old lucked out when a member of his jury, who firmly opposed capital punishment, refused to find the accused guilty.

Murrell's luck ran out during his second court appearance. Almost from the beginning, the judge made it clear what he thought of the accused. In commenting to the jury about a recent change in the law, which for the first time allowed an accused to testify on his own behalf, the judge said that in Murrell's case, giving evidence could not hurt his case. "This case was so black against him that nothing could make it any worse."

In his charge to the jury, the judge stressed that crimes such as the one committed by Murrell had become commonplace. He suggested that the lives and property of people were under constant threat from bandits and gunmen like the accused, who executed their felonious plans and then escaped in motorcars. A member of the jury later confessed that jurors decided Murrell's fate in about 15 minutes, then sat and smoked briefly so it would not look like they rushed to judgement.

Murrell seemed to take his sentence in stride. He shuffled out of court as fast as his leg-irons and manacled hands allowed, taking time only to toss a kiss to his friends.

The day before Murrell was executed, the sentence of one of his partners, who was also scheduled to hang, was commuted to life imprisonment. Murrell wanted to spend some time with him during his last moments. Members of the death watch must have found it a little incongruous to observe two hardened criminals spending their last visit in prayer and song.

Most last visits received by condemned prisoners were with family members, and seldom were they lacking in emotion. Stanislas Lacroix shot his wife to death on a street in Montebello, Québec, in August 1900. Most of his family forgave him and were with him at the end. When Lacroix's son showed up, Stanislas was determined to do or say something that might keep the young man from the path he had chosen. He told the boy that above all else he must get a good education and warned him to stay away from bad company and hard liquor. In fact, before the evening was over, he insisted that all his relatives pledge to abstain from drinking alcohol.

In 1929, John Ivanchuk was sentenced to hang for killing a police officer. He wanted none of the heightened emotion he knew would result from spending his last moments with family or friends. The resident of the Cochrane area of northern Ontario was already depressed about what lay ahead and refused to see three acquaintances from Kirkland Lake who travelled to the town of Haileybury in the hope of meeting with him. Instead of talking to the trio, Ivanchuk spent most of the entire afternoon pounding on the bars of his cell. The noise was so loud that it was clearly heard by people passing by the jail. As his time wound down, Ivanchuk changed his mind about spiritual counselling and asked to see a priest before he began his final walk.

The emotion of last meetings was too much for some prisoners. John Sullivan found that the family visits he received while in a death cell in 1897 for killing a female bootlegger were increasingly difficult to bear. Finally, he could no longer take all the tears and emotion and asked the Dorchester, New Brunswick, sheriff if there was any way he could be executed before his scheduled time. His final request was granted.

As Sullivan learned, some last moments seem to last forever. At least that was the way it must have seemed to famous American slavery abolitionist, John Brown, whose body "lies a-mouldering in the grave." Before he was hanged in 1859, Brown was forced to wait on the scaffold, noosed and pinioned, for more than 10 minutes while government troops paraded back and forth in front of his gallows. Finally, an official went up to him and asked if he was tired. Brown replied that he wasn't, but asked not to be kept waiting any longer than necessary.

LOOKING OUT

It's not surprising that with little to do, and a lot of time to do it, condemned prisoners spent hours looking out the barred windows of their cells. In the last moments of their lives, many hoped to catch sight of a friend or loved one. In July 1931, that was a hope denied an Orthodox Jewish businessman from Toronto.

Abraham Steinberg allegedly murdered his nephew, who was also his business partner, during a dispute over money. Despite two trials and a clemency petition signed by 40,000 people, he spent his last hours in a death cell overlooking a city street. The day before he was hanged, he waved a white towel out of the window as a form of farewell to his wife and one of his sons.

Steinberg was reluctant to allow any of his eight children to visit him in jail. He thought it would be too traumatic for them. When it became clear his death sentence was not going to be commuted, he changed his mind and asked his wife to arrange for them to visit. Because of his towel waving, a last, symbolic meeting was denied the family when jail officials blocked off the window of his cell.

Following Steinberg's execution, his body was released to relatives for burial. When the hearse carrying it arrived at the family home, thousands of friends and supporters swamped the streets, forcing the police to establish order. After prayers, during which the casket was opened, Steinberg's remains were taken to the McCaul Street Synagogue, where more prayers were said, and then a huge line of cars made its way to the Little York Cemetery, the burial place used by the Hebrew Free Burial Society.

Although no one covered the death cell window of Elizabeth Popovitch, her desire for a symbolic farewell was also frustrated.

In early December 1946, both Popovitch and her husband, George, spent their last hours in separate cells of the Welland, Ontario, jail. The couple was convicted of murdering an Italian storeowner, for whom Elizabeth once worked. He was the person she had turned to when she needed to borrow a car, and after her first husband died, the Italian gave her $1000 to pay her bills and clothe her children.

In a bit of irony, the Popovitchs were forced to sell their small home to pay their legal bills. When the new owner started renovating the house, he discovered the murder victim's 18-karat gold watch and a rope and flashlight used in the robbery. Finding those items sealed the couple's fate.

Elizabeth Popovitch's death cell faced the main street of Welland, and in her final moments, the mother seldom left the window, wanting one last look at the only daughter to visit her. Sadly, just hours before she was hanged, a son of Elizabeth was denied a chance to visit his mother. Jail rules said all visits must be over by 10:00 PM, and he could not get to the prison on time. His bus was late.

Nearing the End

It's hard to imagine the anguish felt by prisoners who knew precisely when they were to die. The anxiety of waiting affected them in different ways. Austin Humphrey shot to death his former employer over a work-related dispute. Even before his 1877 trial in Windsor, Ontario, started, he ran as fast as he could toward a prison wall and threw himself at it head first. He survived, and weeks later found himself in a death cell.

Minutes before he was taken from his cell to the gallows, Humphrey and his spiritual advisers knelt in his cell and prayed. During the prayer, he seemed overcome and began to pound on a bench with his right hand, and after a while, with his left. Then he started to shake his head and murmur. Finally, he broke down and wept. Seconds later, his executioner arrived. After that it was over quickly.

Frequently, condemned prisoners spent their last moments in tears. From the time he was convicted of strangling his mother in Québec City, Eugène Bigaouette showed few signs of emotion. Even as his time drew near, he seemed unaffected by thoughts of what was to come. On August 19, 1927, all that changed. When told that it was time to go, the 42-year-old cried like a baby.

Many Canadian jail chaplains witnessed emotional breakdowns like that of Bigaouette, and there was seldom anything they could do to make things better. Reverend Father Jean Paul Regimbal was for many years chaplain at Montréal's infamous Bordeaux Jail. During that time, he ministered to the spiritual needs of 30 murderers who were sentenced to hang. Time after time, their execution was postponed in a process the priest referred to as social sadism. He became so upset at the torture these last-minute reprieves caused prisoners on death row that he spoke up. In doing so, Father Regimbal violated the regulation that required chaplains in federal and most provincial institutions to submit a written request before they could say anything about an execution. Because he did not, in 1965, he was fired. His description of how condemned men were treated, however, was a factor in ending the practice of sentencing prisoners to death and then commuting their sentences at the last moment.

Father Regimbal said what prisoners went through was unbelievable. On the day before the scheduled execution, a contraption was set up in front of the prisoner's cell, consisting of a trapdoor and a bag of sand suspended by a rope from a girder. As everyone watched, including the prisoner and the official hangman, the bag was dropped five or six times through the trapdoor. The bag was exactly the weight of the person to be hanged. Supposedly, the rehearsal was to ensure that the rope wouldn't break.

According to Bordeaux Jail regulations, the last visit a condemned prisoner was allowed took place at 3:00 PM. Three hours later, a warden read the official order of condemnation to the prisoner. Supper was then served, and the jail chaplain was admitted to the death cell at 8:00 PM and could remain with the prisoner for three hours. Regimbal said that by 11:00 PM, most prisoners were completely traumatized and full of anger.

The former jail chaplain noted that every time a reprieve was granted, it arrived less than an hour before the scheduled execution. One convict went through this process 10 times before his sentence was finally commuted.

DINING BEFORE DEATH

Serving the last meal has been a death ritual in Canada since 1867. The tradition is rooted in the belief that because meals are a social act, accepting food from jail officials was an acknowledgement that a prisoner held no grudges for what was soon to happen. It is for the same reason that many executioners sought to shake the hands of those they were about to execute.

For occupants of death row, a last meal was deeply symbolic in another way. It reminded them of much happier times. If they ordered anything special, it was almost always similar to what they had eaten in their youth, though in a much different place. Prison officials encouraged the consumption of such meals. The time spent thinking of the past calmed nerves and directed a prisoner's mind away from thoughts of impending death.

If one excludes the day in early November 1949 that he sexually assaulted and murdered a Vancouver woman, Frederick Ducharme's end started the day before he was executed. A cook from the Oakalla prison farm went to several food shops to select the fare Ducharme requested for his last meal. The 37-year-old mill worker dined on breast of turkey, cauliflower, French fried potatoes, cucumber, tomatoes, celeries stuffed with cheese, fruit salad, vanilla ice cream, bread and butter, and tea. He topped that off with two ounces of Hennessy's Three Star Cognac.

Ducharme entered the Oakalla death chamber shortly after 6:00 AM. He walked unaided through eight uniformed guards stationed across the front and along both sides of the trap, facing outward. The only sound that could be heard was the Latin chanted by the priest. From the moment he walked into the room, Ducharme stared with unblinking eyes at the wall in front of him. Then he was gone.

Ducharme ate well the last day of his life, and for many on death row, eating was all they had to live for. Prisoners often ate so well during their confinement, and exercised so little, that they would put on considerable weight. That was certainly the case with Henry Malanik, Daniel Prokiw and Tomassina (Sarao) Teolis.

Although most of those who gained weight while waiting to be hanged were executed without mishap, that did not happen with Malanik. The Winnipeg plumber killed a city detective during a domestic disturbance in July 1950. The judge who presided over his first trial was not convinced jurors reached the correct verdict when they found Malanik guilty, and he made that clear in a letter he sent to the federal department of justice:

> I must say that had I been sitting as a judge without a jury in a similar case, I would have had a doubt as to whether or not the accused was capable of knowing what he was doing, or of knowing right from wrong. In my opinion, the accused was very drunk. I concluded that he went "berserk" at 19 Argyle Street, otherwise I cannot understand why he would shoot at everyone who came in sight.

The Manitoba Court of Appeal agreed with the trial judge and quashed Malanik's conviction.

On May 28, 1951, the former plumber's luck ran out. The chief justice of the province's Court of Queen's Bench presided over Malanik's second trial. No one charged with murder escaped Headingley's death chamber if they appeared in front of him.

Malanik spent almost two years in jail between the day of his arrest and his execution. During that time, his weight ballooned to more than 100 kilograms, making it difficult for his hangman to estimate the appropriate length of drop. Whatever calculation he made, it turned out to be wrong.

When the man dressed in a black beret and brightly flowered Hawaiian shirt pulled the lever, Malanik dropped like a rock. A very heavy rock. The force of his descent severed his jugular vein and nearly ripped off his head.

If Malanik nearly lost his head because he ate so much, Daniel Prockiw and Tomassina Teolis had theirs removed completely. Like Malanik, Prockiw was a plumber, and during his five-month imprisonment for brutally murdering his common-law wife, he did little but eat. On the day of his execution in late August 1926, no one realized that even though his body had grown substantially larger, his neck muscles remained as weak as ever. When Prockiw dropped through the floor of an outdoor Winnipeg gallows, his body landed some distance from his head.

Montréaler Tomassina Teolis, convicted with her lover and another man of murdering her husband in 1934, also gained a lot of weight on death row. Executioners usually obtained a condemned prisoner's personal data from jail officials, then unobtrusively observed the victim to ensure the calculations seemed right. In the case of Teolis, the executioner underestimated her weight by approximately 18 kilograms, and he had been denied even a glance at the woman. The result was almost predictable. Like Prokiw nine years earlier, Tomassina lost her head.

But prisoners on death row who ate with gusto during their last moments were not representative of the vast majority of those sentenced to hang. Most, like Marion "Peg-leg" Brown, ate sparingly. Brown's meal consisted of three scrambled eggs, three pieces of bread and butter and about a quart of cocoa. He took a couple of bites of his meal, drank the cocoa and then was done.

Brown may have eaten little, but he lived large. Losing a leg early in life did little to dampen his enthusiasm for adventure and crime. When he arrived in southern Ontario in 1898, he was already a veteran of the American prison system. Shortly after he turned up in the London yard of the Grand Trunk Railway, he became involved in a confrontation with a railway watchman and then with a police officer. He shot the constable in the chest, but the bullet hit the man's watch, leaving him alive but stunned. Brown walked over, shot the defenceless officer between the eyes and promptly returned to the United States. He was eventually arrested in the state of Washington and held pending an extradition hearing.

In the late 19th century, the process of extraditing a prisoner to Canada from the States was long and cumbersome, and someone decided that the best way to deal with Brown was to drug him with morphine and ship him straight to Vancouver.

From there it was a train ride to London and a May 1899 date with a hangman.

DRESSED TO KILL

Many killers dressed themselves meticulously, only to die minutes later. The quality of their clothes perhaps explains why, until the 1890s, executioners usually took advantage of their right to the clothes worn by a victim on the day of the execution. That tradition quickly became part of the culture of capital punishment, though we have no clothing stories quite as dramatic as that involving Hannah Dagoe, an Irish woman who was executed at Tyburn, England, in 1763 for breaking into the home of an acquaintance and stealing everything in it.

Hannah was incredibly strong, and when she arrived at the place of her execution, she began struggling with her hangman, shouting that while he might take her life, he would not take her clothes. She then ripped off all she was wearing and tossed the garments into the crowd of spectators. Now naked and noosed, the woman took matters into her own hands. She threw herself off the cart in which she was being transported with such force that she broke her neck, avoiding a slow and agonizing death by strangulation.

In the late 19th century, William Marwood, one of England's best-known executioners, noted that hanging people for a living wasn't profitable, but by claiming and selling the clothing and personal effects of those he dispatched, he could earn a tidy income.

Canada's first official executioner made no apologies for following in the tradition of Marwood, with whom John Radclive claimed to have apprenticed. Although entitled to all of the belongings of Simon Czubej and Wasyl Guszczak, executed in 1899 for killing a family of homesteaders south of Winnipeg, Radclive claimed only Czubej's coat. He said he was sending it to a friend, whose hobby was collecting gruesome relics.

The care with which some condemned prisoners dressed themselves on the day of their execution often hid what the killer truly was feeling. Reginald Birchall was always a bit of a dandy, so no one was surprised when he left his cell in Woodstock, Ontario, dressed as if he was on the way to a fancy party. He was wearing a dark suit, white shirt with cuffs and collar, a black corded tie, white gloves and silk socks. When the procession to the gallows began, Birchall placed himself first in line. He looked as fresh as if he had slept all night and eaten a hearty breakfast. In fact, the 24-year-old con artist hadn't slept a wink, nor had he eaten.

George and Elizabeth Popovitch were hanged in Welland, Ontario, and in the days preceding the couple's early December 1946 execution, both killers had let themselves go to seed. For weeks George did not shave, but on his big day, he decided to look his best and asked for the assistance of a barber. "I don't want to look too bad for this," he said. His wife also wanted to look good, and a local hairdresser curled her short, black hair.

Jail officials allowed the pair a brief meeting shortly before guards came for George. The two embraced and kissed. Forty-five minutes later, the man was dead, and it was time for the woman. As she was standing where her husband so recently stood, Elizabeth shouted to spectators, "Goodbye everybody. God bless you all." Then she, too, was gone.

In a sad bit of irony, the minister who accompanied the Popovitchs to the gallows was the same person who not much earlier had married them. Outside the jail, a car containing two of Elizabeth's daughters by her first husband cruised around even as their mother dropped to her death.

Many prisoners took particular care to dress for their execution, bur few were as determined to die well dressed as Peter Wheeler. In 1896, he tried to sexually assault a neighbour girl, and when she repulsed his advances, he killed her. In antici-pation of his execution in Digby, Nova Scotia, the Salvation Army provided him with a new pair of pants and a white shirt, and a local merchant sent him a brand-new pair of patent leather shoes. Although Wheeler no doubt appreciated the clothes, he was absolutely fascinated by the shiny dress shoes, the likes of which he had never worn.

Shortly before his date with destiny, the shackles welded around his ankles were removed, and Wheeler was allowed to dress himself in his new outfit. He sent word to the sheriff that he wanted to borrow a mirror, so he could see firsthand how he looked. Standing it against the wall of his cell, he dressed as carefully as a bridegroom, turning from side to side and assuming a variety of positions. Satisfied, he turned his attention to his hair, ending his toilette only when he received the approval of his death watch.

Later, during his execution, his left leg kicked out convulsively, and one of the shoes with which he had become so enamoured was thrown from his foot. When his body was returned to his cell for a coroner's inquest, someone noticed that a shoe was missing. A deputy sheriff retrieved it from the scaffold, and it was re-attached to Wheeler's foot. His body was then carried to the death chamber, where an exterior door was opened to allow a public viewing.

Not satisfied to see the well-dressed killer from afar, hundreds of spectators soon made their way into the chamber, where they had a chance to look directly at the surprisingly peaceful visage of a man who only minutes earlier was preening over his shoes. But the story of Peter Wheeler does not end with his burial in the jail yard.

A year after his execution and interment, a deputy sheriff, the same man who retrieved Wheeler's missing shoe, noticed that the earth around Wheeler's grave was disturbed. On closer inspection, he found that not only had it been tampered with, but the coffin was also exposed and its lid opened. When word got around that Wheeler had returned, crowds flocked to the jail to see what the killer looked like in death. And he did not disappoint. Conscious of his appearance in life, Wheeler seemed equally concerned about it in death. His corpse was, in the opinion of most of those who stood over his grave, almost as fresh as the day he was hanged.

The saga of Peter Wheeler's body does not end with his second interment. During construction of a new courthouse in 1909, officials dug up Wheeler for a second time. It was immediately obvious his body was no longer as it once was. Now reduced to nothing but bones, the only evidence remaining of the man who was once a dandy was his patent leather shoes. The footwear, however, did not accompany the bones that were shipped off to Acadia University, where for a fourth time, the body of Peter Wheeler was on display.

Prisoners like Wheeler, who died in new clothes, were the exception rather than the rule. Although prisoners about to be executed could wear whatever they wanted to the gallows, most died in either the clothes they wore at trial or the clothes they wore in jail. When Timothy Candy was hanged in Montréal in 1910, for example, the cop killer was dressed in the same light, checked flannel suit he wore during his trial.

Thomas Collins, on the other hand, had no suit. Instead, the man who in 1906 killed a fellow worker wore to the gallows the clothing he had on when arrested in New Ireland, New Brunswick—a blue serge jacket and a white shirt.

Frederick Ducharme died in his Oakalla, British Columbia, prison clothes—a faded blue-grey work shirt, blue denim pants and worn felt slippers. Both Harry Medos, who killed two Vancouver police officers in 1947, and Davis Houston, the rapist-murderer with whom he was hanged, were executed in standard prison attire. Robert Hoodley and Gerald Eaton, also hanged at the Oakalla prison farm in 1955 and in 1957, respectively, similarly died in their prison uniforms.

SOMETHING TO SMOOTH OUT THE JOURNEY

Keen students of capital punishment are among a select group who know that most of the women and men executed on a gallows in Canada went to their death drugged or drunk. Prison officials in England, the United States and other countries that executed killers historically allowed those sentenced to death access to stimulants before they began their last trip, and for good reason. There was nothing more awkward than trying to subdue someone on the way to the scaffold.

In 1949, for example, a slightly built California inmate was strapped into the gas chamber at San Quentin prison. He slipped out of the chair's arm straps as the poison gas began to circulate, then jumped up and began running around the chamber. As he ran, he screamed and pounded on the glass windows separating him from witnesses. It took three tries before the excitable little man was executed.

A Florida legislator described the problem prison officials have with prisoners like the California inmate. He said those sentenced to death in his state are almost always sedated before being executed, but in the case of drug abusers, alcoholics and people easily excited, the sedation quickly wears off, leaving the prisoners conscious enough to realize they are being suffocated to death.

In September 1910, Edward Jardine raped, murdered and mutilated the body of a teenage girl attending the annual fall fair in Goderich, Ontario. Nine months later, he was hanged. Thirty minutes before he began his last walk, he broke down. Worried officials wanted to avoid a scaffold scene at all costs, and within seconds the killer received an injection of morphine. It worked wonders. Several people who watched him hang commented that he died without showing the slightest sign of emotion.

Everett Farmer was hanged in Shelburne, Nova Scotia, for the 1937 murder of his half-brother during a drunken argument. When he ascended the gallows, he was the calmest member of his death procession. Later it was reported that he was the only one in the group drugged.

Thomas Laplante was executed in January 1958 for beating a man to death on a deserted road near Niagara Falls, Ontario. He walked to the Welland execution chamber without help, greeting spectators with a genial "Hi, boys" and grinning at his hangman until the black hood was pulled over his face. In the opinion of one witness, "He couldn't have been more co-operative if he was committing suicide." A substantial part of his willingness was the result of the tranquilizer administered while he waited for the day's events to unfold.

Just as Canadian jail officials did not hesitate to use sedatives to smooth out the last journey of convicted killers, they were equally willing to help things along with a drink or two. For prisoners, that is.

In April 1924, Clarence Topping, who murdered his girlfriend, and Sidney Murrell, who killed a bystander during a robbery, were hanged together on a London, Ontario, gallows. Each nearly collapsed prior to his execution. Before pinioning the arms of the men, their hangman made a visit to the office of the jail governor. When the hangman re-appeared, he carried two tumblers, each partially filled with liquor. Less than an hour later, the two were standing on the scaffold, calm and emotionless, Topping with a smile on his face.

British Columbia killers Walter Worobec and William Prestyko, who killed a Vancouver couple during a home invasion, were given the option of sedatives, whiskey or both when they were hanged in 1950. They each chose scotch, declining a sedative.

Another pair of killers also seemed to have benefitted from a drink or two before being hanged. Prior to their 1888 execution in Regina for killing the owner of a horse they stole, Moses Racette and James Gaddy ate a good breakfast and drank two or three glasses of wine. On the scaffold, they were the picture of stoicism, though Racette made it clear he did not feel he belonged there. Asked by his hangman if he had anything to say, Racette said he did:

> *I did no murder. I do not think I deserve to have a rope put around my neck. I don't think I got a fair show at the trial. I am not sorry because I have to die, but I had no chance at the trial to explain. It was not my fault because McLeish was killed. I hope God will forgive those who sentenced me to death.*

Gaddy stood beside his partner, patient and penitent. When asked if he wanted to say anything, he replied in a single sentence, "All I want to say is that Racette did all the advising, and I did all the shooting."

VISIBLE EFFECT OF DRUGS OR ALCOHOL

When jail officials refused to disclose whether an executed prisoner had been given drugs or alcohol before the hanging, it was left to reporters to speculate. Typical of suggestive reporting were comments about the gallows conduct of killer Peter Davis, who in 1890 murdered his lover's husband. As he stood on a Belleville, Ontario, gallows, he seemed not to realize the awfulness of the situation. According to news reports, he was as calm as a statue and wore a look of peacefulness that stood in sharp contrast to the blanched faces of those witnessing his execution.

By the time he reached the gallows, Eugène Bigaouette was similarly unaffected by the prospect of hanging. The man who strangled his mother in November 1925 stood on the scaffold with his eyes fixed on the grey walls of the prison in what reporters said was a daze. When his confessor presented the crucifix to him, he kissed it without knowing what he was doing.

Wesley Campbell, who in 1931 brutally beat his father to death, met his end in a similar fashion. According to witnesses, he stood on the scaffold as if in a trance, his face masklike. When a group of rowdies broke into the death chamber of the jail in Barrie, Ontario, he was the only person in the room who seemed not to notice.

Twenty-one-year-old Robert Hoodley looked similarly out of touch with reality when he walked into a British Columbia death chamber in May 1955. Six months earlier, the young logger shot his girlfriend's father, and by the time he started his walk to the gallows, he seemed to have neither the will to live nor a sense of what was to come. He was not given the chance to find out. Less than a minute after he stepped onto the scaffold, his body was spinning slowly at the end of a rope.

REFUSAL TO TAKE DRUGS OR ALCOHOL

Although most condemned prisoners welcomed the offer of drugs or alcohol, not everyone chose the escape aids. Lawrence (Corky) Vincent, a carnival worker who strangled a preteen Quesnel, British Columbia, girl with a shoelace in September 1953, was determined to die before he could be hanged. Vincent attempted suicide the night before his execution, using some contraband poison he'd managed to sneak into his cell.

The McArthur headstone erected in a cemetery near the Welwyn, Saskatchewan, residence where John Morrison slaughtered eight members of the family in June 1900.

●◆●

In an ironic twist, the warden of the Oakalla prison farm, an outspoken opponent of capital punishment, spent hours with Vincent as doctors pumped the convict's stomach in an attempt to keep him alive so that later the same day, the State could kill him. When he was returned to his cell and made ready for his trip to the gallows, Vincent was asked if he wanted a sedative to ease his journey. He refused the offer. Apparently, he'd had enough drugs.

William Petrekowich shot and killed his former common-law wife because, as he told the authorities later, he loved her so much. In January 1939, he shot her in the head with a .22-calibre rifle and then put two bullets in his own chest. He survived, and nine months later stood on the scaffold of the Don Jail. He walked to the gallows with a smile on his face, determined to die fully conscious. Asked if he wanted a narcotic injection, he refused, saying, "I can take it, thanks."

Before he stepped out into the cold of a typical December day in Regina, John Morrison was not coping as well as jail officials hoped, and a stimulant was prepared for him. The man, who in June 1900 killed eight members of the McArthur family in their Welwyn area home, refused it.

Four years later, another man went to his death spurning drugs or alcohol. In fact, William Robinson was offended that he was even offered help dying when he ascended a Kentville, Nova Scotia, gallows to pay the price for murdering his wife.

Robinson ate a hearty breakfast the day before his execution, laughing and chatting with his death watch. "This is my last Sunday morning on earth," he observed, "and what a glorious day it is." Guards were concerned about the 70-year-old prisoner's inclination to become excited, and they suggested he have a drink. Robinson would have none of it.

> *You don't mean liquor. I detest it and would not poison my lips with it. Had I the opportunity of drinking the liquor that would on Monday morning cheat the gallows of its victim, I would refrain from taking it. I would not take any poisonous pills or liquid. God is my comfort and He will support me at the last moment as He is doing now while I am within the shadow of death.*

DEAD MEN WALKING

The walk of those sentenced to death when executions took place in the yards of Canadian jails was dramatically different than when hangings were carried out inside provincial death chambers. In the waning years of Canada's experiment with capital punishment, prisoners were housed just a few metres from where they would be hanged. The walk from cell to gallows lasted seconds, and rarely did it take a hangman more than a minute to execute someone. Until about the 1930s, the death procession was a formal, and dramatic, part of the execution process.

In May 1910, Timothy Candy killed two Montréal police officers when they tried to arrest him for selling stolen property. Six months later, he was led to a gallows in the yard of the city's jail. Just after 7:00 AM, the local sheriff pulled up in a taxi and entered the home of the prison governor. Minutes later, another cab arrived with two of his officers, each carrying a mace. Last to be admitted to the jail was a contingent of 100 city police officers and about 40 witnesses, a third of whom were reporters. The spectators gathered in front of the red-painted wooden gallows, many staring at the rope dangling from the structure's crossbeam or the trapdoor, plainly visible behind an iron railing.

Shortly before 8:00 AM, 20 prison guards under the command of a sergeant, each armed with a rifle, took their places on either side of the route that members of the death procession would walk from Candy's cell to the scaffold. As soon as the guards were in place, the jail doors opened and a sheriff's officer bearing one of the maces emerged. He was immediately followed by the sheriff, wearing his robe of office and cocked hat, who was in turn followed by Candy and his spiritual adviser. Bringing up the rear were the jail governor and the executioner.

Ontario sheriffs adopted a similar formality. In December 1893, Charles Luckey was hanged for murdering his sister, father and stepmother and burning their bodies in a failed attempt to escape detection. Slightly more than a year later, he was escorted to a gallows erected in the women's section of the Brockville jail. The yard was small and narrow, just 15 metres long and 7.5 metres wide, and looked even smaller because of the massive stone walls surrounding it. The scaffold took up almost the entire eastern end of the enclosure.

Just before 8:00 AM, witnesses heard the tramp of feet coming from the main corridor of the jail, and a few moments later, the city's deputy sheriff stepped into the freezing cold. Next came the jail physician, Luckey's spiritual adviser, the executioner, a guard and the man about to hang. Luckey's arms were bound to his sides, his face ghastly pale, but he walked with a firm step, slowing occasionally to glance curiously at the 50 spectators waiting to watch him die.

The death procession in which Chong Sam Bow found himself in early January 1925 ended with much more drama than those of Candy and Luckey. The day before the killer was hanged at British Columbia's Oakalla prison farm for shooting a Vancouver man, he was moved from the main jail to a cell nearer the scaffold. The following morning, his arms were bound and he was led down a short corridor to the gallows. As soon as the door to the death chamber opened, Chong Bow saw the rope that in seconds was to encircle his neck. He immediately began shouting, "The Book! The Book!" presumably referring to the Bible.

The small procession continued on, and the condemned man was guided to the trap. There he began moaning in Chinese, and his knees sagged. Realizing that the killer was about to collapse, his executioner quickly drew a hood over the man's head, adjusted the noose and released the trap. Chong Sam Bow was still crying when he dropped from view.

Some killers were so determined to end the anguish of waiting that they literally tried to run to their death. In 1901, Joseph Laplaine murdered the woman who operated the Montréal boarding house where he resided. When he went to the gallows at the year's end, more than 200 people showed up to witness his execution. What they saw as they entered the jail compound was a crude-looking instrument of death, and a deep pit, into which the body of the prisoner was to fall.

Three minutes before Laplaine was scheduled to hang, spectators heard a door opening. Instantly, a hush fell over the crowd. They were startled to see Laplaine almost bolt from the jailhouse. He trotted the 45 metres between prison and gallows, the pitter-patter of his feet clearly audible as he crossed the frozen ground. As soon as he reached the foot of the scaffold, he started up at a near run. His two priests could not keep up, and for a time, those present thought they were witnessing a foot race between a man with his arms tied to his sides and two pursuers dressed in flowing robes.

Laplaine at least made it to the gallows on his own. That could not be said for others executed on a Canadian scaffold, including Montréaler Tomasso Bernardi. In April 1913, the Italian immigrant was competing with another Italian for the affections of the same woman. When Bernardi saw the two walking along a city street, he pulled out a revolver and shot them both, killing his rival and wounding the woman he said he loved. A year later, the killer was again overcome with emotion, and guards had to carry him to the scaffold.

On August 28, 1926, Thomas McCoskey killed a Kingston Penitentiary prison guard during a failed escape attempt. He became distraught as soon as he got within eyesight of the gallows, and he would have collapsed had not two guards helped him onto the trap. From that point on, everything happened so quickly he did not have time to become more anxious. Thirteen seconds after he left his cell, the bolt was pulled; 14 minutes later his body was cut down, and 10 minutes after that the burial service ended, and McCoskey was interred.

BELLS

According to federal regulations governing executions, a bell had to be tolled 15 minutes before and 15 minutes after an execution. Often the tolling was the first indication that someone sentenced to death was about to die.

When Maurice Lebel, a Québec trucker, was hanged in 1949 for the murder of a bank manager and a taxi driver, an air of secrecy surrounded his execution. Jail officials in Montréal refused to release any information about the execution, and news became public only after Bordeaux residents asked why the prison bell tolled six times. The authorities were forced to admit that Lebel was dead.

Many sheriffs, particularly those in rural areas of the country, found that ringing the bells was an unnecessary reminder to local residents that someone was about die, especially if an execution was to take place during a season usually reserved for thoughts of peace and good will.

In 1903, when Sion Azuhally was executed in Windsor, Nova Scotia, for killing a fellow Syrian peddler, federal officials notified the city's sheriff that the bell of his jail was to toll following the execution. The sheriff refused to carry out the instructions.

A similar refusal occurred in 1942, when Thomas Hutchings was executed for raping and murdering a Blacks Harbour, New Brunswick, woman shortly before Christmas. In a letter to the department of justice, the sheriff of St. Andrews acknowledged that according to procedure, the bell of either the prison or the parish church was to toll before and after the execution. The problem, he wrote, was that in communities as small as his, no one wanted to be reminded of what was about to happen. The response from Ottawa was swift: close application of the rules did not always have to be followed, and for the execution taking place on December 16, the tolling of the bell could be dispensed with.

BLACK FLAGS

Just as a tolling prison bell was often the first sign that an execution was being carried out, a black flag was another visible indication that the hanging was over. As long as Canada executed murderers, it was a tradition that a black emblem be raised to signal their deaths. It was up to local sheriffs, however, to ensure that the custom was followed, but many refused to do so. When Thomas Kane was hanged in 1890 for murdering his common-law wife, the sheriff of the Toronto jail insisted that nothing be done to signal the killer's passing. Local newspapers applauded his decision.

The *Toronto News* noted that Kane's execution was carried out smoothly and "was marked by an entire absence of the gloomy ceremonies that usually accompany executions. No black flags floated over the great stone building. No bells tolled mournfully, and no yawning grave or black box disturbed the last minutes of the doomed man."

Even when the flag was flown, officials often got the procedure wrong. After Walter Gordon was hanged in Brandon, Manitoba, in 1902 for murdering two area farmers, his body was left suspended for a time. While waiting to cut down the dead killer, his hangman walked around the jail compound. He noticed that the black flag flying above the jail was at half-mast and immediately grew indignant. Looking for an official, he shouted, "What the devil is that flag flying at half-mast for? This is no time for mourning." He then rushed into the jail to find the caretaker. When the emblem of death eventually rose to the top of the flagstaff, the executioner's face assumed a look of obvious satisfaction.

Chapter Five

Last Words

~

The last words of a person about to die seem always to interest us, perhaps because they represent a stage in our existence where we will all arrive. We pay attention to the process of dying in no small measure because we are searching for a glimpse of what lies ahead, a place about which those setting out on their final journey are curious. Because the trip is not one we can repeat, words spoken by people leaving one realm for another are usually carefully chosen. They have the sort of permanence at one time associated with death masks.

Mark Twain suggested we should be as concerned about our departing words as we are about our last breath. It's best not to leave their preparation to the last moment, he cautioned, lest we are overwhelmed by the occasion and are unable to die with a witticism or comment of such intellectual depth it both defines our existence and becomes a memorial to the person we were. The worry is that with so much on our minds, we will be unable to leave with just the right comment, and whatever we say cannot be taken back.

Most of us pay attention to last words because of their curiosity value. We want to know how the famous, or infamous, chose to be remembered. The problem for some is that, like Twain warned, nothing comes to mind. After Pancho Villa was assassinated in 1923, a journalist noted his last moments. With posterity looming, the Mexican revolutionary could think of nothing to say. "Don't let it end like this," he implored the writer. "Tell them I said something." A former queen of Romania was also not up to the moment. "You are supposed to say beautiful things," she gasped, "but I can't." Then she died.

Some people say just the right thing before dying. Historians still remember the words of wife-murderer William Borwick, even if they have long forgotten the Englishman. Standing on the scaffold, he looked at the rope that shortly would be placed around his neck. "I hope it is strong enough," he said, "because if it breaks I'll fall to the ground and be crippled for life." The last words of another British killer were in a similar vein. After being placed on the trapdoor of his gallows, the man tapped the trap with his foot then turned to the hangman and said, "Are you sure it's safe?"

Occasionally, killers are remembered for last words that seem almost *too* appropriate. When George Appel died in New York's electric chair in 1928, for example, he said to those around him, "Well, gentlemen, you are about to see a baked Appel." Equally fitting were the closing comments of James French, electrocuted by the state of Oklahoma. "I can see the headline of tomorrow's papers," he said, "French Fries."

The last words of Canadians sentenced to death rarely have been as amusing as those of British and American killers. Very often they are more reflective, occasionally even culturally appropriate. The comments made by Frank Sylvestre, a Shuswap Native executed in British Columbia in 1941 are an example. Before he was hanged for murdering a former member of the provincial legislature, Sylvestre's last thoughts were of his horse: "My horse was the last friend I had. Look after my horse and destroy him as soon as possible. They won't look after him the way I did."

Last words were always an important part of the execution process. Just as we want to know how a killer died, we are curious about what the person said. Scaffold speeches were once a distinctive genre of literature, and long after executions were moved out of the public eye, whatever was said on the gallows was carefully recorded. As a consequence, last words became formulaic. Prison officials and jail chaplains tried to make the killers feel obligated to take responsibility for what they did and to show an appropriate amount of remorse.

Prisoners on death row were also encouraged to exhort others not to follow in their footsteps and to acknowledge that with their deaths justice was served. Above all, it was important that they appeal to God for forgiveness. Part of the reason killers were given a few months to prepare themselves to die was to allow jail chaplains sufficient time to ensure departing speeches made evident their change of heart.

Only through a public act of contrition could those on death row affirm the religious and legal norms of society, thereby helping the public overlook the horror of state-sponsored murder.

Doubts About Authenticity of Last Words

Perhaps it is precisely because we so badly want to remember last words that there is often doubt about their authenticity. It is quite likely that we are overcome by the emotion of the event and remember only what was most appealing, rather than what was actually said.

Many famous people died with several different death-bed speeches attributed to them, leaving us unsure of what words were actually spoken last. As Oscar Wilde lay dying in a dingy Paris hotel, he is reported to have turned and said, referring to the room's awful wallpaper, "One of us has to go." It no longer matters if those were indeed his last words. If they were not, they should have been. What we want is not truth, but legend.

When English prime minister William Pitt the Younger died early in the 19th century, his dying words were recorded as, "Oh, my country, how I leave my country." What many remember him actually saying was, "I think I could eat one of Bellamy's pork pies."

One reason we cannot be certain of the authenticity of last words is because often newspaper reporters recorded them.

For example, in the hours before Nicholas Melady was executed for the 1868 murder of his father and stepmother, he was visited by members of his family, guards, court officials, clergy and reporters. People were allowed to ask him whatever they wanted. The stories that resulted from these visits were detailed but not factually similar. The *London Free Press* told its readers that Nicholas slept soundly the night before he was hanged. The *Stratford Herald* reported he had little or no sleep.

There is also doubt about what was really said when in 1926, rumrunners Owen Baker and Harry Sowash were executed. The men murdered the father-and-son crew of a small freighter working off the coast of British Columbia. Sowash was reported to have turned to his executioner and said, "Step on 'er kid." According to another reporter present at the hanging, what Sowash actually said was simply, "Goodbye, Cannonball," referring to Baker by his nickname.

PROCEDURE FOR LAST WORDS

Although condemned prisoners were usually given the opportunity to say a few last words, not all were spoken on the gallows. News reports of Canadian executions, sometimes graphic in their description of what happened after a prisoner reached the scaffold, often made no mention of the killer being offered a chance to speak. Because prison officials wanted executions carried out as quickly as possible, they felt that giving panic-stricken or drugged convicts a chance to talk needlessly prolonged the execution process.

Executioners usually knew in advance when a prisoner wanted to say something. As a result, some prisoners were not even asked if they had any last words. By the time Fred Rice ascended a Toronto gallows for killing a city constable during a 1901 prison escape, he'd pretty much said all he had to say. As he waited on the scaffold, his hangman went about things in total silence. The usual query about parting comments was unasked.

If a killer had nothing to say, an execution was over pretty quickly. When Wilfrid Bonnin, who killed a teller during a bank robbery in 1926, reached a Winnipeg gallows, it took his hangman just 11 seconds to place him on the trap, pinion his legs, pull a hood over his face, put the noose around his neck and pull the lever.

Occasionally, prison officials worried that a prisoner would make a scene if allowed to speak. To avoid that, an executioner might be told to proceed without permitting any last words. When a Halifax, Nova Scotia, court sentenced William Robinson for the 1904 murder and mutilation of his wife, he jumped up and exhorted everyone to come to his necktie party. Robinson made quite a scene, not one the authorities wanted repeated. When summoned from his cell for the last time, Robinson was told in no uncertain terms that if he had anything to say, he would have to say it before he reached the gallows.

Even if a prisoner made it clear he wanted to speak, the privilege was often denied outright, or if allowed, only a short time was given.

Carlo Battista was executed in Montréal in late December 1912. As he stood waiting to fall, the member of the Black Hand Society, precursor to our modern Mafia, said he had something to say. He never got the chance. As soon as his mouth opened, his hangman yanked a black hood over his face, and without a moment's hesitation, pulled the lever. Officials later told reporters they were warned about the contents of the Italian immigrant's last speech, and to prevent any kind of disruption, decided to hang him before he could start talking.

John Morrison, on the other hand, was allowed to speak, but only for a moment. In 1900, Morrison worked and lived with the McArthur family near Welwyn, Saskatchewan. Depressed by his circumstances, the farmhand decided to commit suicide, and to take the nine McArthurs with him. By the time his murder spree ended, the only survivor, besides Morrison, was the family's 15-year-old daughter. She woke up when the killer lifted her younger brother from their bed, killed him, then climbed in himself. Her pleas for mercy had an effect. Morrison got up, left the house and in a nearby barn shot himself. His death, however, did not come until almost seven months later on a Regina gallows.

Morrison was standing on the trapdoor already pinioned and noosed when he told his hangman that he wanted to say something. The obviously impatient executioner stopped drawing the hood over Morrison's face. "Then look quick about it," he said, turning the mass murderer to face the sheriff.

I would like to say something for the good of the world. I have lived a sinful life. It is foolish to do this and I hope my life will be a warning to others. Although I have been very wicked, yet I know God of His great mercy will forgive the greatest of sins and the deepest of crimes. Life at best is very short and I hope that what I have done will be a warning to others to live that short life in a different way to what I have done. Life, I say, is short and the sword is always hanging over us, and we do not know how soon it will drop. It is not worthwhile to be sinful then. That is all I have to say. Goodbye, and God bless you all.

With that, the trap was sprung, and the perpetrator of the second largest mass murder in Saskatchewan history (Victor Ernest Hoffman killed nine members of James Peterson's family in 1967) dropped to his death.

Some prisoners spent so much time preparing their final speeches, they could hardly wait to deliver them. George O'Brien was that kind of person. He arrived in the Yukon with the intention of becoming wealthy by stealing other people's money. For a while it worked. He camped along a desolate stretch of the Yukon River and spent days watching through a telescope for travellers. On Christmas Day 1899, he saw three victims approach his hideout. Although he only wanted to rob the men, he had little compunction in killing them when they refused to give up their possessions voluntarily.

O'Brien went to trial shortly after the bodies of the missing men were discovered. While waiting to be hanged, he insisted he was not guilty, and he did so using an impressive command of profanity.

When the convicted killer stepped out of his cell for the formal reading of his death warrant, quite a crowd surrounded the sheriff. As O'Brien stood to have his arms bound, he was holding several sheets of paper containing his prepared statement. He started to read it but was immediately stopped by the sheriff. The place to make a last statement was on the scaffold, he said, not in a jail corridor. "This is your warrant of execution, which I am to read to you," explained the sheriff.

"Well, I don't want to hear it," replied O'Brien.

"Then consider it read," said the sheriff, and with that, the procession headed for the gallows. On the way, O'Brien again started to curse all and sundry, until the fed-up sheriff told him enough was enough and to shut up.

After O'Brien's execution, officials released to reporters a copy of the statement he wanted to make outside his cell:

I deny having murdered Fred H. Clayson, Lynn Wallace Relfe or one Oleson as charged against me and for one of which murders I am condemned to death. My defense as written by me and delivered to one George to be published is true in all particulars. I make this declaration as my last statement on the day previous to the day appointed for my execution, and I protest with all my powers that I am innocent of the crimes charged against me and that I am to suffer for the deeds of others.

In 1907, Jacob Sunfield of Hamilton, Ontario, killed a friend during a drunken argument, and he also left behind a written proclamation of his innocence. On the scaffold he explained why he would not be delivering it personally. He had been warned, he said, not to make a statement. That point made, he concluded with a simple, "Goodbye, gentlemen," then was dropped to his death.

INFLUENCE OF SPIRITUAL ADVISERS

One of the important tasks performed by jail chaplains was helping death row prisoners prepare their last words. The influence of spiritual advisers explains why so many scaffold speeches followed a standard format and were delivered with the appearance of sincere regret. In most cases, those about to die declared themselves reconciled to their fate, which they confessed was justly deserved. Occasionally, a career criminal might also confess to having committed other crimes.

Poral Steffoff was a bad man, and no one seemed upset when he was sentenced to die on a Toronto gallows in 1909. But however bad he was, Steffoff had a conscience. Hours before his execution, he sat down with his spiritual adviser and made a clean breast of his past misdeeds. Not only was he guilty of the murder for which he was to be executed, but he also admitted to taking the life of a man in the state of Indiana and murdering two others near Buffalo, New York.

Such last-minute confessions were not unusual. Killers were urged to take responsibility for their past crimes, and declarations like the one Steffoff made served to reaffirm the majesty of Canada's legal system, as well as being an important part of the pageantry associated with executions.

Reporters and, through their stories, the general public, paid close attention to what notorious murderers said on the gallows. Very often the statement crafted by a jail chaplain was a thinly disguised attempt to warn potential evildoers away from some of society's most attractive, and legal, evils, such as cigarettes and alcohol.

Twenty-year-old George Arthur Pearson was an assistant butcher in Hamilton, Ontario, when he attempted to sexually assault the young woman to whom he was engaged. When she resisted, he shot her. Pearson was executed in early December 1900, and in his last days was constantly attended by two local ministers. Their influence is evident in the speech he delivered from the scaffold:

> *I desire to make this statement to the general public, but mostly to young people, as a warning against three things, namely: Cigarette smoking, strong drink, and bad company. I have never had either good example or advice. I was permitted to run the streets at all hours, and with all kinds of companions, where I formed many bad habits that have helped to ruin me. I am not naturally a criminal, nor bad-hearted, but I have been unfortunate, and I feel if I had only had a fair chance, I would not be where I am this hour. I had a fair trial, and am justly condemned.*

On the Sunday evening of the shooting, I made, improper proposals to Annie Griffin. She seemed greatly surprised, and said, "George, I did not think you were that kind of a fellow— this is the last drive we will ever have together. My reputation is all I have." I then felt so ashamed of myself that I shot her. Intending to shoot myself, I shot her twice, once in the buggy, and again after I lifted her out.

ACCEPTANCE OF RESPONSIBILITY AND APOLOGY

Canadian prison officials specifically, and society generally, wanted those sentenced to hang to have a good death. The most obvious way killers could make this evident was through publicly acknowledging their crime and asking for forgiveness. Such statements were often not long.

In February 1890, Nathaniel Dubois used an axe to slaughter his wife, two children and his mother-in-law. Seconds after ascending a Québec City gallows, he started an exceptionally short but well-coached speech. "I regret very much what I did in a moment of temper," he said, "and hope God has forgiven me. Despite my actions, I hope to meet my wife and children in heaven." His speech over, the killer turned his head toward his executioner and said simply, "I have done." With that, the noose was adjusted around his neck, and Dubois was hanged.

When Austin Humphrey died on a Windsor gallows in 1877 for killing his former employer, he too did what was expected of him. The 65-year-old former American cavalry officer listened as his spiritual adviser read a burial service, and then Humphrey dutifully stepped forward to address those present. As was the case with Dubois, his last words were brief and to the point. "My dear friends, I am now on the scaffold to pay the last penalty of the law. I feel that my sentence is just, and I want to warn you all, my dear friends, never, never to touch the intoxicating cup. It was all through liquor that I came here."

British labourer Reginald White was executed in Kitchener, Ontario, in early 1940 for murdering two members of the same family. On the scaffold, he acknowledged his sin was great, and that at first he tried to hide it. Now was time to own up, and he was glad to do so. He told those gathered that he deserved his fate, before concluding with a warning: "I want my horrible experience to serve as a lesson to all young people, so that they won't get into trouble that I did."

A LAST CHANCE TO EXPLAIN

However much prison officials and spiritual advisers wanted condemned prisoners to use their last words to ask for forgiveness, occasionally that did not happen. Some murderers were more concerned about setting the record straight than they were with eternal salvation.

Several months before she was murdered in 1868, 12-year-old Mary Jones was visiting with relatives when a masked man entered the house and stole whatever money and valuables he could find. Mary recognized the thief, and in short order her uncle,

Thomas Jones, was on trial for larceny. The two were never close, but from that moment on, their relationship got much worse.

In mid-June 1868, Mary disappeared while on the way to borrow flour from her aunt. As soon as it was apparent that something was wrong, a search party was organized. Thomas was immediately suspected of somehow being involved in her disappearance. Within hours, more than 100 people were scouring the countryside. When nothing was found, the mob descended on Thomas' 10-year-old son. It was quickly made clear to the boy that if he did not tell all he knew about Mary's disappearance, he could well end up dangling from the limb of a nearby tree.

Mary's body was discovered less than an hour later, partially hidden under a fallen tree. According to the boy, the killers were his father and his older sister. Thomas and Elizabeth Jones were immediately arrested and taken from the village of Delaware, Ontario, to a jail in London where they would be safer.

At trial, Thomas denied his guilt and said his daughter was the culprit. Elizabeth agreed, confessing that she killed her cousin accidently when the two were playing in the woods. She denied that her father had anything to do with Mary's death.

The jury did not believe Elizabeth or her father, and Thomas was sentenced to hang. Two days later, the trial of Elizabeth got underway. This time a jury believed what the young woman had to say. She was convicted of manslaughter and sentenced to 10 years imprisonment.

Thomas Jones was executed in front of the London, Ontario, jail because the authorities wanted as many people as possible to watch him hang, as a kind of macabre warning to others. Asked if he had any last words, Thomas replied that he did.

Looking into a sea of faces not the least bit sympathetic to his cause, he said, "I wish to say that I am Thomas Jones; and I never did good, bad nor indifferent to Mary. Brothers and sisters, goodbye to you all. I don't regret this road, because I have got no guilt to feel. I have nothing to confess or feel repentant for. I never did the deed."

For a few more moments he continued to speak, repeating phrases like "Lord Jesus receive my spirit," and "May the love of God keep me." When Jones finished speaking, his hangman tugged a cloth cap over his face, and the bolt supporting the trapdoor was drawn. Death came quickly for Thomas Jones, it being evident that his neck was broken.

Right up to the moment the trap fell, Antonio Luciano also protested his innocence. During the early part of 1893, the Italian musician and his friend toured western Canada, making what money they could by entertaining homesteaders. Near Grenfell, Saskatchewan, a fellow countryman joined them. The man was earning a surprisingly good living as a scissors and knife grinder. The two musicians decided to relieve him of his savings.

In mid-June, an employee of the Canadian Pacific Railway found the grinder's body, and in short order, Luciano and his companion were arrested and charged with murder. Late 19th-century trials typically lasted a few days, but because no direct evidence connected the musicians to the murder, the trial of the Italians dragged on for nearly three weeks.

Shortly before they were executed, the sentence of Luciano's partner was commuted, leaving Luciano to ascend a Regina gallows alone. As he stood on the trap, the killer made it clear that before being executed he wanted to set the record straight.

"I like everybody not to believe what the papers have said about the crime. I die innocent like Jesus Christ. He died for everybody. I died for my partner, D'Egidio. I made the confession so that both might not die. We are both innocent. I am a stranger in a strange country; nobody believes me but Jesus. Good-bye, I no kill the man; nobody believed but Jesus. I leave my wife and two children." He then told the hangman he was ready, and after the black hood was pulled over his head, he repeated over and over "goodbye," "Jesus" and "innocent," until he dropped.

While Luciano may indeed have been innocent, there is little doubt about the guilt of David Nesbitt, though he, too, used his last words to paint a picture of himself as a victim.

Nesbitt was a carpenter in Lindsay, Ontario, when he met and fell in love with a local girl. His feelings were reciprocated until the young woman discovered that Nesbitt was already married and his wife and child lived in a nearby town. The carpenter was not one to give up on romance and continued to pursue what he could not have. After several days, the woman he wanted lost her patience and told him to go back to his family. She then turned on her heel and entered her home. Nesbitt followed and shot her. When discovered, he was cradling her body in his arms, crying.

Three days before Christmas 1873, Nesbitt was hanged in Haliburton. Just before the trap fell, he turned toward the few spectators present and protested his innocence. He said his alleged victim shot herself. He also suggested she was immoral and lowly, and that the judge and jurors who found him guilty were liars. He felt he was the real victim. All of a sudden, he seemed to run out of energy and stopped talking. After saying that he had nothing more to add, he concluded by asking that God have mercy on everyone present.

LONG SPEECHES

Occasionally, a Canadian sentenced to death used the opportunity to make a few last comments to prolong life just a little more. At least, men on the east and west coasts of Canada seemed to do so.

George Dowie was a cheat and a drunk and kept bad company. The day he was hanged in Charlottetown, Prince Edward Island, for killing a man who paid too much attention to his woman friend, people found him entertaining.

Dowie was taken from his jail cell just after noon in April 1869, as nearly 2000 people waited for him to make an appearance. The militia men on duty were visibly nervous, in no small part because shouts of "Rescue him!" resonated around them. When Dowie finally appeared, members of his guard lowered their rifles and pointed their bayonets at the crowd.

Dowie knew he would be allowed to make a last statement, and he went to the gallows prepared, with eight pages of notes and a 17-stanza poem. He spoke for so long that officials provided him with a chair, from which he continued to read. Early on, he told spectators that he had undergone a religious conversion while in jail, and he wanted to share with them some of his past sins. His main theme, though, was a warning for others to shun "drink, vicious inclinations, evil habits, and dens of iniquity."

Dowie spoke for almost an hour. The more restless in the crowd knew he must have run out of things to say when he thanked the lawyers who tried to save him. Finally, he said he harboured no ill will toward his executioner then stood and faced the rope. In no time at all, the trap was sprung.

What was likely the second longest gallows speech in Canadian history was delivered from a scaffold in Cassiar, British Columbia, in 1880. Attoo was originally from Alaska but became well known in northwest British Columbia for his violent temper. It was also known that his woman had a wandering eye. It was precisely because of the latter that he began beating his wife on the main street of Telegraph Creek. Frustrated when she refused to come home with him, he pulled out a knife and stabbed her. A passerby rushed to her aid, and Attoo tried to shoot him. Although the bullet went wide, the discharge scorched the would-be rescuer's coat.

A second Good Samaritan was not so lucky. Attoo stabbed him to death then fled. He was quickly caught, tried and sentenced to death. The scaffold on which the Aboriginal was executed in 1880 was considerably higher than the fence surrounding it, and when he began to speak, with the noose already around his neck, almost the entire community was in attendance. Likely because of the influence of his spiritual adviser, Attoo seemed determined to make his death an object lesson to others. But perhaps he went on a little too long.

"My dear friends, there are many white men who do wrong to the Indians, and many Indians who do wrong to whites. I should like all this ill-feeling to stop and I want you all to help to bring it about." And so it went, until an Aboriginal woman lost her patience and interrupted. She asked Attoo to stop talking so much and to get on with it. "We are not afraid to watch you die, so make your heart strong, and die quickly."

Angered at being upstaged in the closing moments of his life, Attoo called the woman by name and asked for quiet. He continued with his last words, but the interruption made him uncertain whether his audience was still listening. He shouted the name of a friend, and asked if he was present. From the moment the friend acknowledged that he indeed was there, Attoo addressed his remarks only to him.

While all this was going on, the hangman was growing increasingly impatient. Finally fed up, he grabbed Attoo by the arms and began fastening his wrists together. The Native was not intimidated and insisted that the rope around his neck be slackened so he could kneel and make the sign of the cross. Rising slowly to his feet, he turned to his executioner and said, "Go ahead." He died minutes later.

COMPLAINTS FROM THE INEXPERIENCED

With very few exceptions, prisoners are hanged only once. Many did not know what to expect and were confused, or uncomfortable, with being noosed and pinioned. Some came to the scaffold angry with something to get off their chests. It is perhaps ironic that regardless how well prepared a condemned prisoner's speech might have been, what was remembered were words of complaint.

When Elijah Van Koughnet was executed in Kingston in 1882 for killing his neighbour, his last words were a reaction to his arms being tied too securely: "Not so tight, it hurts my shoulders."

William Welter also complained of tightness. His trip to the gallows with John Hendershott was the result of a plan concocted by John, who many in 1895 St. Thomas, Ontario, thought was William's lover. Hendershott was much older than Welter, and when he began sharing his home with the young man, community gossip lines heated up. A year later they burst into flames when Hendershott's nephew was found beaten to death not long after his uncle insured his life for $11,000.

Before their execution, the partners each confessed to the murder. That did little to slake the thirst of the huge crowd that showed up to watch them hang. Although most were not admitted to the jail compound, they were within earshot, and the sobbing of the men cut through the still of the June day. Those who listened closely probably heard Welter's last words: "Too tight, please! Goodbye everybody. Oh, Lord! Have mercy and compassion, have mercy and compassion."

The last words of Stefan Ogrodowski, though hardly memorable, seemed to capture the moment. Ogrodowski was hanged in 1943 for killing a man during a robbery in Windsor, Ontario. He followed his partner to the scaffold. Uncomfortable with being pushed and shoved by his hangman, Ogrodowski complained: "Take it easy, I'm not used to this business."

Walter Prestyko had a complaint of a different kind that his hangman was not prepared to accommodate. When the unemployed mechanic from Windsor, together with friend William Worobec, broke into the home of an elderly British Columbia couple, they showed their victims absolutely no sympathy. The pair first strangled the man and then his wife.

On the gallows at Oakalla prison farm, the killers saw no friends among the 15 men who showed up to watch them hang. Reports of their February 1950 execution suggested there were no tears, no final statements, no waste of time. But that was not entirely true.

About 5:30 AM, witnesses to the double execution were conducted to a waiting room while the two prisoners each finished a glass of scotch, and last-minute preparations were made. Thirty minutes later, the spectators were led into the execution chamber, an abandoned elevator shaft. Prestyko and Worobec stood outside their cells a few metres away, their hands cuffed behind their backs, waiting for everyone to take up position near the trap.

Prestyko came in first. He walked through the ring of prison guards surrounding the drop and took his assigned spot. Then Worobec entered. The two stood face to back as their executioner buckled leather straps about their ankles and started to pull hoods over their heads. That is when Prestyko complained. He twisted his head to one side to prevent the silk covering from being tugged down. In a small, high-pitched voice, he asked, "Do I have to have that?" The hangman replied, "I guess you do." Then the men were no longer there.

All that could be seen where they once stood were two ropes, both hanging straight down, not moving. The men were declared dead 11 minutes after the trap opened. Minutes later, Prestyko's lawyer received a call from Windsor. The mother of the dead convict wanted to know what happened. The response was brief: "It's all over."

Wife-killer Peter Bordeniuk did not use his last words to complain of ill treatment on the gallows. His complaint was about his trial. In mid-August 1954, the lumberman went to the home of his estranged common-law wife and begged her to return to him. Shortly before he was hanged, he told his spiritual adviser that he was crying when he told his wife of 19 years that if she did not take him back, he would kill himself. She wanted none of it. "She tell me to go away—that I act like a baby." That was when the 60-year-old murdered his spouse. Her body was found on a roadway near her Alert Bay, BC, home.

As the hangman strapped his legs together, Bordeniuk complained about the way he was treated during his trial: "You should have given me a fair trial. You should have let me see my wife." Bordeniuk was still talking when the executioner released the trap. The entire drama, starting from the moment Bordeniuk entered the death chamber until he dropped, lasted less than a minute. The execution did not go unnoticed by Oakalla prisoners. As soon as they heard the trap slam open, they began shouting, "Hang the hangman."

HELPING THE HANGMAN

The realization that they are going to die perhaps explains why so many condemned prisoners tried to help their executioner get things over with as quickly as possible, or, as in the case of Robert Olsen, tried to calm down the hangman.

For several months in 1892, stores around Moncton were broken into, and as was common at the time, detailed descriptions of the stolen goods were printed in area newspapers.

When a store in Chatham, New Brunswick, was burgled, a large quantity of silverware was stolen. A patron of a Moncton brothel read about the burglary, and on reflection, remembered seeing some of the missing loot in a house of ill repute he frequented. The police were informed, and in short order, officers surrounded the brothel. Olsen and his partner ran out the back door as two constables rushed in the front. Almost immediately, one of the officers grabbed Olsen, and several shots rang out. A bullet from Olsen's gun killed the officer who seized him, while a shot fired by the officer's partner struck Olsen in the leg.

The night before he was hanged in the Dorchester jail, Olsen was allowed a last visit with his friend, who was sentenced to 25 years in prison for his part in the robbery and shootout. Their meeting was anything but sad. As they reminisced about past exploits, the laughter of the partners in crime could be heard up and down the corridor. After they parted, Olsen was told that his hangman had just arrived. The prisoner was pleased when he heard the man's name. He wanted the hanging done right.

Although Olsen's hangman was Canada's only official executioner, on this occasion he was nervous. Olsen noticed, and as the black hood was pulled over his head, said in a quiet undertone, "Don't get excited." Seconds later, turning toward where he thought the hangman was standing, he made a final suggestion: "Let her go." In seconds, he was dead.

In the waning days of November 1945, 24-year-old Alec Prince was executed in British Columbia for murdering two fellow trappers. During his stay on death row, he grew close to his spiritual adviser, and as he prepared to depart for the gallows, he handed his rosary to the chaplain, saying, "You are my best friend. I give you this. It is the only thing I own in the world." As his executioner tightened the noose around his neck, the ever-polite young man asked him to "Put it a little lower, please."

As uncomfortable and overwrought as most condemned prisoners must have felt in the minutes before they were hanged, a few had sufficient presence of mind to help their executioner prepare them to die. In 1828, for example, Englishman Robert Hartley was hanged for stabbing to death the captain of a convict ship. He gave his hangman some very precise, and practical, instructions. "Do not be long about it—let me feel what drop you have given me." Leaning forward to see how long the rope was, he said it would do, but suggested that the knot under his jaw was much too tight. His executioner quickly moved it toward Hartley's chin, causing the bound man to complain, "It is now too much under my chin." After the rope was adjusted a second time, he told the hangman he was ready to have the hood pulled over his face. Still not satisfied, Hartley issued a last demand. "Let me draw it off my mouth."

ANXIETY ON THE SCAFFOLD

Antonio Arosha and Leon Sepepil were very much alike. They both immigrated to Canada from Italy in the first decade of the 20th century, both worked as labourers in New Brunswick, and both participated in the robbery and murder of Paddy Green. Their similarities end there. When it came to dying, Leon had it all over his friend.

In December 1908, Antonio and Leon were drinking in Beaver Brook when they fell into conversation with a couple of peddlers. Before long, the Italians decided to wait for their drinking companions outside the village, to relieve them of their money and their lives. Things did not work out the way they had planned. While the labourers succeeded in shooting the peddlers, only Green was killed. The surviving door-to-door salesman made his way to the nearest police station as soon as he safely could do so, and within hours returned with the police.

Finding Green's killers did not take long. Shortly before the shooting, a light snow had fallen, and police officers simply followed footprints to the spot along the Grand Trunk Railway where Arosha and Sepepil were found, nearly frozen to death.

Two and a half months later, the killers went to trial and were sentenced to hang on a Victoria, New Brunswick, gallows. That is where their stories become quite different. Sepepil may not have accepted his fate, but he was at least resigned to it. He stood unsupported while his executioner prepared him to hang. Arosha, on the other hand, was in a near state of collapse. When the hangman started to pinion and noose him, the 19-year-old nearly fainted.

Ten years later, an Ontario killer reacted in a similar way when he too almost collapsed as he was being prepared to hang.

James Giovanzzo died on a Guelph gallows in 1919, and although he'd committed murder with his friends, he died alone. The young Italian and two companions were robbing and beating a man on a city street when they were seen by two passersby. When the Good Samaritans were warned off, they left to call the police then returned to the scene of the beating. As soon as the two men drew near, Giovanzzo pulled out a revolver and shot one of them several times.

Giovanzzo was charged with murder, and his friends with robbery. All three were convicted, and less than five months after the killing, "Jimmie" Giovanzzo found himself on a gallows. A few days before his execution, he stopped eating and drinking, hoping to weaken himself sufficiently that his hanging would be postponed. His efforts were in vain.

While standing on the scaffold, Giovanzzo was over-come, physically and emotionally, and collapsed before he could be dropped. His stay of execution lasted only seconds, as guards quickly pulled him to his feet and held him upright until the trap opened.

A loss of nerves did not always result in the physical collapse of a condemned prisoner. Usually the person about to be hanged managed to regain her or his composure and stay upright until the trap was sprung. An example is the gallows experience of Alexander Wysochan, a 29-year-old hanged in Prince Albert, Saskatchewan, in 1930.

On Christmas Day of the previous year, the Polish immigrant shot his common-law wife to death and then attempted suicide. When he walked to the gallows six months later, Wysochan was determined to die with a semblance of dignity and spent much of his last evening with his spiritual adviser, trying to remain calm. It almost worked.

Comforted by the Mass held in front of his cell, Wysochan was able to walk without assistance to his place of execution. At the foot of the scaffold, he was asked if he had anything to say. Wysochan took the opportunity to once again proclaim his innocence. "I am innocent," he stammered in broken English, "but am ready to die. I am dying for my God and my church."

Finished, he ascended the scaffold platform. But things became too much to bear, and Wysochan started crying. In a few moments, however, he was able to compose himself. He straightened his shoulders and stood ramrod straight, waiting for the trap to give way. Eight minutes later, the first person to be executed in Prince Albert's new death chamber officially was pronounced dead.

CONVERSATIONS

The last words of quite a large number of killers were actually part of a gallows conversation rather than a speech. Usually the discussion included the hangman, but occasionally a witness either spoke to a prisoner about to hang or was addressed by one.

As his hangman was adjusting the noose around his neck, cop-killer Robert Olsen held out his hands toward the dozens of spectators waiting to watch him die and asked, "Do you want to shake hands?" In response, one witness yelled out, "Go to heaven, Buck!" Olsen replied with one word: "Thanks."

In late May 1914, Afancy Sokoloff and two partners tried to steal the payroll of an Exshaw, Alberta, cement company as it was being transferred on foot from the train station to the cement works. The robbery quickly went awry, and Sokoloff shot and killed one of the men carrying the money. He was captured in Calgary two weeks later. The three robbers were convicted at trial and sentenced to hang, though the sentence of one was later reduced to life in prison.

As Sokoloff and Serhay Konuch (better known as Joseph Smith) reached the gallows, Sokoloff asked Calgary's sheriff, "Can't you put this off? I did not do it." Told that the execution would not be postponed, the killer turned to his companion and said, "Well, goodbye, Smith." The sound of the opening trapdoor drowned out any response.

One of the longest one-sided scaffold conversations in British Columbia history was between a 68-year-old man, who had murdered his 35-year-old wife, and the spectators at his 1939 execution. As he stood on the trapdoor of the Oakalla gallows, everyone in the small room could clearly hear the bell-like voice of R.A. Wright.

"My friends," he said, "how many of you here will promise to meet me beyond this vale of tears?" As his executioner stood nearby, politely waiting, Wright continued, his voice taking on a plaintive quality. "Is there one of you here?"

Wright continued even after the hangman pulled the death hood over his face. "Is there one of you here?" For a moment his further words were muffled by the hood, then just as the trap opened, he was heard to moan, "Lord have mercy on me."

LAST WORDS NOT UNDERSTOOD

Sometimes a condemned prisoner's last words could be heard clearly, but not understood. Usually it was because the witnesses could not understand the language spoken.

As he stood on a Brantford, Ontario, gallows in 1880, Benjamin Carrier was asked if he had anything to say. He did, but he wanted an interpreter, and a chief from a local First Nations community volunteered his services. Carrier slowly began to speak, as if he was determined to delay his execution for as long as he could.

Although spectators were aware of the horrific crime that put Carrier on the scaffold, they could not help but be struck by the incongruity of what they were witnessing. The wife killer stood with the noose around his neck, with the greatest part of the rope hanging down his back until it bent upward to an iron ring embedded overhead. The lighting was poor, the atmosphere still and gloomy, and the only sound was a voice speaking in a tongue few present could understand. When Carrier finished, a white cap was pulled over his eyes, and the knot of the noose was moved under his left ear. The Baptist minister attending the killer began to pray, and while he was speaking, the trap opened and Carrier dropped 3.5 metres.

The lost last words spoken by Poral Stefoff were in Greek. In 1909, Stefoff was living in a Toronto rooming house with a number of other men from Macedonia. When one of them became ill, the man's family raised enough money to pay for his passage home. Stefoff wanted that money, and while everyone else was at work, he murdered his stricken friend and stole $104. Stefoff raised the alarm, hoping to divert attention from himself; it didn't work. When he could not tell the police where he got the pocketful of money they found on him, or explain the bloodstains on his clothes, he was arrested.

Eight months later, Stefoff stood on a gallows erected in the yard of the Toronto common jail. He accepted the opportunity to make a few last comments. Indeed, he made more than a few. The irony was, no one understood his words.

Stefoff was for a time remembered by his fellow countrymen, though not because of his last words. A city newspaper article about his execution was used to warn foreigners that it was safer to trust their money to banks than to carry cash on their person, as Stefoff's victim had.

Occasionally, anger and the obvious anxiety of the person standing on a gallows made the meaning of last words difficult to understand. Marguerite Pitre was hanged for her part in the 1949 bombing of an airplane that resulted in the deaths of 23 people. As she stood on a scaffold in Montréal's Bordeaux Jail, she made a final speech in which she likened herself to Christ: "I want to say something, and I have this to say for the sake of my children. Christ was condemned by Pontius Pilate and delivered into the hands of Caiaphas, and now it is your hour. That is all I have to say."

INTERRUPTIONS

Everyone connected to the execution process wanted things to go smoothly and quickly. The longer the person to be executed stayed alive, the greater the likelihood something would go awry. The official most responsible for ensuring that they did not was the executioner, and he was particularly concerned with a lengthy gallows speech. Three Manitoba executions illustrate just how quickly hangmen reacted when they thought an execution was starting to go off the rails.

Simon Czubej and Wasyl Guszczak murdered five members of a homestead family living just north of the Manitoba–United States border. In May 1899, the two killers ascended a Winnipeg gallows. As soon as the excitable Czubej reached the top of the scaffold, he shouted to spectators that it was his co-accused, not him, who had committed the murders.

To emphasize his point, he began beating his chest. Fearing things were getting a little out of hand, the hangman interrupted the diatribe and pulled a black hood over his head. Now in darkness, the murderer grew silent.

Nineteen years after Czubej and his partner were hanged, Frank Sullivan, Philip Johnston and a teenage accomplice arrived in Manitoba from Ontario. The three came to the attention of authorities when they were interrupted while robbing a local hardware store. In the ensuing struggle, a city police constable was killed. Police arrested the trio in a hotel next door, where they rented rooms.

As Sullivan and Johnston stood on their gallows in 1918, they looked out on an unsympathetic audience. Sullivan started to proclaim his innocence. "I want to tell you gentlemen, and I want you to tell my sister, that I am innocent. I know nothing about this. The policeman who said he heard me say I killed him is a liar. The jury and the judge did not give me a fair deal."

That was as far as he got. The hangman wanted to get the execution over with, and Sullivan's rant was delaying it. The executioner stepped up to the killer, stooped to tie his legs together and then snapped a hood over his head. Johnston managed only, "I am in…" before the trap was sprung, and the two men plummeted to their death.

If possible, 26-year-old Peter Piniak was even less liked by Winnipeg area residents than Sullivan and Johnston, Piniak lived in Winnipeg Beach, a community just north of Manitoba's capital city. He was frequently the object of complaints from women who accused him of harassing them. Piniak's mother was among his detractors. At his murder trial, she testified against him, referring to her offspring as a lazy no-good.

Just before murdering Martha Squarok and her son, Piniak's own son died, in part because of his neglect. He accused the Squaroks, who lived nearby, of allowing his child to freeze to death. Obsessed with getting even, he went to the Squarok farm and beat Martha to death with a piece of firewood, then threw her five-year-old into a well.

Piniak was hanged on September 1, 1933. After being placed on the trap, he seemed determined to involve his executioner in a conversation. "What drop are you giving me?" The hangman ignored the question and began pulling the black hood over Piniak's face. The killer objected. "I don't want…" was all he managed before the trap in Manitoba's Headingley Jail opened.

OVERCOME BY THE OCCASION—NO LAST WORDS

Many of those sentenced to hang took considerable time preparing their last words, determined to be remembered for a deeply meaningful comment or perhaps just wanting to set the record straight. Often, however, they were overcome by the occasion. Whether they walked into a death chamber or ascended a gallows, the first thing they saw was a rope, the instrument of their death, and the faces of unsmiling witnesses, some of whom were often family members of their victim. It's no wonder that so many couldn't say their lines.

Michael O'Rourke, at least, had someone to explain his inability to speak. The farmhand worked for almost a year with the man he murdered, then showed his appreciation by killing him with an axe and attempting to cut his victim's head off with a kitchen knife. After dispatching his former employer, O'Rourke murdered the man's daughter and then molested her body.

Before he was finished with the remains, a son of the dead man showed up, greeted at the door by O'Rouke, who was covered head to toe in blood. Raising his axe, the killer taunted the young man, "I'm ready for you too!" This time he was over-matched. The youth struck him with a club and beat O'Rourke so badly the killer was forced to flee for his life.

On a January morning in 1883, O'Rourke started toward a snow-covered Milton, Ontario, gallows. On the scaffold, he was told, "Michael O'Rourke, if you have anything to say, say it now." The man's spiritual adviser stepped forward and explained why there would be no last words. "His mind is too much engaged in this important affair to allow of him turning his mind from his Maker and Judge."

Before going to sleep the night before his 1895 execution, Amedée Chatelle worked hard to prepare the short speech he wanted to deliver to the people of Stratford, Ontario. He intended to acknowledge that his punishment was just, and he was going to ask the forgiveness of both God and the father of the young girl he butchered. Perhaps it was just as well for those present, who included his victim's father, that at the last moment his courage failed him and he said nothing.

SPIRITUAL ADVISERS SPEAK OUT

Many of those sentenced to death did not want to face the pressure of speaking to a hostile audience and entrusted their speechmaking to someone else. Usually that person was a spiritual adviser.

Frederick Lindsley was a man with a chequered past, even before he murdered his common-law wife and shot her pre-teen daughter in Sault Ste. Marie, Ontario. Already charged and acquitted of one murder, the lifelong troublemaker served two years in prison for stealing a horse and failing to tell his new wife that he was already married to a woman living in the United States.

By the time he reached the gallows in February 1902, Lindsley seemed to have convinced himself that he, not the woman he shot six times, was the victim. To further add to the aura of make-believe with which he surrounded himself, the killer told everyone who would listen that he'd found religion. He may indeed have done so, though his version of it did not prohibit lying. He told authorities that his name was Fred Schultz, and when that was found to be untrue, he refused to disclose his real identity.

Of one thing Lindsley was certain, he wanted his last words to be just right, so he wrote them down. When jail officials told him he would not be allowed to deliver a speech from the scaffold, he left it to his spiritual adviser to convey his words:

> *My last dying message is that I am guiltless of this charge. I do not give my life to the Government, but as an example to sinners; for them I freely give it, that they may come to be Christians, as I am today. I can walk on the scaffold and fear nothing, for my Lord Jesus Christ is with me. Trusting in Him I have no fear. They would not let me speak from the scaffold. Good-bye to all. There is love in my heart for everybody.*

While standing on the trapdoor of his gallows, the American murderer defied authorities one last time. Told to say nothing, Lindsley turned to those present and managed to get out, "Well, boys, here goes an innocent soul," before he was dropped to his death.

In late December 1873, Peter Mailman also made use of the services of a spiritual adviser, though no one would have stopped him had he decided to speak from the scaffold himself.

Four months before he was executed, Mailman and his wife spent an August morning picking berries in the woods near their home in Lunenberg, Nova Scotia. The couple fought constantly, and that day was no different. As usual, the argument was about money, and it was one discussion too many. In the middle of their screaming, Mailman snapped and began beating his wife with an axe handle. By the time he was done, she was barely recognizable.

Mailman buried his wife's body under a tree, and on arriving home told his young daughter that her mother was off visiting friends. The girl saw through the lie and confronted her father. Mailman explained that if anyone found out about what he had done, he would hang. That did nothing to make his daughter feel any better, and she eventually told a neighbour about her father's confession. A search party quickly found the body of the missing woman.

Three thousand people turned out to watch Mailman hang. On the surface, he seemed to be the least affected person present. As he stood emotionless on the trapdoor, never moving a muscle, he was asked if he had anything to say. He replied that he didn't, that he wanted to keep his mind fixed on heaven. Then he handed his spiritual adviser a piece of paper. On it was his confession, which the minister promptly read. After a short prayer and a quick drop, the wife killer was dead.

Like Peter Mailman, Henry Smith was executed for killing his wife, and like him, the resident of London, Ontario, also used a spiritual adviser to deliver his last statement. Unlike Mailman, however, Smith died neither quickly nor well.

Sheriff's officers came for the condemned man shortly after 6:00 AM in June 1890. When Smith saw them, he almost fainted and had to be held up while his arms were pinioned. That was a foretaste of what was to come. Jail guards virtually carried the distraught man to the gallows, and once there, he would have collapsed had they not grabbed him in time.

On the scaffold, Smith showed obvious signs of collapsing and again needed help from the officers. When order was restored and Smith managed to regain his composure, his spiritual adviser told the 100 witnesses present that he was going to read the prisoner's written confession. That done, the killer managed a last "God have mercy" before he was hanged. But he did not die right away. Smith was suspended for almost 30 minutes before being pronounced dead. During that time, several spectators threw up, and one fainted dead away.

LAST WORDS IN THE FORM OF A LETTER

Some killers wanted their last words to reach a much larger audience than would be attending their execution, and they sought to have their parting comments published in a newspaper.

In 1869, Nicholas Melady was hanged for murdering his father and stepmother. During his months on death row, the killer received frequent visitors and responded to hundreds of questions. In the end, he decided to set the record straight and wrote a letter to the editor of a local paper. The first part was an expression of thanks to those who were kind to him during his imprisonment. Then he apologized for committing the murders and told readers what he thought about the way his trial was conducted.

Now Mr. Editor, as I wish to make no public speech, permit me through the medium of your columns to make one last atonement to an outraged society. The evidence on which I was found guilty was weak and insufficient, it is true, but notwithstanding in that conviction I perceived the judgement of a just and hold God who has commanded us to honour father and mother, and whose name is never to be taken in vain. Nicholas Melady, Goderich, December 7, 1869.

George Louder and Joseph Thomset were likely not guilty of the murder of Peter Lazier for which they were hanged in 1884. Louder's last words, in the form of a letter, are steeped with the frustration felt by someone about to die for something he did not do:

I thought I would write you a few lines before I die. I do not suppose anything I might say will cause you to change your minds regarding my guilt or innocence; and even if I could it would be too late to rectify mistakes and bring me back to earth again. God is my witness, I am innocent of having had anything to do with the murder of Mr. Peter Lazier, and when I am hung for that crime the innocent is punished for the guilty. I die, bearing neither spite nor malice against any one; and my wishes are, that all my enemies may be forgiven as truly as I hope to be forgiven for all my sins.

Believe me, I do not die a murderer, nor with a murderer's heart. If I knew who were guilty of the crime for which I am to suffer death, I would make it known. I have not owned a revolver for two years past, and I have not fired one off for upwards of one year. I did not have a gun in my hands for six weeks prior to my arrest, and I was not in Mr. Gilbert Jones' house nor on his premises in my life, to my knowledge. These are my last and dying words. George Louder. Picton Gaol.

Peter Lazier was visiting at the farm home of friends a few days before Christmas 1883. When two masked men entered the house, intent on robbery, he rushed to the aid of his friends and was shot in the heart during a struggle. Police followed a combination of cart tracks and footprints in the snow and ended up at the homes of Louder and his alleged partner. The two were promptly arrested and, six months later, hanged back to back at the Picton, Ontario, courthouse.

Unlike the last words of George Louder, those of 24-year-old Charles Russell were an apology for past crimes. Before the former auto-mechanic was executed in 1936 at the Oakalla prison farm for murdering a Canadian Bank of Commerce teller, he wrote to a Vancouver newspaper.

His letter began simply enough:

My dear friends, trusting that you will forgive the informality of this missive, may I make this sincere, but inadequate effort to thank you and yours for all you have done on my behalf. I am sorely at loss for words which would fully express the deep feeling of reverence and gratitude which I have.

At the hour of writing I have, as far as I know, but a few hours left in this world. A desire paramount, almost to the point of becoming an obsession, grips firmly, a desire to prove to those of you who have supported me at this great hour of need that the confidence and faith has not been misplaced. My conscience is clear and although I am unable to understand it, if it is His will, there must be a purpose. May I say again in closing that no words will express the gratitude that I do feel. God bless you and yours. Yours respectfully, Charles Russell.

Russell may have written with humility, but in his last moments, he showed a little of the arrogance by which he was known during his life of crime. He was executed with Eneas and Richardson George, brothers sentenced to hang for the murder of an Aboriginal police constable.

When the brothers entered the death chamber, they were positioned on the trap face to back, their bodies almost touching. Russell came in last, smoking a cigarette, with a faint smile on his face. Before stepping onto the scaffold, he spat out the cigarette. Moving so quickly witnesses barely followed what was happening, the hangman pinioned, hooded and noosed the bank robber, then in a calm voice directed at the three killers, said, "You may pray."

No sooner had a major of the Salvation Army started to pray than the trap was sprung.

LAST WORDS IN THE FORM OF AN AUTOBIOGRAPHY

The last words of two British Columbia killers were among the longest gallows speeches published by Canadian newspapers. Both were intimate autobiographies. At times sensitive, each was written as a warning to others.

The first story was that of Joseph Ouelette, a 22-year-old farm worker sentenced to hang for killing two Chinese vegetable gardeners in a shack near the Vernon airport.

To the Young men starting a life of crime: I am writing this because I've been through it all and I feel that I should pass on what I know, that someone will see what is wrong with crime.

I started out young. The first thing I ever stole was a pair of ice skates; then it got worse, until now I have only a few days to live. You see, kids, if you play you must pay.

I've always lived my life my way and never thought how wrong I was. As I sit in my cell I ask myself how many more of the young men will follow in my footsteps? I hope and pray there are none as it is not the fellow in the death cell who is getting hurt; think of the pain you are causing your mother, wife and children.

Death is nothing: but it is the waiting and wondering if you will go to Heaven or Hell. I often wonder what it is like in the next world and where I will spend eternity. I hope it is with the Lord, but I must first believe in Jesus Christ and pray to Him.

It never pays to be a tough guy and say: "I don't care"; I tried that and I realize it is not toughness but just to cover your weakness. You may think I am a sissy and afraid of death. I don't claim to be a tough guy. It takes more than toughness to tell your friends that you believe in the Lord.

In a way I'm lucky because I have the time to prepare myself to meet the Lord, but you never know when you're going to die and then it will be too late. I have only a few more days to live now and there is no one to blame but myself, because if I had done the things God wanted I may have lived to be an elderly man. I wanted easy money and you see what I got.

The night before he was hanged, Ouelette took advantage of the offer of a last meal. For himself and a member of his death watch he ordered turkey, two kinds of salad, strawberries and cream, strawberry shortcake and soft drinks. A few hours later, he was equally thoughtful. As he was being prepared on the scaffold, Ouelette turned to a guard who waited out his final hours with him and murmured a simple, "Thanks very much."

Joseph Ouelette was hanged in late May 1951, six years before another Joseph suffered a similar fate. In the hours immediately preceding his execution, a 37-year-old cop killer kept his mind off what was to come by laboriously writing his autobiography. A Vancouver newspaper published it after his death, as the story of Joe Gordon:

> *Whatever good I can do before I depart this world of pain and tears, let me do now.*
>
> *Juvenile delinquency begins in the home, and expands on the street. From the path of juvenile delinquency is but a step to the road of crime. For some it is a means of experience; for others a career.*
>
> *I was born in Montréal. There I had my first taste of bitterness, sorrow and pain. Mine was a heart yearning for the love I felt was denied by father.*
>
> *You believe your father indulges the whims of your brothers and sisters, but you are scolded or taste the strap. Perhaps, because you seem more mature, you are left to your own devices and consequently, not having reached the age of reason, emotions rule. You feel unwanted.*
>
> *In 1929, my family moved to Vancouver. I was six when I first entered the juvenile detention home. My crime—running away from home. My punishment: the strap—the reason I ran away in the first place. The first night in the detention home was*

a terrible one. Thrust among older boys than myself—all complete strangers—led to my first step into crime. Fear is a strange emotion. You may cringe from pain, but despite this respect is lacking. In its place bitterness and rebellion is born.

At the age of 12, I was sent to the Boy's Industrial School. It was far different than from what I understand it is today. I was sentenced three times to the Industrial School for petty offences. Each time I learned more of crime. Punishment succeeds very well in making criminals. It also keeps you on the road of crime and in the company of criminals.

Those poor unfortunates who were to be my friends welcomed me. Why not? Misery like company. Also the most compassionate people are criminals, for they have suffered the rejection of the society. You learn from them how to steal a car, break into any sort of dwelling, blow open a safe, and become a drug addict, a drug connection and a gun man. You become brutal at times and bitter always. You are also soft and sentimental—championing the underdog.

You are not yet 15 when sentenced first to Oakalla Prison farm, for possessing burglary tools. In prison I learned what a drug addict was. I was given my first taste of drugs in Oakalla.

Guided by understanding and parental love, these juveniles may well be tomorrow's leaders and go on to help create other good citizens.

The only friends I have in life are criminals. Due process of law brought me into contact with them in the first instance. Where no one else I had met showed any interest in my behaviour, these criminals offered me friendship and understanding which I eagerly accepted. Drug addicts, gunmen, pimps and prostitutes— those denizens of the underworld outcast by society—proved to be more humane than their socially acceptable counterparts.

No one is entirely good or entirely bad. We all excuse our own failures but seldom, if ever, do we excuse the failures of others. The archaic and medieval statutes protecting society are reprehensible. The question of today is: Who shall protect a delinquent or for that matter, a criminal, from society?

Oscar Wilde wrote: "The easiest way to resist temptation is to yield." Can we blame immature kids for falling prey to temptation in their paths? If adults cannot resist, how can we expect adolescents to do otherwise? Instead of breaking a kid's heart why not give him a break and help him. Help him now. Don't wait while irreparable damage is done to their growing personality traits.

Joseph Gordon was executed on the Oakalla prison farm on April 2, 1957.

Chapter Six

Witness to an Execution

~

H istory is full of stories of people mounting the scaffold trembling in fear, and certainly there is some truth to that suggestion. When England hanged five pirates in 1865, one was too faint to stand and was executed seated in a chair. But the stories in this chapter suggest that while the decorum of those put to death in Canada varied from panic stricken to stoic, most prisoners sentenced to death seemed to have learned their parts in this brutal drama of death and to have acted them out well. Those who died prayerful and determined significantly outnumber the few who grovelled in terror. Until banned from execution chambers across the country, Canadian newspaper reporters filled their stories with references to courage and determination in the face of death, perhaps inappropriately lionizing killers at the expense of their victims.

EXECUTIONS AS COMMUNITY EVENTS

Until well into the 20th century, executions in Canada were big events. Peter Wheeler's hanging in 1896 in Nova Scotia, for example, not only drew a huge local crowd, but it also attracted people from all over the province and beyond. Steamers from Saint John, New Brunswick, sold excursioners on the prospect of a pleasant outing, topped off with the spectacle of watching a man die in Digby. Hotels and private homes were filled to capacity, and local newspaper social columns were full of details of the comings and goings.

The Montréal execution of Thorvald Hanson was typical of the extent to which hangings were important community events. In October 1901, an eight-year-old boy was on his way home when he passed the vacant lot where Hanson was lounging. The sound of the coins in the young man's pocket attracted the attention of the out-of-work drifter, and in an instant, Hanson attacked. Holding his victim with one hand, he stabbed the helpless boy several times in the neck. The next morning, Hanson turned himself in to the police, and after a brief trial, was sentenced to hang.

Although the Danish immigrant was not scheduled to hang until 8:00 AM, hours earlier, people began gathering around the Montréal jail. When the building's front doors were finally opened, the densely packed crowd reached most of the way across the street. A squad of police officers struggled to control the pushing and shoving among the 200 people with tickets. Another corps of armed officers was stationed along three sides of the waiting gallows.

Prior to leaving his cell, the deeply repentant killer again confessed to the murder and apologized to those affected by his crime.

The moment is fast approaching when I shall atone for my sin on the scaffold. I am sincerely repentant for the odious crime I committed under the cursed influence of liquor. I also beg the parents of my innocent victim to forgive me the great sorrow I have caused them. Mingling my tears with theirs, I have every day and night prayed Almighty God to comfort and strengthen them in their sad bereavement.

Montréalers were forewarned that one among them was about to die when a neighbourhood church clock began tolling the time. Just before it struck the top of the hour, a door in the western wing of the jail opened, and the death procession emerged. Leading the group was the city's magnificently dressed sheriff, adorned in a cocked hat and the official robes of his office, and carrying a sword. He was followed an appropriate distance behind by Hanson and the rest of the death-walk participants.

Hanson was dressed in a brown sack coat, dark pants and a red necktie. He walked to the scaffold without obvious emotion and quickly took his place beneath the dangling noose. Once he was in place, the hangman went to work. Seconds later he stepped back, and with an almost imperceptible motion of his foot, released a lever, springing the trap. Before the echo of the falling doors faded, Hanson dropped into the open pit, his head instantly thrown to one side.

Two minutes later, witnesses saw the muscles of his legs jerk, and then it was over. Hanson's death was announced to the community by the ringing of a bell and the sudden appearance of a black flag hoisted over the jail.

EXECUTIONS AS SPECTACLES

People have always been drawn to spectacles, and the more gruesome the sight, the larger the crowd. When English women and men were hanged in public, as many as 50,000 people turned out for the day's events. In Canada, crowds were smaller, but no less enthusiastic. That was especially the case if the person was notorious, and in 1919, few were more infamous than Toronto cop-killer Frank McCullough.

The charismatic career criminal captured the imagination of Canadians when he broke out of his death row cell, then sent friendly but taunting postcards to Ontario prison officials. Following his capture, the public continued to find him fascinating, and as his June 13 date with destiny drew nearer, that fascination grew.

In the days before he was hanged, McCullough regularly was seen at his cell window, which overlooked the streets of downtown Toronto. He communicated with spectators by waving his arms, often keeping time to the music blaring out from the mob, and on occasion motioned for silence so he could sing alone to those assembled below him.

Police drove away crowds when violence threatened; with more than 500 people milling about, that happened often. The day before McCullough was to hang, demonstrators started gathering in front of his cell as soon as their workday was over, and before the evening ended, 13 were arrested and two police officers injured.

Shortly before dark, the noise of the crowd grew substantially louder as nearly 1000 people started cheering, clapping, shouting and singing as one. McCullough was attracted by the sound, and in the light flooding his cell, he was clearly outlined behind the bars. He waved his arms, reached out and waved again. After a while, he stopped, threw a few kisses, clapped his hands together and was gone. He repeated the same performance every 10 minutes or so, until after midnight.

Around 2:30 AM, officials feared things might get well and truly out of hand, and police reserves from across the city were rushed in to keep order. Their appearance was greeted with enthusiasm, and the singing and noisemaking grew louder. Before the morning was out, however, McCullough was no longer alive to hear it.

Rowdy Crowds

Although crowds often grew rowdy outside Canadian jails, occasionally they brought their rowdiness inside, even to the scaffold itself. An example is what happened when William Robinson was executed in Kentville, Nova Scotia, in September 1904.

For a reason he refused to discuss, the 70-year-old Robinson murdered his wife. He was quickly arrested, tried and sentenced to hang, without a recommendation for mercy. His last days were unsettling, in no small measure because the gallows was built right outside his cell. Despite objecting to the constant hammering, he could not help but spend hours watching the construction.

Shortly after midnight on September 12, an official involved in Robinson's execution made his way through a large and growing crowd. The last to arrive was the country's official hangman. Within minutes of his appearance, the Englishman threatened to call things off. The gallows was attached to the side of the jail, and to get to it, witnesses were required to pass through a second-floor room. So many crowded into the passageway that it was almost impossible to move. The hangman wanted the situation rectified.

Just before 1:30 AM, the executioner entered Robinson's cell and advised him it was time. Before they left the ward, however, the hangman made it clear that there were to be no last words from the gallows. If you have anything to say, he told the doomed man, say it now.

Without further ado, the executioner handcuffed Robinson's hands behind his back, and he and his victim started off. Nothing had changed in the antechamber leading to the scaffold, and the hangman was forced to push his prisoner through the room, avoiding several fistfights that had broken out. The scaffold itself was packed with men shoving and pushing to get a better view, and officials had to elbow the mob aside to make room for Robinson.

Once the white-haired killer was on the trap, his life quickly came to a crashing end. Within five seconds he was noosed and dropped. Four minutes later he was declared dead, and his body laid out in a coffin lying ready beneath the gallows floor.

As raucous as the hanging of William Robinson became, it was nowhere near as chaotic as the execution of Cordélia Viau and her lover, Sam Parslow. After the two were sentenced to die for the 1897 murder of Cordélia's husband, the notoriety associated with their double hanging attracted more than 2000 people to the jail at St. Scholastique, Québec.

Shortly before the breakfast-time hanging, a mob rushed the huge front door of the prison compound, attempting to break into the jail yard. Only after police officers drew their revolvers and started firing into the air was peace restored. The calm, however, did not last long.

When the crowd inside the yard heard the thunderous bang of the dropping trapdoor, some among it surged to the scaffold, perhaps spurred on by cheering from beyond the jail walls. As rowdies began ripping apart the black cloth encircling the well into which the two lovers fell, the couple's priest leaned over a scaffold railing, shouting, "Shame, shame, for decency's sake. Have you no decency?"

His words had no effect. Determined to see the bodies, more of the crowd pushed forward, and what cloth remained nailed to the gallows was ripped down. There, exposed for all to see, were Viau and Parslow. Finally satisfied, the mob quickly dispersed.

In January 1932, an execution crowd in Ontario succeeded where the Québec mob failed; it actually broke into an execution chamber where a killer stood, about to be hanged.

Right up until he stepped on a Barrie gallows, the wheels of justice had turned pretty quickly for Thomas Wesley Campbell. Two months after murdering his 88-year-old father, he was tried, convicted and sentenced to hang. Less than three months later, he was standing on a gallows built in a jail yard coal shed. That's when everything started to go sideways.

Three years earlier, a rowdy crowd disrupted a Barrie execution, and local authorities were determined not to let that happen again. They not only kept the time of the hanging secret, but they also carefully boarded up places where someone could look into the building in which the hanging was to take place.

Their efforts did little to deter a pack of men and youths who prowled the outside of the jail looking for an opening, and it was not long before they found one. A small, rectangular cover was used to close off a chute used to fill the gallows shed with coal. The gang had just finished prying it off when a car driven by Campbell's son pulled up, headlights flooding the scene. As soon as he got out of the car, the son was told about the opening, and he immediately rushed to it, peering over the heads of those already crowding in, trying to get a glimpse of the scaffold.

Before long, news that a breach was opened caused a stampede. The more aggressive among the crowd jumped onto the shoulders of those in front, fighting to see the gallows where Wesley Campbell stood.

The noise attracted the attention of a traffic officer, one of the extra men brought in to prevent what was just about to happen. He rushed to the opening, squeezed through, and stood, loaded gun in hand, facing the mob. He quickly made his intentions clear. "Let any man of you come back to this wall again and I will shoot." When the crowd pulled back, the officer re-entered the shed, and the execution resumed, soon watched by a dozen men who returned to the shed opening.

In the years immediately preceding the abolition of capital punishment, Canadian executions continued to attract large crowds. Ontario killer Peter Balcombe was hanged in 1954 for the sex slaying of a 21-year-old woman, and the top of his canvas-covered gallows was easily visible from Cornwall streets. Two hours before the execution, residents surrounded the jail and began shooting off fireworks. Only after the police moved in was calm restored.

Dying Alone

For every Canadian execution that attracted a crowd, rowdy or not, there were dozens in which a killer died almost unnoticed. The 1939 hanging of William Petrekowich is an example.

The 29-year-old coal miner shot his former common-law wife in the head because he loved her, he said, and then he tried to commit suicide by firing two bullets into his own chest.

Few in Toronto knew either the killer or his victim, and just six people showed up in front of the Don jail the evening he was to hang. Like the man he put to death, the executioner, too, was unknown. The rookie hangman simply showed up, presented his credentials, carried out the execution then rushed off in a taxi.

Like Petrekowich, Dominico Nassa died almost alone when he was hanged in the death chamber at British Columbia's Oakalla prison farm. The 25-year-old, described in provincial newspapers as the "passion slayer," killed the father of his teen-age fiancée when his future father-in-law refused to consent to moving up the wedding date.

The wedding was to take place as soon as the young miner had saved the few hundred dollars his prospective in-laws felt he needed to support their girl. Nassa agreed to the terms, but just before Christmas 1928, he called at the Agostino home and demanded that the marriage take place right away. When he was refused, Nassa lost his temper. He shot his fiancée's father then tried to kill his fiancée and her brother before fleeing. The next morning he was arrested.

Nassa's execution was set for late July 1929. In the three months he spent on death row, he grew increasingly resigned to his fate, and the night before his execution, he slept peacefully. In the morning, he ate breakfast, prayed briefly with a priest then sat down to wait. As soon as his hangman appeared, the slightly built Calabrian was hustled out of the jail and into the light of a grey dawn. Ten steps later he was on the scaffold.

While being prepared, Nassa told the guards tying his arms to "Fixa good so maka no mistake," then before the black hood could be pulled over his head, he asked permission to say a few words. "Wella, gentlemen, I was always a nica boy, but I made onena mistake. The guards was good to me. The time is come for me to go. I ama ready to go. Thanka you, gentlemen. Gooda bye."

Once the short speech ended, the executioner adjusted the hood and noose, and snapped open the trap.

With the exception of prison officials, fewer than 14 people, mostly reporters, witnessed the hanging. That made the execution among the most private in British Columbia's history. The prison warden refused to let more spectators into the jail compound because he wanted to eliminate any possibility that the execution would become a "Roman holiday," as so many were in the past.

EVEN MURDERERS HAVE FRIENDS

Despite killing his wife and two daughters, William Harvey was a man nearly everyone liked. While in jail, he befriended the local sheriff, who refused to allow his prison staff to agitate Harvey by asking him about the murders. The sheriff also did not want anyone to talk to Harvey because he worried such conversations might affect the prisoner's appeal. Two local ministers persisted in their attempts to speak with the killer, but Harvey refused to see them.

His execution was scheduled to take place in Guelph, Ontario, on November 29, 1889, and Harvey spent his last day and night quietly. He was a little upset that he had nothing to leave one of his death watch, a man he regarded as a friend. Desperate to be remembered by something, however small, he finally gave the guard the buttons from his shirt cuffs. On one condition. Harvey did not want the man to sell the gift as a curiosity or to show the buttons around. Harvey added, "I have nothing else to give you. If you want a piece of the rope, you will have to ask the hangman for it."

On his way to the scaffold, the killer asked the sheriff to go first, in case his nerves gave way and he stumbled. The procession moved slowly through a mantle of snow, a remnant of the previous evening's storm. As the group neared the gallows, built in the yard of the Guelph jail, spectators silently made way. Most were Harvey's friends, who said they wanted to attend so he would not feel alone in his darkest hour.

Even Harvey's son, the only member of his family he did not succeed in killing, was in a forgiving mood. He asked friends to claim his father's body and have it buried beside those of his mother and sisters.

In a scene that deeply touched everyone present, Harvey stood on the scaffold with two scraps of paper held in the palm of his hand, kept in place by an elastic band. One was part of a letter written by his son, in which the young man told his father that he had forgiven him for what he had done. The other was the last letter written by his youngest daughter, in which the 12-year-old told her father how much she loved him.

Harvey's execution apart, the deaths of few killers were witnessed by friends. A Victoria, British Columbia, lawyer was one of the exceptions. He attended the April 1959 execution of Leo Mantha at the request of the former tugboat operator, who wanted someone present he knew would help him maintain his courage. Mantha was among a handful of men executed in Canada for killing a male lover. When the young sailor with whom he was infatuated ended their relationship, Mantha crept into his lover's barracks at Esquimalt and stabbed him in the throat.

Refusing all but a small dose of morphine administered to lessen the terror of his last moments, Mantha walked into Oakalla prison farm's death chamber with grim determination. As he took his place under the rope dangling from a beam in the abandoned elevator shaft, he looked around for the face of his lawyer-friend. Nearest him were the hangman, his priest and seven guards, who stood in a loose semi-circle around the trapdoor. The remaining few witnesses stood farther back, their faces obscured by shadows in the dimly lit, yellow-painted room.

When the trap snapped open, Mantha dropped so quickly that a speck of white phlegm remained suspended even as the thud of his body being jerked to a stop echoed throughout the chamber. A guard above the room heard the sound, and he reached over to close the telephone circuit that was held open in case of a last-minute reprieve.

FAMILY AND FRIENDS OF THE VICTIM

It was long a Canadian tradition that members of a victim's family could attend the killer's execution. Occasionally, their presence was noticed.

In late August 1908, John Pertella beat to death a Vancouver woman and dismembered her body. Four months later he was hanged for the crime, going to the gallows with two men not connected to his offence. A few dozen spectators watched the execution, all invited guests of the city's sheriff. Among that number was the husband of Pertella's victim. While the killer stood on the scaffold, he caught sight of the man, and to the consternation of everyone present, began laughing.

Usually the chance to mock on such occasions belonged to family members of the victim, not the other way around. More normal was the execution of Amedée Chatelle, a killer whose brutal crime horrified the nation.

In mid-October 1894, Chatelle met his 13-year-old victim on a road near Listowel, Ontario. He grabbed the young girl and tried to sexually assault her. She resisted, and Chatelle knocked her unconscious with a rock. He then carried her across a field to an isolated bush, where he slit the girl's throat and cut her into pieces. When the teenager's body was found, it was discovered that her internal organs were missing. It later turned out that Chatelle wanted them for himself.

The father of the murdered young girl wanted to witness the execution of his daughter's killer, not out of a sense of revenge, he said, but to satisfy himself that the killer did indeed pay his debt to society.

Chatelle spent his last night alive in a cell that looked onto the yard where the gallows stood ready. As his execution neared, everyone within earshot could hear him pacing up and down his jail corridor.

Two hours before the morning hanging, spectators began to gather around the Stratford, Ontario, jail. Although hundreds applied for permission to witness the execution, only 50, invited by the local sheriff, were allowed in.

Even before the death procession formed, the bell of a nearby church began tolling. Fifteen minutes later, a jail door opened about 27 metres from the unusual-looking gallows, and the doomed man, supported on each side by a guard, covered the distance in no time. Chatelle's grizzled, iron-grey beard heightened the paleness of his face. His hollowed eyes and sunken cheeks gave him a haunted, haggard look in testimony to the mental anguish of his last days.

Two minutes after the death procession entered the jail yard, the weight attached to the jerk 'em up gallows fell, and Chatelle appeared to leap into the air. Almost at the moment his body reached the end of the rope, it plummeted down, stopping with his feet just centimetres above the ground. As his muscles relaxed, Chatelle's body appeared to shudder; for all intents and purposes, the child killer was dead.

DOCTORS AND LAWYERS

Apart from friends and family of either the victim or the killer, the two individuals, by profession, most often seen at executions were doctors and lawyers. Reports of late 19th- and early 20th-century executions routinely referred to their presence. Doctors used such events as teaching aids for medical students, who often gathered in large numbers around the corpses of those recently hanged to watch either a post-mortem examination or a dissection.

The execution of Thomas Kane is an example. He resided with his former sister-in-law, but the relationship was not a happy one, and the pair lived in poverty. On the day Mary Kane was murdered, the two fought, and in a fit of alcohol-fuelled anger, Thomas beat her with a plasterer's trowel, an iron, a fire shovel, a hammer and a spittoon. For the rest of that day and part of the next, he walked around Mary's body, until finally telling his neighbours that she was dead.

Contemporary accounts of his execution offer a glimpse into the pathetic life, and death, of the very poor. "Thomas Kane was hanged this morning," reported a Toronto paper. It said that no one knew why he committed murder, and that no one was sufficiently troubled to look for a reason. According to the paper, the murderer was poor, illiterate and uncultured, and died unregretted by anyone.

While it may have been true that Kane was friendless, his death did not go unnoticed. Of the nearly 100 people who attended the February 1890 execution, 44 were doctors or medical students.

Lawyers, too, often attended executions. At the hanging of Joseph Laplaine, 300 people crowded Montréal's jail, and prominent among them was a group of lawyers.

In 1901, Laplaine was deeply in love with the woman who ran the boarding house where he lived, but he feared his feelings for her were not reciprocated. Uncomfortable with the attention other boarders paid his landlady, he killed her in a jealous rage. His execution nine months later went off without a hitch.

The presence of a large number of lawyers at Laplaine's execution, and many others, was never explained. Most probably came out of curiosity and because their connection to the legal system guaranteed them a ticket. Admission to a high-profile hanging was much sought after, especially when it involved a woman. In 95 years, only 11 females were executed, and the rarity of such an event meant it attracted a lot of attention.

Phoebe Campbell suffered considerable abuse at the hands of her husband before she killed him in July 1871. At her trial, the issue was not whether she committed the murder but whether she had help. Shortly after her arrest, Campbell accused her husband's hired hand of the axe killing then recanted. The Thorndale, Ontario, prosecution lawyer introduced in evidence a letter from Phoebe to the hired man. She refused to explain what she meant when she wrote, "I never shall say you done any such thing again—if I have to die for it."

Her jury took just an hour to find her guilty. The hired man was acquitted at his trial and promptly left for England. That was perhaps a good thing. After it was made clear to her that there would be no commutation of her sentence, Phoebe confessed that she and the hired hand did indeed kill her husband because they wanted to marry.

Campbell was just 25 years old when she was executed. Despite the anxiety that must have made her last days difficult to endure, she freely chatted with her death watch, laughing at their anecdotes and behaving nothing like someone about to die. Instead of bemoaning her fate, Campbell spent her time making cloth souvenirs, to which she attached locks of her hair.

The morning she was taken to the gallows, Phoebe was the single vision of peacefulness among the wailing crowd. Not once amid the weeping did she show the slightest sign of nervousness, even when her executioner came for her. At his approach, Campbell got up from her bed to greet him. Before her arms could be tied, a jail matron insisted Phoebe be bound while on the scaffold, so she could walk to her death unaided. And that was where she was pinioned.

In a ground-floor corridor leading to the jail yard and gallows, Campbell shook hands with the witnesses she recognized, warmly wishing each farewell. She then walked directly to the scaffold, stopping for a moment to gather the skirt of her long black dress, and stepped up. On the platform, Campbell turned her back to the spectators standing below. Without a tremor she waited to be pinioned, all the while watching with apparent curiosity the executioner's movements.

As Phoebe's time wound down, her spiritual adviser began reading what he said were the young woman's last words. "I thank the jury for bringing me in guilty, and hope I will meet them in heaven," she said, "and I thank the judge for my right sentence, and say for a truth they done what was right in the sight of God and man." Continuing, she went on to thank the Queen's Counsel for his kindness and said she hoped to meet him in heaven. "They all done their best to find out the murder, and I say it would have been wrong to let me free after that dreadful crime."

While many last statements read from the gallows were actually scripted by the spiritual adviser, Campbell's words were clearly her own:

> *Oh my dear friends, I hope you will take warning by what you see and hear. The judgment of God is dreadful to face if not forgiven, but if your sins is forgiven, the thought of dying is sweet to a believer's ear. My dear fellow creatures, I pray seek the Lord while he may be found. Oh I am so happy. This morning is the happiest morning I ever spent for I am a day's march nearer home.*

Her statement finished, Campbell was led to the trap, where she knelt and started to pray. A few moments later, the sheriff gave a signal, and the trapdoor opened. The rope connecting Phoebe to the scaffold beam was too long, and although it turned out her neck broke at the drop, her feet dangled barely 2.5 centimetres above the ground. The distraught hangman immediately grabbed the rope and hauled her body up a few feet, where he held her until death was pronounced.

Because Campbell had no one to claim her body, even were that possible, she became increasingly anxious in her last days that her corpse not be given to attending doctors for dissection. In the end, Phoebe was buried intact in the jail yard after she was able to extract a promise from officials. In death there was little change in her appearance but for a raw-looking mark caused by the noose. Her face was pale but tranquil and gave no hint that she'd suffered any pain.

Although hundreds of people sought admission to the execution, and the banks of the river running by the jail were crowded, prominent among those who actually witnessed the hanging were members of the legal profession.

COULD NOT WATCH

Hangings seemed always to have fascinated people, and it was not uncommon for Canadians by the hundreds to seek admission to executions. Occasionally, those who attended such events found them too stressful, and at the last minute they could not bear to watch someone's life ending. That's what happened in June 1890, when Ontario's Henry Smith was hanged for murdering his wife of 22 years.

Smith was the sort of prisoner jail officials agonized about executing, not because they felt sympathy for him or were particularly empathetic, but because they worried he was going to panic and cause a scene. Jail officials were given ample reason for feeling that way. Smith was clearly nervous as the hours to his execution wound down, and he nearly fainted when guards arrived to take him to the scaffold. He was so terrified about what was to come that officers were forced to hold him up while his arms were tied together.

By the time his death walk got underway, Smith was surrounded by four guards, each ready to grab hold if he collapsed. And he very nearly did, both during the walk and when he reached the gallows. The obvious panic Smith experienced seemed to affect those watching his execution. One witness fainted, another threw up and several turned away.

Thirty-seven years later, many who watched the execution of John Barty reacted the same way. Barty was sentenced to die for a hammer murder committed during the robbery of a Hamilton, Ontario, convenience store. He was not a nice man, and few attending his execution worried about what he would endure.

The room in which Barty was hanged was a whitewashed enclosure where witnesses stood crammed for some time prior to the actual execution. The jail surgeon was summoned to the cell of the prisoner shortly before the death procession was to set out, and it is likely that the blank expression spectators saw on Barty's face was the result of sedation.

Although the killer died quickly, and there were no last-minute theatrics of the kind seen during Henry Smith's execution, one witness never saw what actually happened. Overcome at the oppressive nature of the scene, the man rushed from the room well before the lever was pulled. In a similar vein, when Bow River, Alberta, farmer John Fisk was hanged in late June 1911, members of his coroner's jury were allowed to watch the execution. Five of the six jurors refused to do so.

No Press Is Good Press

For part of the period during which Canadians were hanged, reports of what happened during executions were full of generalities and euphemisms. Newspaper stories were filled with phrases like "launched into eternity" or "death was instantaneous." Sheriffs were advised not to keep track of how long it took prisoners to die, and if pressed, to respond with vague references to events happening quickly and uneventfully, and that everything was carried out with dispatch.

This failure to report, or at least report accurately, was the result of a refusal on the part of Canadian sheriffs to allow reporters into death chambers. Stories of executions attracted a lot of attention, especially the reports of botched hangings. Better no report at all than one that reflected poorly on jail officials. While no one asked prisoners what they thought about dying in anonymity, it may well be they felt as Voltaire: "Nothing is more annoying than to be obscurely hanged."

Much data relating to capital punishment in Canada was either not kept or not yet put into usable form. It is nonetheless likely that the 1911 execution of 22-year-old Edward Jardine was among the first from which newspaper reporters were banned.

Jardine and Elizabeth Anderson, a girl of 16, both lived in the area around Goderich, Ontario. When the nude body of the young woman, her throat slit, was found near where she was last seen in Jardine's company, the young man was arrested and ultimately convicted of her murder.

While awaiting his execution, Jardine maintained an almost stoic demeanour. In his last hours, however, he began to disintegrate emotionally. Fears he might collapse before his sentence was carried out were realized when, 30 minutes before the hangman made his appearance, he broke down. Jail officials were ready. Within minutes, the prostrate killer was given an injection of morphine. It worked.

Jardine walked unaided to his death. Less than a minute elapsed between the start of the death procession and the trapdoor dropping. Death was pronounced a little over eight minutes later. At least that was what local newspapers reported. No one knows for sure exactly what happened, since news reporters were not allowed onto the jail grounds.

When John Fisk was hanged in Calgary in 1911, the same policy was followed. That did not stop newspapers from recounting his last moments. They told readers that as he stood on the trap, noosed and pinioned, with his last breath he protested his innocence. Reporters accepted as accurate everything Sheriff Van Wart told them. Officially, however, even he was not supposed to report what happened on the scaffold. According to a directive of Alberta's Attorney General, no official discussion of the execution was permitted. All newspapers could report with accuracy was that well before the hanging got underway, a large and "morbid" crowd gathered near the police barracks, attracted by the scaffold that rose threateningly above the jail's walls.

Members of the press were not happy about being excluded from executions. Particularly incensed was an Oshawa, Ontario, reporter assigned to cover the hanging of George Norman Bilton, who battered and murdered his lover and her daughter near Ajax in mid-1946. The 25-year-old welder was hanged inside the local jail on an improvised gallows built on the second floor of the building, with a hole cut through the floor to provide the necessary drop.

Reporters were expressly forbidden from entering any jail building prior to the execution, including the home of the prison governor. That did not stop Elmer Ross. Although the newsman slipped through an unlocked door in the residence, his entry did not go unnoticed. Minutes before Bilton was to hang, the front door of the governor's home swung open, and a man came flying out, landing with a crash on the front veranda. Startled witnesses looked up to see a few articles of clothing follow, then the door slammed shut. Two police constables quickly seized the reporter and started to hustle him down the steps. Ross, however, broke away, staggered across the lawn and left the compound, presumably the same way be broke in.

On one occasion, efforts by officials to keep reporters in the dark about what happened during an execution were the cause of considerable embarrassment.

When the body of a Lachine, Québec, taxi driver was found in a ditch near Montréal in July 1927, the police immediately suspected he was murdered by George "Cross-Eyed" McDonald and his wife, Doris. A few months after the couple was captured in Butte, Montana, both were sentenced to hang for killing the cabbie. Doris' sentence was commuted to life imprisonment two days before the couple's scheduled execution, and George went to the scaffold alone.

That was what reporters were told. All they were certain of was what they heard. The first sound was the voice of a priest, presumably walking with McDonald to the gallows. Of the second sound there was no doubt—it was the thunderclap of a dropping trapdoor.

The problem for officials was that more than an hour before the execution was carried out, a peace officer appeared at the door of the adjacent courthouse and announced that McDonald had been hanged. The words were barely out of his mouth before another officer ran up and denied the report.

From there, what should have been a sombre event turned into a farce. When reporters refused to disperse, searchlights were turned on them, and a platoon of armed guards arrived to escort newsmen away from the jail. By the time McDonald was actually hanged, most were back in position, and if they did not witness the execution, they at least heard it.

Chapter Seven

On the Scaffold

~

Nothing in his life
Became him like the leaving it; he died
As one that had been studied in his death
To throw away the dearest thing he ow'd
As 'twere a careless trifle.

—Macbeth, Act 1, Scene 4

The decorum of the women and men who died on a Canadian gallows varied from abject grovelling to heroic stoicism. Although a handful of those sentenced to death appeared unaffected by their surroundings, most met their fate with a sense of resignation, if not acceptance.

An example of how different two individuals acted on the scaffold occurred early in 1935. Teenager Angelo Donafrio and his partner Leone Gagliardi were hanged for the insurance murder of Nicholas Sarao, whose battered body was found a year earlier near a Montréal racetrack. Donafrio met death bravely, walking to the scaffold with his head erect. Gagliardi, on the other hand, staggered several times before finally collapsing. In the end, two guards supported him on the trap while he was pinioned and noosed before dropping to his death.

CROWDS ON THE SCAFFOLD

For much of the period during which Canadians were hanged, the most sought-after ticket at an execution was one that permitted a spectator to stand on the scaffold with the person about to be hanged. When George O'Brien was executed in the Yukon in 1901, the first 35 people to show up at the jail were allowed on the gallows platform, perhaps as an incentive to arrive early.

In the case of O'Brien, the lucky 35 were in addition to members of the official execution party. Such groups typically included the sheriff of the town where the hanging took place, his deputy, several officials from the jail, several guards, three or four spiritual advisers, reporters, the hangman and his assistant, occasionally police officers, and always one or more condemned prisoners.

Although the executioner prepared the prisoner, permission to pull the lever was given by the sheriff. That some-times presented a problem because sheriffs gave the signal to go ahead in a variety of ways. Some nodded their heads, others raised a hand and a few snapped their fingers. The shuffling of feet and whispering on the scaffold meant a hangman was required to be especially vigilant, lest he open the trap with someone in addition to the condemned prisoner on it.

The crowd that gathered to watch the execution of Thomas Collins in 1907 was about average size for a hanging in that era. His scaffold was 2.5 metres square and supported by posts three metres high. The trapdoor, roughly two-thirds of a metre square, was located in the centre of the platform. A bar ran under both doors. The bar was connected to a lever that the hangman pulled to release the trap. The scaffold was enclosed by walls 5.4 metres high, ensuring that only ticketholders witnessed the hanging. Surrounding Collins on the Hopewell Cape, New Brunswick, scaffold were a deputy sheriff, a jailer, three constables, two ministers, the coroner, a second doctor and six reporters.

Collins' eyes were red from weeping, his face pale, but he walked with a steady step toward the gallows. Until he reached the foot of the scaffold, he stared straight ahead. Then he looked up and, never missing a step, ascended. Everyone present heard his steps, as the heavy planks of the scaffold creaked under his weight. When he reached his destination, Collins stopped, and for just a moment, looked at the dangling noose.

The hangman moved with experience and purpose. He positioned Collins on the centre of the trap. Collins could not see it, but his executioner gathered the slack of the rope, coiled it into short loops, and then to prevent them from becoming caught up in Collins' falling body, tied the coils out of the way with a thread. It would snap when the trap opened, releasing the rope. The witnesses surrounding Collins watched in silence, occasionally shuffling their feet.

As soon as the hangman stepped away from the bound man, the prisoner's spiritual adviser began the Lord's Prayer. Part way through the prayer, the executioner pulled the wooden lever. The doors opened with a heavy grating sound, smashing into the lower frame of the platform with a sharp thump. In the blink of an eye, Collins vanished. Although no one saw the thread break, the coils suddenly separated, and with a snap, the rope straightened. It then began moving in very small, declining circles.

Seven minutes later, the life of Thomas Collins was pronounced extinct.

KNEELING ON THE GALLOWS

If Canadians were to imagine what a gallows execution would look like, most would envision the condemned prisoner noosed under a beam, standing over a pit into which he would drop when the trapdoors snapped open. Parts of that scene reflect the reality of executions—the beam, the dangling rope and the trapdoor. Standing, however, was not always a component of executions.

In the early 19th century, eastern newspapers referred to condemned prisoners dropping to their death while kneeling. Not only was kneeling on the trap a North American phenomenon, but it also was primarily an eastern way of doing things, no doubt evolving out of the notion of prayers said on bended knees. An example of the tradition can be seen in the execution of John Traviss, the first person hanged in post-Confederation Toronto.

Three months before the 20-year-old was executed, he became annoyed with John Johnson, a farmer he felt was frustrating his efforts to win the heart, if not the hand, of a local woman. Traviss bought a pistol, practiced with it, and on November 23, 1871, shot Johnson with it. After killing his victim, Traviss ran to his sister's house, where he confessed to the murder. At his trial, she was one of the principal witnesses to testify against him.

The evening before he was executed, some friends came to visit Traviss, and after they left, four ministers remained with him until morning. He went to bed about 11:00 PM and slept for almost three hours. He awoke feeling chilled and got up to cover himself with a few coats. He hugged them around his shoulders while he warned himself by the stove that heated his cell then went back to bed. Three hours later he woke up for the last time.

Traviss washed, dressed himself, drank a cup of coffee, participated in a religious service and then walked to the gallows. It was erected in the east yard of the Toronto jail and stood 3.5 metres high. A pit several metres deep was dug below the trapdoor, to ensure a drop sufficient to snap the prisoner's neck. When he reached the steps of the scaffold, Traviss at once started up. He proceeded to the front of the platform, where he spoke to those gathered to watch him die:

> *Brother and I undertook to build a house for Mr. John Johnson,*
> *about a mile and a half from our own house. While I was work-*
> *ing at Johnson's, I formed an intimacy with Miss Elizabeth*
> *Nichole, who lived quite near Johnson. After a time I learned*
> *that he was in the habit of slandering me there, until he brought*
> *about what he threatened, and the family showed themselves*
> *very distant toward me. Naturally violent when wronged,*
> *a spirit of revenge gradually possessed me.*
>
> *About eight o'clock Mr. Johnson started for Queensville, and*
> *as the road lay for a mile in the direction in which I wanted*
> *to go, I jumped on the sleigh and accompanied him. I discharged*
> *the pistol behind his ear. I am the man that killed him.*

When he finished speaking, Traviss shook hands with those standing beside him on the scaffold and then knelt on the trap. As soon as he did, his hangman pulled a black hood over his head. He also adjusted the noose around Traviss' neck, being careful to secure the knot beneath his left ear. Traviss fell almost two metres. After a few convulsive twitches, his arms remained motionless. Moments later he died.

Désiré Auger was a young but experienced criminal the year he left his home in the province of Québec to begin a new life in Ontario. It did not take long, however, before he reverted to his old ways. When an 80-year-old Polish woman was found raped and murdered in Pembroke, Auger was soon arrested. Two trials later, he was sentenced to hang, and on December 27, 1873, he was escorted to the gallows.

The condemned man knelt on the scaffold platform and gave a brief speech: "I am going to tell the truth now, as before

God, in whose presence I am about to appear. What I said about O'Keafe when I accused him of the crime was false. He is innocent, as I am also, of that crime."

Auger finished his statement and remained on his knees, praying for mercy, until the trap was released. Although his drop was less than two metres, he died almost instantly. The only movement spectators observed was a slight twitching of his hands and feet and a drawing up of his shoulders. His body remained suspended for almost an hour before it was cut down and given to his spiritual adviser for burial.

SOUND OF SILENCE

Occasionally, reports of a killer's execution seemed to capture the drama of the event perfectly. In 1902, Walter Gordon was hanged in Brandon, Manitoba, for killing two area farmers. A reporter attending his execution observed that the silence that enveloped Gordon was as deep as the forest, and when Lawrence Deacon was put to death in the same province 46 years later for murdering a taxi driver, it was reported he was executed in a silence you could hear.

Many executions were just as quiet, including that of bank robber Sidney Murrell and girlfriend-killer Clarence Topping, who in 1924 were hanged in the yard of London, Ontario's Middlesex jail. It took their hangman about a minute to pinion, noose and hood the men. During that time, not

a word was spoken by anyone. The only sounds were the footsteps of the executioner as he walked across the scaffold.
Although the quiet ended in a heartbeat, when the bolt of the
trapdoor was drawn and the killers dropped with a thud, it was
the unnatural silence that witnesses spoke of later.

Executions on Canada's west coast were just as silent as
those in the east, and every bit as quick. The 1953 hanging of
Alexander Viatkin is an example. He dropped to his death alone,
sick and unrepentant five seconds after he stepped onto the trapdoor of the Oakalla prison farm gallows.

The 24-year-old engineer had an acute case of tuberculosis when he was hanged for murdering an elderly Vancouver
man. The execution chamber was deathly still as Viatkin
entered. The only sound was the executioner's heavy breathing,
and the terrible rasp of the knot being drawn into position
behind the killer's left ear.

Robert Alexander Hoodley was executed at the same
British Columbia prison in 1955, with neither drama nor delay.
When witnesses attending his hanging walked along the jail's
death row, Hoodley had not yet left his cell. Yet so quick did
his death procession form that they had barely taken their places
when a door opened and Hoodley was led in.

A railing nearly encircled the trap, and witnesses stood
behind it. Hoodley looked at them briefly. What he saw were six
members of his coroner's jury and half a dozen guards. Hoodley
seemed not to believe was he was seeing. When he lowered his

head, he almost gasped at the sight of the yawning pit clearly visible through the gap between the trapdoors.

While Hoodley fought to hold his sense of panic at bay, his executioner went to work. The brow of the plump, bald, pimpled hangman was beaded with sweat as he strapped his victim's feet together. Hoodley could not take his eyes off the man and was still looking at him when a black hood was pulled over his face and a noose tightened around his neck. No one said a word.

The silence continued even as the witnesses filed out of the death chamber after Hoodley was hanged. The quiet was disturbed only for a moment as a solitary cry of protest echoed from somewhere in the prison, but beyond that, silence was everywhere.

Speed Is of the Essence

Even before death sentences were carried out indoors, it did not take long to hang someone. An example is the hanging of Henry "The Flying Dutchman" Wagner. After an incredibly colourful life of crime, during which the killer claimed to have ridden with Butch Cassidy and the Sundance Kid, Wagner died before he fully realized what was happening.

The beginning of the end of The Flying Dutchman's criminal career began in 1913, when two undercover police officers tried to arrest a burglar they thought was responsible for a series of break-ins up and down the British Columbia

coast. Their miscalculation cost one of the constables his life.
The burglaries were committed by two men, not one, and the
perpetrators were armed and dangerous.

The moment the officers opened the door of the store
they were staking out, Wagner shot and killed one of them and
injured the other. With a little help from his partner, Wagner
probably would have gotten away, but in the ensuing one-on-one
fight with the surviving officer, Wagner was overpowered.

The Flying Dutchman was certainly not reluctant to talk
about himself. Already wanted for murder in the state of Washington, he not only claimed to have ridden with the duo of
Cassidy and Sundance but also said he actually led the Hole in
the Wall Gang before deciding to retire to Canada.

The colourful killer did not do well in jail, and on several
occasions tried to commit suicide. He first attempted to strangle
himself, and when that failed, he slit his wrists. That too accom-
plished nothing, and he was reduced to running full speed
toward one of the walls in his exercise yard, hoping to break his
neck by lunging head first into the bricks. Nothing worked,
although ironically, the closest he came was the evening before
he was to hang, when he suffered a seizure.

Only 30 seconds elapsed from the time The Flying
Dutchman started his walk across a Nanaimo courtyard to the
time his executioner released the trapdoor on which Wagner
stood. Attired only in an undershirt and overalls, his face

unshaven and his hair uncut, the prisoner looked every bit the wild man he claimed to be.

Things happened just as quickly in Edmonton three years later, when it took only 14 seconds to hang George Leek. In the fall of 1915, Leek was released from an Alberta jail and made his way to the small town of Junkins. In a robbery gone wrong, he attacked a local man, leaving him dead. Days later, Leek started selling his victim's possessions, a move that helped pave his way to a Fort Saskatchewan gallows. Once the authorities heard that a man was hawking goods clearly not his own, it did not take them long to catch up with one of the few black men in a very white province.

In February 1920, Stockyo Boyeff also had a very brief stay on a gallows—exactly seven seconds. Nine months before he was executed, Boyeff and Ivan Petcoff were approached by a third man, who told them a story of gold being found just outside Kitchener, Ontario. The three quickly made their way to Galt, and from there to the gravel pit where the gold was supposed to be found. Whether out of disappointment at discovering the story was not true or because of some personal grievance, Petcoff and the third man started arguing. Their disagreement quickly turned violent, and the third man was beaten to death with a rock. Or at least that was Boyeff's version of events when he testified at his friend's murder trial.

As soon as Petcoff was convicted and sentenced to hang, it was Boyeff's turn. This time it was Petcoff doing the testifying. He accused Boyeff of committing the murder and robbery, and of burying the victim's body under a pile of stones. The jury was convinced.

Boyeff slept most of his last night alive and ate a big breakfast before settling in to await the arrival of his executioner. Although he was nervous while his arms were tied, the killer walked on his own to the gallows erected in a woodshed. A few jail officials, members of a coroner's jury and three reporters witnessed his execution. Barely a handful of minutes passed from the time Boyeff left his cell to the official pronouncement of his death.

Over the years, it wasn't unusual for newspapers describing the execution of a killer to suggest that the hanging was the fastest on record. Such claims were likely untrue, since there was no absolute uniformity to Canadian executions, and keeping track of how long it took to hang a prisoner was never part of our culture of capital punishment. Still, there is little doubt that things happened quickly, particularly in the case of Thomas McCoskey.

In August 1926, McCoskey killed a guard at Kingston Penitentiary during a failed escape attempt. Eight months later, he found himself in a death cell in the same city. He remained calm until he was within sight of the gallows, where he would have collapsed were it not for the assistance of two guards. Only 13 seconds elapsed from the time McCoskey stepped from his cell to the time he plummeted to his death. Fourteen minutes more went by before he was declared dead, and then an additional 10 until he was buried.

Yet another robbery gone bad resulted in the speedy execution of Ray Cortland in mid-October 1930. Almost 10 months earlier, he and a female companion were seen at the home of a Richelieu, Québec, man, whose body was discovered after the couple departed. The victim was lying on the floor beside his bed, with a mattress thrown over him. The dead man's hands were tied behind his back, an improvised garrotte wound was found around his throat and his skull was fractured. A week after the murder, Cortland and his friend were arrested.

The day before he was executed, Cortland was transferred from Montréal's Bordeaux Jail to a death cell at St. Hyacinthe. Because the small community did not have a gallows of its own, and anticipated no future need for one, local officials arranged to borrow a scaffold for a few days.

When Cortland's parents made the trip from their home in southern Ontario to see their son for the last time, the prisoner's mother was overcome with emotion the moment she stepped into the St. Hyacinthe jail. She was rushed to a local hospital, but before long recovered sufficiently to spend the afternoon with her son.

The evening before he was hanged, Cortland wrote three letters—one to his mother, another to his wife and a third to the woman who was with him at the time of the murder. At dawn, the town sheriff entered his cell and announced that the time had come. Without any fuss, Cortland rose, shook hands with his death watch and whoever else was standing nearby and started for the gallows.

At the foot of the red-painted scaffold, the killer stopped, and in a tone of resignation, said, "It has to be done—I must go through with it." Even allowing for a brief hesitation at the top of the steps, only 47 seconds elapsed from the time Cortland left his cell to the pulling of the lever.

Once Canadian scaffolds were moved indoors, and death cells relocated as near them as possible, the time it took to hang someone was dramatically reduced. The execution of a Fernie, British Columbia section foreman was typical of a speedy process that suddenly became much quicker.

In February 1936, Vincent Macchione, a 36-year-old married man, killed his mistress' husband. Two and a half years later, he was hanged at the Oakalla prison farm. His hangman tightened a strap around his legs, slipped a black hood and a noose over his head and pulled the lever in less than five seconds.

HANGING WITH OTHERS

Canada has never had a national policy dealing with how many people could be executed at the same time. The largest multiple hanging occurred in late November 1885 when eight Native men were put to death for the part they played in the North West Rebellion.

The government of John A. Macdonald was determined to send a very visible message to potential troublemakers in the west and decided to execute the men at the same time, and in front of as many people as possible. It was a macabre sight. A lone hangman stood on a huge scaffold, surrounded by 150 police officers, while one after another his victims were led to their places. As the executioner walked from man to man, preparing each in turn, the sound of eight death chants could be heard by spectators standing as far away as a hill overlooking the Saskatchewan River, where eight bodies were moments later interred.

The second largest mass execution in our country's history took place in mid-December 1946 when four German prisoners of war and a pedophile were hanged in Lethbridge, Alberta.

In September 1944, Canadian authorities were sufficiently concerned about the growing violence in the Medicine Hat prisoner-of-war camp that they transferred leaders of the inmate population to other camps, where they would have less influence. A day before the transfers were made, Sergeant-Major Bruno Perzonowsky, a dyed-in-the-wool Nazi, instructed a group of underlings to execute a known camp informer. The former teacher was lured to a hall he once used for inmate lectures where he was then beaten and hanged.

Four Nazis were charged with his murder. They were tried separately, and each was convicted. All gave statements admitting their involvement in the killing, though one man maintained that he was less complicit than his co-accused, convinced that his cooperation would result in the commutation of his sentence. It was no surprise then that he was the only one of the POWs not to attempt suicide one day prior to the scheduled execution.

Shortly before the Germans were to hang, a 29-year-old Canadian army veteran joined the Germans on Lethbridge's death row. He was convicted of the sex slaying of a young Calgary boy, and his addition to the roster of condemned prisoners guaranteed that the execution would be of historic proportion.

In the few days following the arrival of the Canadian at Lethbridge, the Germans refused to speak to or acknowledge the newcomer. They regarded him as a thug, something much less than they were. Ironically, all five shared a common grave in the yard of the Alberta jail, just a couple feet from the gallows on which they died.

Often two killers were hanged at the same time not because they committed a common crime, but because a double hanging was a money saver. An example was the execution of two British Columbia men. Forty-one-year-old Alexander DeBortoli had killed the woman with whom he was living. The second man was a Costa Rican longshoreman sentenced to die for the brutal murder of a nurse. Benito Pasquale was visiting a friend at the hospital where she worked, and for no apparent reason, he suddenly attacked the woman, slitting her throat with a razor.

On July 14, 1926, DeBortoli went to the gallows first. After he was placed on the trap and pinioned, Pasquale was brought in, supported by two guards. After a few hurried words between officials, the trapdoor was sprung, and the two strangers dropped to their deaths.

Usually, however, when people were executed together, they knew each other. On occasion, as in the case of Norman and Lawrence Menard, they were even related.

The Menard brothers killed a man when they held up the Charcoal Supply Company of Québec, and in December 1929, they were together hanged in Montréal. The chaplain of the Bordeaux jail spent the better part of their last day with the young Menards, and as the hours ticked by, he said they became increasingly resigned to their fate. Eighteen-year-old Lawrence even told the chaplain that he was satisfied that he would die with his 22-year-old brother.

HANGING BACK TO BACK

Just as there was no rule of thumb about how many people could be executed at one time, there was no established procedure for how condemned prisoners were positioned on the gallows. Some, like the Menards, stood side by side, but others were hanged back to back.

Leonard Jackson and Steve Suchan were members of Ontario's infamous Boyd Gang, and in early 1952, they were wanted by police for a number of bank robberies. In March, two officers on car patrol recognized the pair as the men drove down a Toronto street. The pursuit ended in a gun battle and the death of a city police sergeant. Nine months later, the two killers occupied separate cells on the Don Jail's death row, 40 steps from the gallows.

An hour before the men were to hang, they heard Mass. Jackson was born Jewish, raised as an Anglican and while on death row became a Catholic. Before the cop killers were handcuffed and led by pairs of guards to the death chamber, the condemned men's spiritual adviser anointed their eyes, ears, lips, hands and slippered feet with sacred oils. Then they moved into the corridor, and the death possession started toward the gallows.

In the death chamber, Jackson and Suchan were greeted by their executioner and two knotted ropes lying coiled on a beam. The men shuffled their feet impatiently as guards moved them into position on the trap, back to back. The hangman then pulled black hoods over their faces and tightened a noose around the neck of each man. As soon as that was done, he quickly moved to a lever a few feet away and gave it a slight tug. The hinged doors dropped only slightly faster than the men.

The last two people executed in Canada were also hanged back to back at the Don Jail. Ronald Turpin was convicted of killing a Toronto police officer in 1962 while trying to escape arrest, and Arthur Lucas was sentenced to hang for the knife murder of an informant working for the Detroit office of the United States Bureau of Narcotics.

HANGING SIDE BY SIDE

On October 17, 1919, three Québec men living in Saskatchewan were hanged as they stood side by side on a single trapdoor in the yard of the old Prince Albert jail. What brought them there was both sad and surreal.

Two years before his execution, Joseph Gervais, a medical doctor practicing in the province of Québec, accepted 17-year-old Victor Carmel and 27-year-old Jean-Baptiste St. Germain as patients. Gervais was well known as a hypnotist, and both Carmel and St. Germain later maintained that from the time they met the doctor he exercised almost absolute control over them through the power of suggestion.

A year after the three first met, Gervais persuaded his much younger friends to accompany him to the Steep Creek area of Saskatchewan, where he owned a farm. Almost as soon as they arrived, the men began building and provisioning an underground fortification, which Gervais explained would be used by men from Québec who did not want to fight in World War I.

In 1918, Gervais decided he wanted a neighbour's farm, so he and his two young followers murdered the farmer and burned his house to make the death look like an accident. That seemed to establish a pattern of lawlessness for the trio. Before the year was out, Gervais had purchased a pair of horses. When he took delivery but refused to pay for the animals, the owner of the horses obtained a court order to repossess them. The bailiff serving the warrant no sooner arrived at the entrance to the Gervais homestead than he was shot by Carmel and St. Germain.

A search for the missing bailiff began almost at once, and it did not take long for two members of the provincial police force to make their way to Steep Creek. As one officer spoke with Gervais, another noticed the entrance to the underground fortification and went to investigate. In a matter of minutes, he lay dead, the second victim of Carmel and St. Germain. The surviving police officer immediately arrested Gervais, and soon the farmyard was full of reinforcements. After a siege lasting several days, Carmel and St. Germain were flushed from their hideout.

The Crown prosecuted Gervais first and then his two partners in crime. Whatever chance the doctor might have had disappeared when members of his Prince Albert jury learned that he used his influence over Carmel to force the young man to engage in homosexual acts with him.

A week after Gervais was sentenced to death, it was Carmel's and St. Germain's turn to learn their fate. In what is believed to be a Canadian first, their judge was asked to find them not guilty of murder because their crimes were committed while they were hypnotized. That defence did not work, though the judge accepted as fact the argument that Gervais was a hypnotist and had the ability to control the actions of the accused. The judge, however, was not persuaded that this information relieved Carmel and St. Germain of responsibility for the murders.

As the trapdoor the prisoners were standing on snapped open, Gervais got in the last word, shouting, "The King of England stole Québec, I die for my country." The drop broke the necks of all three men, and in 12 minutes, each was officially declared dead.

Hanging Face to Back

In early November 1936, two Aboriginal brothers and a stranger were hanged on an Oakalla prison farm gallows as the trio stood in line, one behind the other. Two years before they were executed, Eneas and Richardson George, together with a third brother whose sentence was commuted, brutally murdered two police officers. The constables were sent to the Canford Reserve in south-central British Columbia to investigate the stabbing of Eneas' wife. After they were beaten to death with sticks and rocks, the bodies of the officers were thrown into the Nicola River.

The third member of the trio hanged at Oakalla was Charles Russell, a young bank robber who shot and killed a teller while holding up a Vancouver branch of the Canadian Bank of Commerce.

Eneas was taken into the death chamber first. He stared straight ahead, not once blinking. His executioner promptly bound his ankles and pulled a black hood over his face. Then Eneas' brother came in. Richardson stood directly behind his brother, facing the same direction. Unlike Eneas, he kept his eyes closed. Last was Russell. He entered the room smoking, his hair evenly parted on the left side. He quickly spat out his cigarette and took the last available spot on the trap. Moments later it was all over.

TWO, THEN ONE

Probably because the trapdoors of some Canadian gallows were too small to accommodate more than two people at a time, condemned prisoners were occasionally hanged in odd combinations. The execution of three Manitoba men was one such occasion.

On May 14, 1938, Peter Korzenowski, Dan Prytula and a friend consumed nearly three litres of homebrew before deciding to rob Anna Cottick and her 91-year-old husband, Elko. Around midnight, the three men roused a sleeping William Kanuka and insisted he come with them to the Cottick farm.

When the men arrived, Korzenowski and Prytula got out of Prytula's car, and Kanuka drove about four kilometres down the road from the farm, where he and the fourth member of the group waited. Armed with two revolvers, Korzenowski and Prytula smashed the glass of a ground-floor window of the house, fired two warning shots and crawled in.

They were immediately confronted by Elko Cottick, whom Prytula attacked with a large flashlight. Korzenowski, meanwhile, rushed to the adjoining room, where Anna was sleeping. After knocking her unconscious with a blackjack, he started kicking her, breaking nine ribs before he finally beat her to death. The men then carried Elko out of the farmhouse, but once outside, seemed to change their minds. They re-entered the tiny residence and threw the Cotticks down a fruit cellar, where their grandson found Elko barely alive the next morning.

Rumours that the two elderly Fishing River district farmers kept more than $1000 in their home proved untrue, and Anna's killers departed with only $23.

After leaving the farm, the four men drove west, where Kanuka, Korzenowski and Prytula robbed and nearly beat to death another octogenarian farmer. Part way through the assault, one of the men noticed that the sun was beginning to rise and insisted that it was time to go.

Within 24 hours, all three were arrested, turned in by the friend who was with them during the two break-ins but who did not take part in any of the beatings. The process of finding enough corroborating evidence to obtain murder convictions against the killers was the stuff of a modern crime drama.

As soon as the RCMP arrived at the Cottick farm, members noticed fresh tire tracks entering and leaving the yard. The officers tracked the men to within 137 metres of Kanuka's residence, and from there to the Gilbert Plains home of Prytula's sister. The tire marks perfectly matched the treads on Prytula's 1929 Ford. The vehicle was confiscated, and while casts were taken of its tires, Prytula was arrested and his

The grave marker of one of the three men executed on February 16, 1939, for the brutal murder of Anna Cottick. The cemetery where the killers are interred is located just west of Headingley Jail.

•—◆—•

bloodstained clothes, boots and three .32 calibre bullets seized and sent to the RCMP crime lab for testing.

As one group of officers arrested Prytula and Korzenowski, another searched the Cottick residence for additional evidence. They noticed what appeared to be finger-prints on the window glass smashed by the killers, and the glass fragments were sent to experts in Winnipeg.

The RCMP also searched Korzenowski's residence and yard, located a few hundred metres from where Kanuka was staying. They found the revolvers used in the break-ins, hidden in a pile of stones. Korzenowski was promptly arrested, and several days later, he and his two friends were part of an identification line-up paraded in front of the hospital bed of Elko Cottick.

While the police waited for the results of forensic tests being carried out in Dauphin, Winnipeg and Regina, they held the alleged killers on a coroner's warrant. That changed on June 1, when the three men were formally charged with murder. The proceeding seemed to amuse Kanuka, who entered and left the courtroom with a broad grin on his face.

His amusement turned to concern, however, when he learned that conversations between he and his co-accused were recorded by a dictograph hidden in the ventilators and registers of their cells.

When those recordings were introduced at trial, it became clear that the men were surprised at the amount of scientific evidence the police had gathered. On one occasion an obviously perplexed Prytula was heard complaining that despite eight years' experience robbing people, "I got caught with the tires. I do not understand it." His other complaint was the cost of his lawyer. "No wonder one has to go robbing."

A combination of eyewitness testimony, scientific evidence and the accused own words sealed their fate. After a weeklong trial and four hours of deliberation, a Dauphin jury found them guilty of murder. Kanuka was the only one to receive a recommendation for mercy, and he alone reacted to the verdict: "I did not enter the house, and I killed no one, and I do not think I should hang."

Once previously, a Manitoba court sentenced three people to hang for taking part in a single murder, but in 1918 the sentence of the youngest was commuted to life imprisonment.

Korzenowski and Kanuka were hanged side by side in the Headingley jail just after midnight on February 16, 1939. While life slowly ebbed out of their bodies, Prytula awaited his turn. He did not wait long. It took jail officials exactly 14 minutes to take down the corpses of Kanuka and Korzenowski and spring the trap on Prytula, five minutes longer than it took him to die.

Chapter Eight

Mistakes Happen

~

Canadian hangmen seem to have come by their inclination to bungle hangings honestly, sharing with their English counterparts a long tradition of mistake-making during executions. Mary Queen of Scots was neither the first nor last to suffer during her last moments, though no one knows for sure which one of the three blows to her head actually killed her.

Cornelius Burleigh set a Canadian precedent for scaffold errors when in 1831 he staggered around in front of hundreds of horrified spectators after he was hanged for killing a police constable. After Burleigh fell through the scaffold floor, the jolt of his body being jerked to a stop drop snapped the rope, and for several minutes he walked around with what was left of the noose dangling from his neck. Only when someone had the presence of mind to get a new rope from the local hardware store was the dazed man seized and returned to the gallows. This time everything worked perfectly, for everyone other than Burleigh, that is.

Two Canadian historians recently claimed that as many as two-thirds of Canadian executions were botched. Depending on your perspective, that suggestion is exaggerated. While it is true that most of the people hanged in this country died as a result of strangulation, rather than a broken neck, that does not mean their executions were bungled. Prison officials typically regarded an execution as "normal," regardless whether it resulted in a broken neck or not, if the person hanged was immediately rendered unconscious and subsequently died without incident.

A DIFFERENT KIND OF MISTAKE

It was not always the case that a bungled hanging caused pain or had anything to do with the execution process itself. Some mistakes occurred in the courtroom.

During the 1890 murder trial of Thomas Kane, it was clear to everyone that at the time the accused beat to death his common-law wife, both killer and victim were drunk. Although the evidence against Kane was entirely circumstantial, jurors had no trouble agreeing that he brought about the woman's death. They mistakenly believed, however, that when they attached to their verdict a recommendation for mercy, Kane's sentence would automatically be reduced to manslaughter and he would go to prison rather than to the gallows. Jurors later complained that if the law was better explained to them, they would have returned a verdict of manslaughter, since none of them wanted Kane to die. But, in 1890, die he did.

Thirteen years later, a British Columbia killer suffered the same fate as a result of a similar error. Until mid-1903, Alfred James Frith worked in a government dockyard in Esquimalt. After he was fired, he grew increasingly bitter toward the dock's chief storekeeper, whom he felt was responsible for his dismissal. Frith's sense of resentment came to a head in late June when he walked into a building and shot the storekeeper in the head.

Frith seemed to accept his fate without complaint. When the Victoria sheriff arrived shortly before the scheduled execution with word that the federal cabinet turned down his request for a reprieve, Frith received the news without emotion. He said only that he was ready to die and wished for the sake of his family that he might be hanged sooner. Then he walked back to his cell, whistling.

Ironically, members of the jury who sentenced him to death said they had no idea Frith would hang. Had they known their verdict would result in his death, they said they would have made a different decision.

IT TAKES TIME TO DIE

Most proponents of capital punishment no doubt believe in the Biblical adage of an eye for an eye. That does not necessarily mean, however, that they believe the process by which a life is forfeited to the State should be prolonged anymore than necessary. Which raises the question: how long does it take a hanging victim to die?

Usually, suspending someone by the neck dislocates the vertebrae supporting the person's head, depriving the brain of oxygen. This process does not happen instantly, because neck muscles are powerful and the arteries supplying blood to the brain are relatively well protected. Victims of hanging, therefore, likely live long enough to suffer pain as a result of their skin being stretched, their neck dislocating, and strangling. But they cannot make their pain known, because the rope suspending them constricts their vocal cords. That is why it is probable that someone with abnormally strong neck muscles may take considerable time to die, during which the victim is likely very much alive.

To measure how long it takes a hanging victim to die, a test was carried out on two murderers executed in the Philippines. According to a 1955 newspaper article, a sphygmographic tracing of their pulse rate was obtained by attaching a small revolving drum to the men's wrists As the two walked to the gallows, the tracing was rapid, and remained so while they stood on the scaffold. When the killers dropped, each struggled for a few seconds, then quieted, apparently unconscious. The sphygmograph recorded a pulse for 18 minutes, though those administering the test concluded that for all intents and purposes, death was immediate.

Even with this information, it was no doubt upsetting to Canadians to read reports of the length of time it took a condemned prisoner to die—more than half an hour in the case of Toronto's William Newell, executed in 1942 for killing his wife; 45 minutes in the case of farmhand Thomas Fletcher, hanged in Manitoba in 1918; and an hour and seven minutes for Québecer Antonio Sprecarce, executed a year after Fletcher, for killing his former boss.

The Noose Slipped

Botched executions usually occurred when the noose encircling a condemned prisoner's neck was not placed under the victim's left ear, or if it was placed properly, the noose was not tightened enough and it slipped. In either case, the result was often horrific.

Frederick Mann was not a good person. On January 2, 1883, he was working for a family of farmers near Hawkesbury, Ontario. For a reason never explained, he raped and strangled the young daughter of his employers. When the girl's mother heard the commotion, she rushed to her daughter's aid, and she too was strangled. Next was the girl's father, killed with an axe. Mann then went into the house and murdered one of his first victim's brothers, who was asleep. His attack on another sibling failed, and the wounded boy woke his two surviving sisters. With the help of a passerby, the children forced Mann out of the house, and he was arrested the next day.

The man hired to hang Mann had two shortcomings: he was a novice, and he was nervous. The former fact became apparent almost as soon as Mann mounted the gallows. Although the killer stood motionless to have his legs tied together, the executioner did not know how the procedure was carried out. Frustrated at the hangman's fumbling, the sheriff took charge. Mann tried to speed things along by moving his legs in whatever way he was asked. When the sheriff told him to be patient, the mass murderer simply smiled and nodded slightly.

After tightening the noose, the hangman turned and tapped the spring holding the trap in place. Mann dropped like a rock, coming to rest less than 2.5 centimetres from the ground. The noose, however, slipped, its knot hitting Mann's chin before it whipped around to stop at the back of his neck. Five minutes after dropping, Mann's pulse was measured at 103 beats per minute. After being suspended for more than eight minutes, the killer was finally pronounced dead.

The only person who seemed not to have been affected by what he witnessed was the hangman. Almost the instant the trap was released, he disappeared into the jail. When the crowd started to disperse, many in it taking with them a piece of the rope used in the hanging, the executioner returned to watch the post-mortem.

The hanging of Fritz Randolph Dubois in a Québec City jail was no better handled than the execution of Frederick Mann. On a fateful day in February 1890, Dubois began quarrelling with his wife and her mother. The women accused him of being lazy and belittled him for relying on handouts from his father-in-law to survive. He seemed to snap, and without warning, attacked them with an axe. He then turned on his two children. He hid all four bodies in the basement before cleaning up as much of the blood as he could and fleeing. Dubois was quickly apprehended, and in April was convicted of his wife's murder. He was sentenced to die two months later.

The morning he was to hang, Dubois got up early, and as was his custom, loosened up by turning somersaults and handsprings in the jail corridor. By eight o'clock, the games were over, and he was standing on the gallows. His hands were strapped to his sides by a leather belt, and his legs tied above his knees. Once his pinioning was complete, Dubois spoke briefly, in English, saying that he regretted what he had done and hoped to meet his wife and children in heaven. No mention was made of his mother-in-law. Then turning to his masked executioner, he said he was done. With that the hangman tugged a black hood over the face of Dubois, adjusted the noose around his neck and pulled the lever. As soon as the killer's body jerked to a stop, the knot slipped behind his head. As 100 spectators held their breath, he began choking. In a state of obvious panic, he drew up his legs and struggled to free his hands.

For more than three minutes, Dubois writhed, periodically drawing up and straightening his legs. Spectators stood transfixed by the body swinging to and fro in front of them for 20 minutes, blood oozing from under the death hood.

Finally, everyone was told to leave the jail compound, and the corpse of Dubois was lowered to the ground and placed in the plain black coffin lying ready under the scaffold.

LENGTH OF ROPE

In 1918 it took Carberry, Manitoba, farmhand Thomas Fletcher three minutes to walk from his cell to the scaffold, and the same length of time for the hangman to bind his legs, slip a hood and rope over his head and spring the trap. Then it took nearly an hour for him to die. A Winnipeg newspaper headline accurately described what happened: "Revolting Scene at Execution, Hangman Makes a Bungle."

Fletcher had worked on the Spence farm southwest of Carberry for five years before 10-year-old Gordon Rasmussen moved in as the Spences' foster child. Rasmussen quickly became a favourite of Mrs. Spence and her 15-year-old daughter, and an object of jealousy for Fletcher.

The Spences spent April 14, 1917, in town, leaving Fletcher and Rasmussen to do chores. Around 6:00 PM, Rasmussen met his foster parents on their way home and started toward Carberry. Before he had gone far, Fletcher caught up with him.

At his trial, Fletcher testified he and Rasmussen decided to shoot rabbits while they waited for the Spences. When he saw one, Fletcher raised his shotgun to his shoulder and was about to place the stock next to his cheek when the gun went off.

The blast knocked Fletcher on his back, and it was only after he struggled to his feet that he realized Rasmussen had been hit.

The jury did not believe Fletcher's version of events, partly because he fired not once, as he testified, but twice, and also because of what he did next. When Fletcher got back to the farm, the Spences were finishing the day's chores. The four walked to the house together, mother and daughter to head upstairs, and the two men to sit in the living room. As soon as they sat down, Fletcher told his employer that he had something important to say and asked that the women join them as witnesses. Although Mr. Spence said he doubted anything his hired man had to say could be very important, he called for his wife and daughter.

After everyone settled in, Fletcher said that Gordon was dead, and that he had shot him. He then jumped up and ran into the kitchen, where he left his shotgun. Despite being startled by both the announcement and Fletcher's sudden departure, the Spences had sufficient presence of mind to head for the stairs. For the next two hours they remained barricaded in a second-floor bedroom, pleading with Fletcher not to shoot them.

While the standoff continued, the oil in the lantern lighting the ground floor ran out, and Mr. Spence suggested that Fletcher refill it from a can he left in his buggy. When the farmhand left to get the fuel, his employer, who had been watching him through a crack in the bedroom door, seized his chance and ran down the stairs and outside.

The Portage la Prairie jail where Thomas Fletcher was hanged in 1918. His remains are interred in an interior courtyard of the jail.

Mr. Spence rushed to the home of a neighbour and phoned the police. Within minutes, two police officers arrived and took the hired man into custody without incident.

Although Fletcher took the stand in his own defence, neither his judge nor jury believed his claim that the shooting was an accident. After deliberating for an hour and a half, jurors returned a verdict of guilty.

On the last Tuesday in February 1918, Fletcher went to his death. He did not, however, go easily. Provincial employees built his scaffold in the Portage la Prairie jail yard where Fletcher was to hang, but it was the hangman's responsibility to supply and test the rope to be used in the execution. Unfortunately, he didn't do that.

This failure meant that when the trap was sprung, the weight of Fletcher's body dropping 2.5 metres stretched the untested rope, and the condemned man came to rest on the ground in a kneeling position. The hangman immediately began pulling him up, but although he got Fletcher off the ground, he could not hold him suspended. Two guards promptly grabbed the unconscious man and held him aloft while he slowly strangled.

Thomas Fletcher died sometime between 8:08 AM and 8:53 AM on February 26, 1918.

Trapdoors That Wouldn't Open

In late November 1875, Hamilton-area farmer Abel Macdonald sold a load of barley, then on his way home stopped in a small hotel for a drink. There he met 35-year-old John Young and his 28-year-old nephew, James. The Youngs soon came to the realization that their drinking companion was flush with money and decided to relieve him of it. After Macdonald left the hotel and passed the village limits, the Youngs jumped onto his wagon and within minutes left him dying beside the road. At trial, uncle and nephew were both sentenced to hang, but shortly before their scheduled execution, the sentence of James was reduced to life in prison.

John's cell faced the scaffold being built especially for him. When carpenters began putting the structure together, the jail warden asked Young if he wanted to move to another part of the prison or perhaps have his window boarded up. Young refused both offers and spent hours gazing through the bars of his cell at the gallows as it was gradually assembled.

The day he was to hang, the 50 people who would witness his execution entered the jail compound around 6:00 AM, while dozens of the less fortunate milled around in front of the Cayuga, Ontario, jail. The younger and more agile of those lacking a pass climbed the trees that overlooked the prison yard to get a better view.

Young's feet were heavily shackled, and an hour before he was hanged, a blacksmith arrived to remove the rivets that held his iron anklets in place. Young cooperated as much as he could, and as the minutes ticked down, he grew steadily more calm, though he sighed heavily every few seconds. Shortly after the shackles were removed from Young's ankles, the masked hangman entered the death cell and bound the prisoner's hands behind his back. Once that was complete, the two men walked a few metres to a small opening that looked into James Young's cell. Uncle and nephew spoke briefly, and then John joined the already-assembled death procession.

The group was not small. Included in its number were the local sheriff and deputy sheriff, several clergymen, a number of police constables, a few city magistrates, the prisoner, his death watch, the hangman and an assortment of other individuals. They quickly made their way along the jail corridor, down a flight of stairs and across the jail compound to the scaffold. After the deputy sheriff formally read to Young the warrant for his execution, the prisoner was asked if he had anything to say.

Young hesitated briefly, before using his last moments to warn others not to follow his path. "I hope it will be a warning to you young fellows not to take my tracks. I don't think I am hardly worthy of this thing, but of course as it is I have to put up with it, and I don't blame anyone. What I did do I didn't intend to do. I hope you will take warning, gentlemen, one and all, and not come to a place like this."

When he finished speaking, Young shook hands with everyone on the gallows, moved to the trap and stood to have his feet pinioned. He was then told to kneel, facing north, and the noose was adjusted under his chin and slightly to the left. Looking around at the hangman, Young asked, "Do you think I will get down there sure?" Without replying, the executioner tugged a white hood over Young's face, drawing yet another heavy sigh from the still kneeling killer.

Perhaps sensing that Young was becoming anxious, one of the clergymen standing close at hand urged him to think only of Christ. The hangman and Young then shook hands, the intensity of Young's clasp suggesting to spectators that the killer was feeling the terrible intensity of the moment.

The trapdoor of the gallows in the Headingley Jail, as seen from the basement room into which an executed prisoner dropped. Directly below the doors, a pit was dug in the cement floor of the room.

On a signal from the deputy sheriff, the hangman jerked the trap lever. Nothing happened. The suddenness with which the executioner yanked the lever caused the hasp, which held the trap in place, to break. While Young continued to kneel where he was placed, no doubt confused about what was happening, a police constable was sent to fetch a hammer. When the officer returned, the hangman used it to hit the broken bolt. The heavy blow had no effect, but after a series of smacks, the hasp at last broke free, and the trap fell. After that, it was all over in minutes. Young dropped just over 2.5 metres and rebounded slightly, his neck broken. When his body was lowered and his death hood removed, the dead man's face gave no indication that his death came painfully.

That may well have been a source of disappointment to the wife and daughter of Young's victim. They showed up at the jail, dressed in black, just after Young plummeted through the trapdoor. Officials allowed them a close-up view of the still suspended killer, prompting the widow to note that while she and her daughter were satisfied with what they saw, they would have been happier had they arrived in time to see Young actually die.

In 1900, a British Columbia man suffered the same inconvenience as Young. Forty-five-year-old Yip Luck was hanged in mid-November for murdering the police officer who showed up at his isolated cabin to question him about the theft of tools from a local farmer. In the days before Luck's execution, it had rained steadily in Vancouver, leaving the outdoors gallows covered in moisture. As the Chinese immigrant stood patiently waiting to die, his hangman pulled the lever, which should have released the trapdoor. But it didn't. The executioner gave the lever one tug after another, until finally the city sheriff stepped forward and pulled. He was as surprised as everyone else when the trap dropped with a deafening thud, and for a moment he did not realize what happened. Then he turned to look at Yip Luck. All he saw was a rope, moving almost imperceptibly in the morning mist.

STRUGGLING TO THE END

Few people executed in Canada died after such a long and heartbreaking struggle at the end of a rope as Cyrus Pickard, who was hanged in 1871 for murdering his former employer.

Pickard worked on a farm near St. Mary's, Ontario, but quit three months into a 12-month contract of employment. When he could not find other work, he returned to confront his old boss. The two argued over whether Pickard was entitled to his pay, since he had walked off without notice. The disagreement became more heated when the farmhand accused his employer of interfering in his efforts to win the hand of a neighbour girl. Fed up, the farmer finally turned to resume his field work, at which time Pickard shot him in the back, killing him instantly.

Three days after Christmas of that same year, Pickard stood on a London, Ontario, scaffold. Through his spiritual adviser, he asked reporters in attendance not to write sensational accounts of his execution, preferring that they simply state the facts. No one could possibly have guessed just how sensational those reports were going to be.

Pickard's executioner was covered in a dark gown and a mask of black crepe, but some of those attending the hanging recognized him from an execution he carried out three years earlier. Even with that experience, Pickard's executioner was nervous. When he placed the noose around the convict's neck, he did not adjust it properly, and even before Pickard dropped, the rope ended up under his chin. Worse, the hangman had not tightened the string binding Pickard's wrists, and the shock of the prisoner's body being jerked to a stop when it hit the end of the rope snapped the twine, and the man's hands were freed.

Pickard promptly grabbed the noose with his left hand and tried to loosen it. At the same time, he drew up his legs and tried to brace them against one of the gallows' support beams, all the while groaning and gasping for breath. Pickard's fight for life went on for 15 minutes before he became too exhausted to continue and was strangled to death.

Like Cyrus Pickard, Elijah Van Koughnet died a horrible death at the hands of his executioner.

In 1882, the Buck Lake, Ontario, farmer murdered his neighbour as the unsuspecting man returned to his home. He then stole his victim's horse, exchanging it for a much less valuable animal of his own, and burned down the barn, horse and all. The following morning, Van Koughnet tried to sell his neighbour's horse, but the body of his victim was already discovered, and Van Koughnet's actions were regarded as suspicious. By the time the police arrived to arrest him, he was gone. Three days later, he was captured, and shortly after that, was tried for murder and sentenced to hang.

When Van Koughnet was informed that the hour of his execution was at hand, he picked up a white handkerchief and joined the death procession. Almost immediately he burst into tears. When he reached the staircase leading to the second storey of the jail, where he would be hanged, he again started to cry.

After a moment he stopped and asked guards if his brother was present, saying, "Is not that he at the door?" Told it was not, the killer began to sob yet again. Finally, his spiritual adviser put his arm around the distraught farmer, and the procession continued.

The gallows was built in a room at the top of a short stairway. To prevent anyone outside the jail seeing in, the local sheriff shuttered the windows, and the gloomy room was lit by lamps. The trap, painted black, was about a metre wide by two metres long.

Spectators stood on one side of the room, while the chubby executioner, wearing a mask of crepe, stood alone on the other. The hangman adjusted the rope around Van Koughnet's neck, leaving a slack of about two metres, and tied his arms behind his back with bed cord, prompting Van Koughnet to protest, "Not so tight, it hurts my shoulders." While his legs were being tied, Van Koughnet started to cry, and when he turned to speak to those gathered to watch him hang, he could barely sob, "Goodbye to you all, gentlemen."

Van Koughnet dropped about two metres. His body rebounded with a sudden jerk, causing the knot to slip from where it was placed to a spot under the chin. Van Koughnet seemed to realize he still had a chance and began struggling for breath. Between gasps, he groaned, and his body was wracked with convulsions, which shook loose the rope that held his legs together. At the end of eight minutes, the man's breathing was less laboured, but he was still alive. For some unknown reason, Van Koughnet was not wearing the hood traditionally pulled over the head of someone being executed, and the killer's facial expression was seared into the minds of witnesses. Fourteen minutes after he was hanged, the Buck Lake murderer was declared dead.

A post-mortem examination revealed that Van Koughnet's neck had not broken when he fell through the trap, and that the noose likely did little to interfere with his ability to breathe. It did, however, exert enough pressure on the sides of his neck, rendering him unconscious, and eventually, dead.

When Robert Neil stabbed and killed a guard in Toronto's Central Prison in January 1888, he earned himself a unique place in Canadian history. His execution came just 46 days after his crime, thought to be the shortest time between crime and capital punishment in Canadian history, and his struggle for life very nearly matched that of Cyrus Pickard and Elijah Van Koughnet.

Neil was a career criminal with a long history of violent crime. The only person who outwardly appeared upset over his pending execution was the judge who sentenced him to hang. While Neil stood unmoved by the occasion, the judge nearly broke into sobs as he read the death sentence.

Neil's last hours were spent in prayer and in the singing of hymns. When his hangman entered his cell to ready him for execution, Neil helped him as much as he could, complaining only a little when the rope around his wrists was tied too tightly.

Shortly before Neil left for the gallows, the crowd assembled to watch him hang was allowed into the yard of the Don Jail. The gallows, built in Welland, Ontario, was shipped to Toronto, where it was attached to the west wall of the city jail. When Neil stepped from the prison, he glanced briefly at the scaffold then walked to it without slowing. On his arrival, his hat was removed and he was asked if he had anything to say. Neil was never one to apologize, so it came as a bit of a surprise to those who knew him that he said he was sorry for killing his guard. More in keeping with his character were his remaining comments.

"Gentlemen," he said, "I am here, although I ought not to be. I didn't mean to kill that man." That out of the way, Neil went on. "They used me at the Central Prison so bad I didn't know what I was doing. They abused me like a dog. I could not stand all that. I am, however, sorry I killed the man."

When Neil finished speaking, his spiritual adviser opened his Bible, read a brief passage and then knelt in prayer. As soon as he was done, the executioner stepped forward, fitted the black death cap and adjusted the noose around Neil's neck. The minister then started reciting the Lord's Prayer. Spectators could hear Neil following along, his voice muffled by the hood. At the words, "Forgive us our trespasses," Neil was hanged. But he did not die.

Initially, his body did not move so much as a muscle, but soon witnesses began to notice Neil's hands twitching and he appeared to raise his arms to his head. When he could not move them, his struggle stopped briefly. Then he started to move his legs, which were left untied by the hangman. After a few minutes, his movements became spasmodic, then his body quieted, and Neil hung motionless. Finally, a violent trembling seized him, and as soon as it ended, Neil was dead. While his executioner collected his $50 fee, Neil was buried in the yard of the jail, a few feet from where he died.

The execution of Antonio De Lena was another, and certainly not the last, execution bungled by a Canadian hangman. In early fall 1914, De Lena murdered a fellow Italian during a drunken brawl, and slightly more than eight months later, he was hanged at Montréal's Bordeaux Jail.

Although De Lena submitted to being pinioned without making a fuss, neither his arms nor his legs were tied properly. When he dropped, he instinctively kicked out, throwing one of his slippers into the crowd, and in the process freed his legs from their pinioning strap. This seemed to enervate the convict, and he began struggling to loosen the strap tying his arms to his body. That too eventually came loose, and De Lena immediately grabbed the rope circling his neck. As he desperately tried to loosen it, he drew his legs up to his chest and began thrashing about, presumably in an effort to find some kind of purchase that would take pressure off the noose. Several guards at last seemed to realize that their prisoner was almost free of his rope and pulled De Lena's hands from the noose. In one last attempt to break free, the suspended man kicked his attackers, but his struggle for breath sapped so much of his strength that he could do little. As shocked witnesses looked on, De Lena's hands dropped to his sides and he strangled to death. Ten minutes after his final battle started, the fight was over.

In 1946, Michael Vescio sexually assaulted and murdered two 13-year-old boys. He went to trial a year later, and during his subsequent months in jail, grew into a caricature of his former self. He gained 40 pounds and was soft and pudgy, with puffed cheeks and drooping jowls, when he stepped into the death chamber at Manitoba's Headingley Jail. Foreseeing that if his victim dropped too far his head might come off, Vescio's hangman erred on the side of caution.

The sheriff presiding over the hanging realized what happened as soon as Vescio went through the trap. The rope attaching the pedophile to the scaffold started jerking in all directions, and the sheriff immediately told witnesses they would not be permitted into the pit below the gallows where the killer was suspended. Vescio's body continued to jerk for nearly 15 minutes while he slowly strangled.

Winnipeg reporters were not allowed to watch as Vescio fought to stay alive. That was just as well, if what they would have witnessed was anything like what some of them saw four years later. Henry Malanik shot a city police sergeant during a drunken domestic dispute, and his execution was well attended by colleagues of the dead officer. His death was not a textbook hanging.

The rope ruptured the killer's jugular vein, and as he swung back and forth below the scaffold floor, blood poured from the under the hood covering his face, splashing the walls and literally cascading onto the floor.

BOTCHED EXECUTIONS

The hanging of an 18-year-old in February 1914 was among a handful of Canadian executions so badly mismanaged that a coroner's jury refused to certify that the victim was actually hanged by his neck until he was dead.

The story of William Jasper Collins first attracted media attention in the Calgary area of Alberta in May 1913 when the young criminal murdered the man who in every sense of the word was his benefactor. Not only was he the lawyer who helped Collins fight a robbery charge in Braymer, Missouri, but he was also the guy who agreed to take the American teenager with him when the lawyer-turned-farmer decided to make a new start near Cereal, Alberta.

To suggest that Collins did not appreciate the help is an understatement. When he was advised that the former lawyer's wife would be joining them in Alberta, Collins decided he wanted the man's money belt, bursting with more than $3000. He first hit his victim on the head with a hammer, hoping to steal his bankroll and be gone before the lawyer regained consciousness. It didn't work. Although stunned, the older man managed to get to his feet and fight back with a razor he kept in his pocket. Collins responded by shooting him twice in the chest.

If Collins had been a little more patient, he might have gotten away with the murder. He covered up his crime perfectly by dousing oil on the body and the shack in which it was placed, then setting fire to both. Officials did not feel an autopsy was necessary, and at the end of a brief inquiry, the death was ruled accidental. It was at this point that Collins should have exercised a little discretion.

The killer and his victim returned to Missouri—the victim for interment, his killer to spend considerably more money than he should have. The extravagance of the spending attracted attention, and in due course, suspicion. When the body of the murdered man was exhumed, it quickly became evident that his death was not accidental. In no time at all Collins was arrested, confessed and was extradited to Canada for trial.

When it became apparent to Collins that he was neither going to escape from the Royal North West Mounted Police barracks in Calgary nor have his sentence commuted, he took matters into his own hands. He tried to starve himself to death. It almost worked. When the city's sheriff arrived at his cell in mid-February 1914, Collins weighed just 70 pounds.

Officials anticipated that the young man would be too weak to die without assistance and made arrangements to execute him while he was strapped into an armchair. Although Collins managed to walk to the scaffold on his own, ignoring the crude coffin he passed on the way, and ascended the gallows stairs, the effort exhausted him. Almost as soon as he reached the top of the scaffold, he was seated in the waiting chair.

It was immediately apparent that the hangman hired to dispatch Collins was nervous. Although a veteran of numerous Canadian executions, he took so long to noose his victim that witnesses, many of them police officers, began openly disparaging his efforts.

When the noose was at last adjusted over the hood covering Collins' face, his Christian Science spiritual adviser stepped forward and read a short prayer, loud enough for only the seated youth to hear. He then asked Collins if he had any last words. As soon as the hangman realized that there would be no gallows speech, he pulled the lever holding the trapdoor in place.

Perhaps because Collins was tied to a chair, or maybe because the noose was simply adjusted improperly, his neck was thrown back in an unusual way and he was still very much alive after the drop, albeit unconscious. The hangman insisted that Collins be cut down five minutes after the trap opened.

Even as the killer was laid out beside his coffin, witnesses could hear him groaning. The sounds continued for nearly 10 minutes, while off to one side the jail surgeon and hangman argued about what to do next. Five minutes later, they decided to examine Collins again before making a decision. Because he was no longer moaning and his pulse rate was much slower, and his breathing more shallow, the two men agreed to let Collins die on his own rather than return him to the gallows. A few minutes later, the killer was dead.

Their decision did not go over well with members of the coroner's jury. While they agreed that Jasper Collins died in Calgary at the barracks of the Royal North West Mounted Police on February 17, 1914, they refused to confirm he so did pursuant to law.

> *In our opinion, the sentence of the court was not carried out, owing to the fact that the said Jasper Collins was not hanged by the neck until dead, but was contrary to the sentence of the court cut down by the executioner before life was extinct. We further desire to express our dissatisfaction with the manner in which the execution was carried out by the hangman, and we feel that, in the interests of justice and of the public weal, there should be an investigation in order that future executions should be carried out properly.*

LOSING ONE'S HEAD

While Thomas Cook was not the first victim of a Canadian execution to lose his head, he is very likely the best remembered.

Cook was blind, and in 1862, he and his wife earned a subsistence living, begging in the area around Woodstock, Ontario. After one such trip, they returned home with a neighbour, who joined them for a few hours of drinking.

When Cook said he was turning in for the night, the couple's companion announced that it was time for him to go home. But he did not.

Later, Cook thought he heard sounds coming from somewhere in the house. When he got out of bed to investigate, a window opened and someone climbed out of the shack. The angry and very drunk beggar suspected what was going on, caught his wife and beat her to death.

Spectators attending Cook's execution got substantially more than they bargained for.

The rope used to hang him was too long, and Cook's neck far too weak. When he dropped, Cook fell all the way to the ground, his headless body landing below the scaffold and his head coming to rest in the crowd.

The now-topless torso continued for some time to spout blood in all directions. The sight of the body's torn muscles and gaping arteries sickened many present, and for several minutes no one did anything to cover it or even pick up the head. There is some dispute about what happened next. According to local lore, before the execution, friends of Cook made arrangements to sell his remains, and when his body was finally put in a coffin, they collected it and did so. About one thing there is no doubt. When Cook's head was finally located, someone used it to make a death mask. That rendering was eventually built into the doorway of the jail, where it remains.

No one knows for sure just where the head of Daniel Prockiw ended up, but most likely it was returned to him following his execution in August 1926. For a decade, the Winnipeg plumber was in an abusive relationship with Annie Cardno, a woman Manitoba newspapers described as a well-known underworld character. However she was known while alive, she gained the attention of much of the nation following her brutal death. First Prockiw beat her, breaking all her ribs but two, then as she lay on the floor, he poured boiling water over her head. When the police found the woman, part of her face and scalp was completely detached from her skull, hanging by the side of her head. Thankfully, she was likely dead before being parboiled.

According to a former *Winnipeg Free Press* reporter, there was an unofficial agreement on the part of local papers to avoid mention of bungled executions. Never was there a hint of a mistake, he said, unless you knew enough to read between the lines, comparing the time the trap was sprung with the time that passed before the prison doctor pronounced the prisoner dead.

The day before someone was hanged, Canadian executioners were expected to use both an official chart and their own best judgment to determine the length of rope used in the execution. Although the main criterion was weight, executioners were allowed to depart from the formula if they felt the neck muscles of the killer were abnormally strong, or as in the case of Prockiw, weak.

His execution was one in which the unofficial prohibition against reporting bungled executions was ignored by Winnipeg reporters. Although buried deep in most papers, and despite their brevity, most reports spoke volumes. One said much by simply noting that the execution was bungled in a horrible manner. "Too long a drop was given by the hangman and the head of the doomed man was severed from the body."

The media attention associated with the decapitation of Prockiw paled in comparison to what happened when Tomassina (Sarao) Teolis and her two companions, Angelo Donafrio and Leone Gagliardi, were executed in 1935 for the insurance murder of her husband.

Donafrio and Gagliardi were executed first. Montréal's Bordeaux Jail has two gallows, and while the two men dropped standing back to back on one, Teolis was being prepared to die on the other. They may well have died at the same time, but jail officials decided to save money by having the same hangman handle both executions.

When Teolis made her way to the gallows, she was accompanied by two matrons and a prison chaplain. She walked without assistance, smiling as her hangman pulled the black death hood over her face. Three minutes after the trap was sprung, she was declared dead. She actually could have been pronounced dead earlier, since her fall through the scaffold floor caused her head and her body to end up in very different places.

According to the executioner, when jail officials supplied him with the weight of Teolis, the figure they used was what she weighed on the day she was sentenced to hang. They did not take into consideration that by the time she was executed, she had ballooned to almost 18 kilograms more than her normal weight. The hangman said he probably would have noticed that she looked different had he been allowed to see Teolis before the execution, but officials felt his presence would be upsetting and denied him access to her.

In the decades leading to the abolition of capital punishment in Canada, most newspapers refused to print detailed stories of executions, making it difficult to determine whether a hanging was bungled. Occasionally, evidence that a mistake occurred became public in other ways. The January 1946 execution of Byron Potter for the murder of the woman he loved is a case in point.

The Vancouver lawyer hired by Potter's daughter said that when he claimed the body on her behalf after it was released by officials at the Oakalla prison farm, he could see stitches under a band of adhesive tape, which was wound around the neck. He said he later learned that Potter's execution was bungled, and that Potter was decapitated. His comments about the hanging were contained in a newspaper story about the possibility that the executioner would be sued for negligence. That story spawned others, as well as a debate over whether decapitations during executions occurred more often than previously thought.

HANGED THREE TIMES

In April 1869, an Englishman killed a fellow sailor in a fit of jealousy over the affections of a woman. He was hanged in Prince Edward Island, three times.

George Dowie was only 23 when he ascended the gallows in the last public execution in the island's history. After finishing a lengthy address to the assembled throng, he stepped onto the trapdoor, forgave the executioner for what was about to be done and then waited patiently as the noose was adjusted. When the trap opened, he dropped like a log, all the way to the ground, a broken rope lying beside him.

For a moment, Dowie lay stunned, then he was seized and quickly carried back to the jail. An hour later, he ascended the gallows again, noosed with a new rope. When the trapdoor was released, he plummeted down and once again landed in a heap on the ground. This time the rope had become detached from a cleat, and it came loose from the gallows beam.

But after twice being embarrassed, the local sheriff was not going to be embarrassed again. Grabbing the rope, he began hauling the stunned Dowie off the ground, noose still tied securely around his neck. When it became apparent that the sheriff could not hold Dowie up by himself, several constables rushed to his aid. Together they hoisted the befuddled sailor up. Forty minutes later, Dowie was pronounced dead and cut down.

In 1899, another double hanging occurred in Canada, this time in the northwest. Two men were shot while prospecting in the Yukon. One was killed instantly, while the other managed to hide in the bottom of a canoe. After the boat floated out of sight of his attackers, he made his way to the nearest camp.

North West Mounted Police officers found some of the miners' equipment in the possession of the four Nantuck brothers, Dawson, Jim, Joe and Frank. The trial of the men was the first murder hearing in the Yukon. Although all four men were convicted, Frank's sentence was commuted to life imprisonment and Joe died of tuberculosis before his scheduled execution date.

When the two surviving brothers were hanged, Jim was neither killed nor rendered unconscious by the drop. He worked his left hand free and frantically tried to loosen the noose that was slowly strangling him. His gurgling sounds attracted the attention of the hangman, who pulled the struggling man up through the trap then dropped him again, this time breaking his neck.

Canada's most famous double hanging of a single victim is no doubt the 1922 execution of Benny Swim in Woodstock, New Brunswick.

The 20-year-old lived for some time with one of his two victims, a young cousin, and when she left him to marry another man, Swim was devastated. After brooding for days, he bought a revolver and confronted his former lover and her husband.

He shot them both then ran into the woods near Woodstock. There he fired a bullet into his own head, but it deflected off a bone, leaving him very much alive.

Although Swim confessed to the killings shortly after his arrest, at trial he pleaded not guilty by reason of insanity. It didn't work. He later admitted that his ploy was the result of a suggestion made by a fellow prisoner. After all, he was told, what have you got to lose?

Swim walked to the gallows on his own, though for part of the way he held onto the arm of his executioner. Actually, two hangmen were on hand, one hired to assist the other. It soon turned out that the services of both were needed.

The more senior of the executioners was responsible for executing Swim the first time. When he placed the noose around the young man's head, however, he miscalculated and failed to adjust it properly. As a result, although the drop rendered Swim unconscious, it did not break his neck. To compound that error, before the jail surgeon had time to declare the killer dead, the hangman insisted on cutting his victim down. Swim was taken to a cell and placed upon a cot. Almost immediately it was obvious to jail officials that Swim was not only alive, but he also appeared to regain consciousness.

The presiding sheriff promptly put the second hangman in charge of returning Swim to the gallows and hanging him a second time. After a delay of nearly an hour, all was finally ready, and the still unconscious Swim was for a second time noosed and dropped. This time the fall broke his neck. Out of an abundance of caution, Swim's body was left suspended for 19 minutes. Only then did the four doctors in attendance agree that he was well and truly dead.

Chapter Nine

Please Help Me Kill My Husband

~

The chances that a woman sentenced to die by a Canadian court would actually hang were slight, compared to the 50–50 likelihood for male killers. Of 58 women sentenced to death, 11 were executed. Of this latter group, five women killed their husband with the help of a male lover.

Most of the women hanged in the province of Québec were motivated to kill by the desire to rid themselves of a husband so they could marry a lover. Their promiscuity offended the sensibilities of residents of a deeply religious, and very Catholic, province where sexual impropriety was looked at askance. For example, when Marie Beaulne was sentenced in June 1929, the judge condemned her infidelity as much as he did her deed. He said that while she had been found guilty of murder, she also had been shown to have broken her wedding vows. "You loved another man who was not worthy of your husband. You now see what this has done for you."

CORDÉLIA VIAU AND SAMUEL PARSLOW

Isidore Poirier left for California in 1895 to pursue his carpentry trade, leaving behind his wife, Cordélia Viau.

In his absence, she fell in love with Samuel Parslow, a young farmhand. Their affair scandalized the small village in which both resided, especially when it continued following the return of Isidore.

Two events of significance occurred with his reappearance. Cordélia took out a large life insurance policy on her husband, and Poirier became depressed and increasingly upset about playing second fiddle to Parslow. Poirier began drinking heavily, so much so that his St. Canut, Québec, neighbours were not totally surprised when he apparently committed suicide. To the police, however, his death was anything but self-inflicted. Not only was his throat cut almost from ear to ear, but he was also stabbed multiple times. Worse, at least for Cordélia and Samuel, officials quickly learned that shortly before Poirier died, his wife asked her insurance agent to confirm that she would receive the proceeds from her husband's life insurance policy if he died violently.

As soon as Viau and Parslow were arrested, both confessed to participating in the murder. Each, however, blamed the other for carrying it out. In the end, it didn't matter who actually committed the crime; they were both sentenced to hang.

The execution of the killers attracted hundreds of people. Crowds from as far away as Montréal began descending on St. Scholastique days before the hanging, jamming the train station. Hotels were quickly filled, and accommodation of any kind was rented at a premium. Latecomers were not deterred, and they contented themselves with sitting up all night.

The scaffold on which Viau and Parslow were to die tow-
ered above the huge stone walls of the St. Scholastique Jail. It
was built in the rear yard, its steps near the door from which the
two were to exit the prison. Two short flights of stairs led to the
top of the scaffold, where officials erected a blanket barrier so
the couple could be hanged back to back without their bodies
actually touching. Black cloth enclosing the area below the gallows prevented witnesses from seeing them suspended.

Almost the entire night before the execution, city streets
were filled with revellers. With daylight, the size of the crowds
grew substantially, as dozens of one- and two-horse sleighs began
arriving from outlying villages. An hour before the pair was
hanged, nearly 3000 people were milling around the jail. Another
600 had passes and were permitted inside.

The evening before the execution, witnesses with tickets
were given a kind of preview and were allowed to walk by the
death cells and gaze at the doomed pair. At one point, the jail
corridor was so crowded that Viau's father had to elbow his way
through the throng to have a final visit with his daughter.

On the morning of March 10, those walking into the jail
compound were immediately confronted by the gallows, a thin
coat of frost covering its brown paint. That a drama of death was
about to begin was made visibly evident by two hemp ropes
dangling above the scaffold and the heaps of frozen dirt scattered around the pit that had been excavated to ensure that Viau
and Parslow did not touch the ground when they dropped.

Both prisoners slept soundly their last night alive. At 5:00 AM, a small group of priests arrived to prepare them for high Mass and to administer the last rites of the Catholic Church. Throughout the hour-long service, Viau was kept in her cell and Parslow in the corridor, so the two could not see each other. Parslow alternately stood or knelt, his head bowed and his face devoid of colour. His sister was beside him, occasionally so overcome with emotion that several times she was given a chair, lest she collapse completely. In all, about a dozen people participated in the service.

After the Mass, the prisoners ate breakfast, and each drank a glass of brandy to smooth out their journey. Then they started for the scaffold. The sheriff was the first to emerge from the jail, followed closely by Cordélia and the priest supporting her. The widow was dressed entirely in black, a thick leather belt encircling her waist. Her hair was tied in a knot, and her arms were bound behind her back. Although it was obvious that she was struggling with her emotions, Cordélia walked without hesitation to the gallows, lifting her skirt slightly so she did not trip, and when she arrived, she immediately started up the steps.

Next was Parslow. He wore a yellowish-coloured suit with cutaway coat, an open vest partially covering his blue shirt, and slippers. Unlike Viau, he needed help walking across the compound, and his body trembled slightly with every step.

As soon as Cordélia reached the top of the scaffold, she went straight to the trap, turned away from the crowd and stood under one of the nooses. When she was in place, the hangman positioned Parslow on the right side of the gallows, his back to the blanket screen put up to prevent the killers from seeing each other. Parslow's legs were quickly strapped together above his ankles, and a black hood was drawn over his face. Only then was the noose placed around his neck.

Once Parslow was prepared, the executioner moved to Viau. Before he started to tie her legs together, the woman shook hands with everyone on the platform, with the exception of her lover. As the hangman bent to bind her legs, Viau closed her eyes, and without so much as a single sign of fear, submitted to being pinioned, hooded and noosed.

The hangman then asked if the priests were ready. The two nearest the killers stepped back, and in an instant, the bolt holding the trap in place was drawn, and Viau and Parslow dropped.

The four doctors in attendance gathered around the two bodies almost as soon as they fell. Cordélia Viau was pronounced dead after being suspended for slightly more than six minutes; Samuel Parslow died a few minutes later. The bodies were left hanging for nearly 30 minutes, then cut down. After a brief coroner's inquest, each body was claimed by relatives.

MARIE-LOUISE CLOUTIER AND ACHILLE GRONDIN

Unlike Cordélia Viau, whose guilt was quickly apparent, Marie-Louise (Brochu) Cloutier almost got away with murder. She made only one mistake; she married her husband's hired man just five weeks after she told the authorities her spouse died from an illness.

Although Vilmont Brochu, a peddler and part-time taxi driver, and Achille Grondin, the man who worked for him, lived in the backwoods of Québec's Frontenac country, their neighbours were sufficiently sophisticated to wonder whether the relationship between Cloutier and Grondin may have started before Brochu's very sudden and unexpected August 1937 death.

When relatives of the dead man went to the police with their concerns, Brochu's body was exhumed. It was soon learned that he had died from arsenic poisoning, not an illness.

The hired man and his new bride were tried separately, but the result for each was the same. Their executions originally were to have been carried out in the yard of the local jail, but residents of the village worried about the carnival-like atmosphere associated with Québec hangings and petitioned the province's Attorney General to have the couple executed in Montréal's Bordeaux Jail. It was there that 40-year-old Cloutier and her 44-year-old husband met their end.

PETER DAVIS AND MARY EMORY

In 1886, Peter Davis seemed to have everything going for himself. He had a good job and was madly in love with the beautiful, 30-year-old wife of his employer. Davis first met Mary Emory when he lived with her family after serving 10 years in prison for theft. When the slightly older woman left home to marry William Emory, Davis followed and quickly got a job on the couple's farm. The closeness of the relationship between Peter and Mary did not go unnoticed by William, and the farmer eventually fired his hired man. Davis vowed he would get even, and perhaps by continuing his affair with Mary, he managed to do just that.

Events came to head in mid-September 1889 when Mary told her father and brothers that she was worried about her husband, who had not come back from cutting hay in a secluded marsh near their home. Emory was quickly found, shot in the chest with his own rifle. Before the day was out, the police learned about the affair of Peter Davis and Mary Emory.

Although nothing tied Davis to the murder, it took a Belleville, Ontario, jury just an hour to find him guilty. A month and a half later, he went to the gallows. Mary, meanwhile, had better luck. A jury agreed that while no doubt she knew what was going to happen before the murder was committed, since she did not take part in carrying it out, she was guilty of no crime.

For Davis, death did not come easily, prompting one paper to complain about the horrible spectacle that made strong men turn pale and walk away.

DAVID DUBÉ AND MARTHA MOONEY

Although David Dubé was hanged in Québec in 1900, and Peter Davis was executed in Ontario 10 years earlier, the men had three things in common. Both had fallen in love with another man's wife; both were convicted of killing the woman's husband; and in each case the person who instigated the crime went free.

Thomas Adams Mooney and his wife, Martha, did not get along, and around Lac Beauport, Québec, their constant quarrelling no longer attracted the attention of neighbours, which probably explains why few were surprised when the couple separated. People did take notice, however, when Mooney was found near his rural home, his head mutilated by the bloody axe lying next to his body.

A few years before his murder, Mooney had worked in the United States. During that time, he employed Dubé to do chores around his small farm in Québec. It was not long before the hired man and Martha became intimate and their relationship was noticed. When he returned home, Mooney was told about the affair, and he made his irritation known to both Martha and her much younger lover. That did little to quell the couple's passion, and their affair continued.

Following the discovery of Mooney's body, the police made a beeline to Dubé's home, in part because he was an obvious suspect, and in part because that was where the dead man's wife now lived. Dubé confessed to the killing, telling the police that Martha was continually after him to murder her husband, which was the only way the two could marry, since Mooney refused to give his wife a divorce. Martha was also arrested, but as was the case with Mary Emory, she was found not guilty of being an accomplice in her husband's death. In April 1900, a Québec City jury convicted Dubé of the murder, and he was hanged three months later.

ÉDOUARD THOMAS AND MRS. ARTHUR NANTEL

In 1931, a 25-year-old Mont Laurier, Québec, lumberjack joined Davis and Dubé in a Canadian club of infamy where membership seemed to be on the rise.

The precise nature of the relationship between Édouard Thomas and the 59-year-old wife of the man he murdered is a little unclear, but there was no doubt it was intimate. The evening Arthur Nantel was murdered, Thomas was waiting outside the home of the restauranteur. As Nantel walked to a stable to feed his horses, the two argued. When Nantel left the stable some time later, Thomas shot him in the back.

Almost as soon as they arrived, the police noticed that tracks from the scene of the crime led along a railway line for 90 metres then broke off opposite the home of Thomas. In his house, officers found a pair of boots that corresponded exactly with the tracks. Confronted with the evidence, Thomas confessed. He and the victim's wife were immediately arrested; Thomas was charged with murder, Mrs. Nantel with being his accomplice.

Throughout his trial, Thomas sat with his head bowed, the picture of despair. When jurors announced their verdict, all he could do was call out, "Jesus, come to my help!"

As he left the courtroom, the convicted killer said only that it truly saddened him to leave behind his mother and young brothers.

A petition seeking clemency was sent to the Minister of Justice by the Canadian Prisoners' Welfare Association, and a meeting between Thomas' mother and the minister was arranged. Neither of these efforts changed anything.

The lumberjack mounted the scaffold with a firm step, praying aloud during the short trip from his cell to the gallows. Twelve minutes after the trap was sprung, Thomas was declared dead. The execution was almost unnoticed. The only people present were members of the coroner's jury, whose attendance was required by law, and a handful of police officers.

Mrs. Nantel was tried after Thomas. And, like Mrs. Emory and Mrs. Mooney, she was found not guilty.

FRANK HAYNES AND TENA ATKINSON

Two days before Frank Haynes was executed for murdering a Sydney, Nova Scotia, hotelkeeper, he decided to confess. What he had to say caused quite a stir, and a local Crown prosecutor turned up to hear his story firsthand. Before he began, however, Haynes wanted to know whether by making the statement he was likely to have his sentence commuted: "On your word of honour, is there any chance for me? Can I secure a postponement?" Told that a reprieve was unlikely, Haynes asked why he should say anything. The prosecutor said the reason was obvious: to find peace in the hereafter, he must first do what is right in the here and now.

Haynes then told his story. He said he first met Tena Atkinson on the West Coast and well and truly was smitten by her. Shortly after their paths crossed again in Sydney, he became totally infatuated, and while in her company possessed no will of his own. Knowing this, he said, Tena asked him to kill her husband, suggesting it was the only way they could ever hope to be together.

But Haynes had his doubts, not about his feelings for Atkinson, but about whether he could commit murder. He told the prosecutor that only when he was away from Tena did he have time to think about what she wanted him to do. Again and again he told Tena that as much as he loved her, he was not up to killing someone.

It was about this time that he met John Donalds. The two soon became close friends, and when Donalds told Haynes that he would do anything for money, Haynes saw his chance. He told Donalds that Tena Atkinson wanted someone to kill her husband, and that she would pay to have the job done.

The deal the three struck was that Atkinson would pay Donalds $1000 to help Haynes commit the murder. When it was done, Haynes would immediately leave town, and as soon as Atkinson cleared up her husband's estate, she would follow. To seal the bargain, Atkinson paid Donalds $300.

In mid-August 1913, Donalds and Haynes hid along a road on the outskirts of Sydney, waiting for Benjamin Atkinson. He was allowed to drive past Haynes, but when Benjamin got to where Donalds was hiding, both men attacked. They quickly overpowered their victim, dragged him from his carriage into a wooded area nearby and killed him. To make it more difficult to identify the body, Donalds mutilated Benjamin's face with a rock. The two killers then turned the dead man's horse around so it would return home, signalling to Tena Atkinson that her husband was dead.

Haynes was seen near where Benjamin's body was discovered, and after being questioned by police, he was charged with murder. Shortly before his May 8, 1914, execution date, the condemned man made a statement. What he said did nothing to delay his execution. Hours before it was carried out, crowds flocked to the Sydney jail, and streets were jammed with carriages, automobiles and people wanting to see what was going on inside the compound. The largest part of the crowds congregated at the rear of the jail, where the scaffold was clearly visible.

As soon as Haynes noticed the crowd, he became anxious, realizing that the presence of so many people could mean only one thing—his application for a reprieve had been turned down.

Shortly after 5:00 PM on the day Haynes was to die, Sydney's deputy sheriff announced that the execution would take place within the half hour. With that the hangman picked up a hood and two pinioning straps and started for the death cell. Moments later, the death procession emerged from the jail.

As Haynes made his way along the jail's corridors, he staggered slightly, perhaps because his face was obscured by the hood partially drawn over it. The bars in a second-storey cell that looked out into the yard had been removed earlier and the window enlarged into a doorway to allow Haynes and the official party to step out of the jail directly onto the scaffold.

The lower part of the gallows was completely enclosed, ensuring that spectators outside the jail could not see what was going on. The platform measured about 2.5 metres by 3 metres. Above the trapdoor a rope was attached to a bar, approximately 4.5 metres above the scaffold.

The first indication that something was amiss occurred when, in a low voice, Haynes asked to speak with the jail surgeon, who was standing nearby. The doctor seemed to anticipate the summons and immediately placed a morphine pill in the mouth of the bound man. That done, Haynes stood quietly while his black hood was pulled all the way down and the noose was adjusted around his neck. The prisoner's spiritual adviser started to recite the Lord's Prayer but was overcome with emotion, and there was a brief pause while he regained his composure.

Haynes was a large and heavy man, and when the trapdoor opened, his fall broke almost every bone in his neck, very nearly ripping off his head.

Two weeks later, Tena Atkinson and John Donalds stood trial, Donalds for being an accessory before the fact and Atkinson an accessory after the fact. Both charges were thrown out.

MARIE (VIAU) BEAULNE AND PHILIBERT LEFEBVRE

When Marie Beaulne was sentenced to hang for poisoning her husband, the judge presiding over her trial was incensed. Zephyr Viau was considerably older than his wife, but he worked hard in the hinterland of Québec chopping wood, and in the opinion of the judge, was well respected by his Montpellier neighbours. During one of Zephyr's frequent absences, Marie fell in love with Philibert Lefebvre, a young trapper who resided in the area. Determined to take their relationship to the next level, the two decided to kill Zephyr, collect on his life insurance and marry.

Their plan almost worked. Over several days, Marie put strychnine in her husband's food. The sicker it made him, the more she ministered to his needs with soups and broths, all laced with the poison. When he finally died in January 1929, area residents were saddened, though not surprised. After all, he had been sick for days. The only person not convinced that the death was natural was Marie's parish priest. He years earlier saw a man die of strychnine poisoning, and Zephyr's symptoms were identical.

What results when domestic unrest turns violent. In 1946, Elizabeth McLean was sentenced to death for murdering her abusive husband when he attacked her during a drinking party. Her sentence was later reduced to manslaughter.

• ◆ •

Because of the priest, provincial authorities started an investigation, and the body of Viau was exhumed. Two weeks after Zephyr was poisoned to death, his widow and her lover were arrested. At their trial, no attempt was made to deny the facts. Instead, their lawyer suggested that because the couple lacked even a rudimentary religious education, and neither knew anything of the law, they were ignorant and intellectually inferior, and therefore unable to appreciate the horror of what they had done.

The judge who imposed the death sentence on the pair made it clear he felt that Lefebvre was the real culprit. It was he who facilitated the murder by furnishing his lover with the means and motivation to commit the crime. The judge told the accused that he felt justice was not truly being done in this case, even though Lefebvre was going to hang. Zephyr was killed over two or three days, he said, and was denied the chance to make peace with God, adding that Lefebvre, on the other hand, had almost two months.

During most of the time they were held in Montréal awaiting execution, the couple seemed oblivious to what their future held. In fact, it was only when they were transferred to Hull, where they were to hang, that they seemed to realize the significance of their crime and the severity of their sentence.

Marie held up the better of the two. During her last days, she stoically waited for death, writing messages of love to each of her eight children, and to her mother and other relatives. None of her missives were answered. Lefebvre wrote only one letter. In it he asked his father to forgive him. Then Lefebvre collapsed in tears. In her last moments, Marie wanted to see her lover one more time. He refused.

For a while, a slim ray of hope appeared for the convicted woman. It was rumoured she was with child and that a reprieve or commutation of her sentence was possible. A medical examination, however, disclosed that Marie was not pregnant.

The scaffold to which the poisoners walked was painted red, a longstanding Québec custom, and was sufficiently tall that it could be seen from the Peace Tower on Parliament Hill. The lovers ascended the gallows 20 minutes apart, neither knowing which of them would be the first or the last to do so. Officials decided to start with Lefebvre. He may have been a murderer, but Philibert at least was loved. His body was claimed by his father and taken to Montréal, where a funeral service was held. Marie Beaulne's corpse was unclaimed.

ELIZABETH ANN TILFORD

Like only two other women hanged in Canada, Elizabeth Tilford did not need anyone's help to kill her husband.

Tilford was born and raised in England and married for the first time when she was only 16. Six months later, her husband left. Not one to wait around or get hung up on legalities, she promptly moved in with her cousin, William Walker, and started raising a family. The couple arrived in Canada in 1928 through the sponsorship of the Salvation Army.

This is where the facts get a little murky. Within a year of settling near Woodstock, Ontario, William went blind. A short while later, he died. At the time, rumours circulated that William suspected his wife was poisoning him, but nothing came of the stories. Elizabeth soon collected on the insurance policies she had placed on her husband's life, and despite not being legally married to Walker, applied for and received a widowed mother's allowance. In the end, she acquired a considerably better lifestyle than she had before Walker's death.

For much of the next year, Elizabeth tried to secure some kind of permanent employment. She was rejected by the

Salvation Army, who decided her history of living with one man after another suggested she lacked a moral compass. As she became increasingly desperate to find some meaning in her life and to earn some money, she turned to spiritualism and began travelling around the countryside as a fortune teller. Keeping her company was a man known only as Professor Blake.

It was during this period that she met, and almost immediately married, Tyrell Tilford. He had quite a few positive attributes: he was easily manipulated, he was more than 20 years younger than Elizabeth and he came from a good family. Like her first two marriages, however, this one quickly turned miserable.

According to the police investigation that followed Tilford's death, Elizabeth and Tyrell lived in abject poverty. Two sons from Elizabeth's relationship with Walker detested the weak-willed Tilford and made his life at home worse by continually beating him up. He retaliated by mistreating his new wife's youngest daughter whenever he thought he could get away with it.

To further complicate matters, Professor Blake reappeared and began making frequent visits to the Tilford residence. Before the couple celebrated their fifth wedding anniversary, two events occurred that, taken together, were sufficient to put Elizabeth on death row. First, she began making enquiries about the amount of insurance she could collect if her husband died; second, Tyrell was already concerned about his wife's straying ways and complained to family members that he was sure he was being poisoned.

He was right. Soon after Elizabeth began insisting her husband take her homemade tablets to improve his health, he became ill and in short order died.

The authorities immediately heard from Tilford's family members. They told the police that a few days before Tyrell died, he had told his mother he was being poisoned. The following day, said the family, Tyrell confronted his wife and told her that he was not about to become the third husband she poisoned and that their marriage was over.

The police were now sufficiently suspicious about Tyrell Tilford's death that they decided to exhume his body. Shortly thereafter, Elizabeth was charged with his murder. No one had much doubt about her guilt, but little physical evidence actually linked her to the crime. It took jurors six hours of deliberation before they returned with a guilty verdict.

It was snowing lightly when Elizabeth made her way across the yard of the Woodstock jail to the shed where her execution was to take place. Reporters were not allowed to witness the execution, and newspaper accounts the next day contained scathing criticism of the prohibition.

Toronto's *Globe and Mail* was particularly incensed, referring to the decision to hang her in private as indefensible and arbitrary. When public hangings were abolished, the paper noted, the press was invited to attend because officials recognized that hangings were just as much a matter of public concern as trials. It said secret hangings were but a step from the adoption of secret trials:

If the Provincial authorities adopted this new procedure as a means of eliminating the sensation and wholly undesirable news story, they have surely carried the censorship a step too far. It is difficult to understand why the government would adopt a practice that tends to shroud future executions with mystery. The best such efforts can achieve is the encouragement of that most distasteful form of attack, namely, malicious and irresponsible gossip.

Reporters were advised that Elizabeth Tilford began her short trip to the gallows a few seconds before 1:00 AM on December 17, 1935. Two guards escorted her through the first stage of a blizzard, and five minutes after stepping onto the scaffold, she was declared dead.

Members of the coroner's jury who viewed her remains were still on their way home when a small cortege made its way through thickening snow to the town's Baptist cemetery. Automobile headlights and flashlight beams cast weird shadows over rows of headstones as Tilford's prison chaplain and his wife, together with a jail matron, a gravedigger and two undertakers, struggled through knee-deep snowdrifts to an open grave beside the last resting place of William Walker.

Elizabeth Tilford was a woman nearly everyone heard about but few knew. She was either 56 or 50, the mother of anywhere between nine and 19 children, the lover of dozens of men and, very likely, the killer of a few.

Chapter Ten

What Comes After?
Bodies and Burials

~

D uring the period the federal government executed murderers, it alone determined where the bodies of Canada's killers ended up. No one seemed to object, perhaps because the Bible is not much concerned about what happens to the temporal home of criminals.

On occasion, how a body was disposed of became a source of embarrassment to federal officials. They were not amused when the bodies of those they hanged were converted into symbols of injustice and carried off to a fine funeral, like that accorded Nicholas Melady in 1869. The irritation experienced by Canadian authorities when that happened, however, was nowhere near as great as that felt across the ocean.

The funeral of a young English woman believed wrongfully hanged, for example, grew into a huge pageant after she was put on public display. For three days, the curious flocked to the home of the man who claimed her corpse. London newspapers made little reference to the circumstances that brought the woman to the gallows, preferring stories about the hundreds who stood in line to see her as "she lay in her coffin seemingly as in a sweet sleep, with a smile on her countenance."

Before federal law required that post-mortems be carried out on the bodies of those hanged in Canada, families were given two options: they could either claim the body, or it could be left unclaimed and revert to the State. In the latter case, the body was interred in the jail where the deceased was hanged, or else it was buried in the pauper's section of a local cemetery. In 1914, the stepmother of Jack Krafchencko, who was executed for killing a bank manager during a robbery a year earlier, did the former. She and five helpers then tried to bring him back to life. Among those in attendance were two witches, a warlock, a soothsayer and a voodoo priest. Their efforts, however, were in vain, and Krafchencko was eventually buried in an unmarked Winnipeg grave.

ROLE OF DOCTORS

Before the bodies of the executed could go anywhere, they were attended to by a doctor. Having a physician on site during an execution served two purposes: it ensured a killer was well and truly dead, and it minimized the barbaric reality of a hanging. The presence of a healer, even at such a macabre scene of death as an execution, made state-sponsored murder palatable for the Canadian public.

Historically, doctors did more than declare condemned prisoners dead. Until almost the 20th century, they used bodies of convicts for scientific and teaching purposes, and when they were done with them, the doctors doled out what remained to local practitioners. Negligent surgeons who did not make their requests known sufficiently early for a body part weren't guaranteed a prime piece of anatomy.

The first use of a convicted killer's body by a North American doctor is thought to have occurred in 1839, when a prisoner on an American death row sold his body to a pair of physicians who were to use his cadaver for scientific purposes. With the money he was paid, the killer spent his remaining time dining on delicacies. According to legend, on the day of his execution, the man still had a dollar left, which he placed between two slices of bread and ate.

In 1862, a prisoner executed at the Woodstock, Ontario, jail made a similar arrangement, or so his friends said. It's not certain if they sold the body of the still alive Thomas Cook with or without his knowledge. When the friends came to collect Cook's body after he was hanged, they had a problem—it was in two pieces. The hangman of the blind wife-killer had miscalculated his drop, and when Cook's body reached the end of the rope, his head landed in one place and his body in another. His friends recovered the greater part of the dead man, but someone else got Cook's head.

As late as the 1920s, Canadian doctors complained that not enough people were being executed to keep medical schools supplied with cadavers. While addressing the Private Members

Committee of the Canadian Parliament, the dean of the Faculty of Medicine at Queen's University warned that if schools like his did not get access to more bodies, students would be forced to "go to the country graveyards and break open the vaults and obtain their material."

The dean told committee members there was a strong market in Ontario for the remains of killers and others whose bodies were not claimed. Provincial inspectors, he said, trafficked in such bodies. "They are allowed a fee of $5 for distributing such body and any expenses in addition. In spite of this, they are demanding $25, $30, $50, $60 and even $75 a body, and bodies are being shipped out of Kingston to Toronto. We need 15 or 16 bodies each year to divide amongst our students, but in 1907, we got only one and four in 1908."

The Anatomy Act of Ontario stated that unclaimed bodies in public institutions were to be handed over to the chief inspector of anatomy, who was to divide them among medical schools in proportion to their number of students.

In the 19th century, the bodies of executed prisoners were used in a variety of ways all over Europe. Sweden is a case in point. After one 1868 execution, the body of a murderer was frozen then placed in a secure place, where it remained for several years. The body was to be thawed at some point, and if all went well, the prisoner would be revived. Whether the experiment was successful was not made public.

DISSECTION

For most of the 19th century, the bodies of executed criminals were often delivered to local physicians for dissection, and thereafter used for teaching purposes. By tradition, such corpses were cut up in public by surgeons who often took pieces of the recently departed. In 1883, for instance, a doctor from Plantagenet in eastern Ontario left the Ottawa execution of Frederick Mann with the mass murderer's heart. Quite a few others took a piece of the hangman's rope. The luckiest of all got the killer's brain, which weighed a healthy 1.4 kilograms.

That same year, a specialist from Toronto or Montréal (no one seemed to know exactly where the doctor came from) was given the brain of Michael O'Rouke, hanged in Milton, Ontario, for murdering his former employer.

Because stories of the dissection of killers' bodies were rampant, some of the condemned used their last request to ask that their bodies be buried, rather than cut up and spread around. One such request came from murderer Phoebe Campbell, executed in London, Ontario, in 1872. Even when dissections were not done, the bodies of murderers occasionally were put to good use. An example occurred a year after Campbell was hanged. Authorities in Peterborough, Ontario, worried that the strange mannerisms of James Fox were different from those of other eccentrics and were perhaps an indication he was insane. To settle the matter, prison doctors carried out a post-mortem after he was hanged. They were relieved to find no evidence of insanity, though they did discover he had suffered from meningitis. Beneath the membrane of his brain, doctors also found a fibrous deposit and places where the brain adhered to the skull.

In 1881, 100 doctors and medical students attended the Montréal execution of Hugh Hayvern. The son of Irish immigrants was a considerable disappointment to his hardworking parents. That became clear during his trial for murdering a fellow inmate of St. Vincent de Paul Penitentiary. Hayvern's mother testified against her son, suggesting he never earned an honest dollar in his life and that from the age of 15 he was rarely sober. The autopsy done on the body of the career criminal revealed that his brain weighed less than normal.

Like James Fox, Benjamin Parrott was a killer whose sanity was in doubt—not enough doubt to persuade federal officials to order that his sentence be commuted, but they had doubt nonetheless. After he was executed in 1899, but before his body was buried in the yard of the Hamilton, Ontario, jail, Parrott was autopsied. Doctors determined that his brain was strong and healthy and weighed more than normal. They said this proved that he was not insane.

A year later, the body of George Pearson, another killer hanged in Hamilton, was autopsied. This time it was discovered that the brain examined was abnormally small, although it, too, was judged healthy.

FACES OF THE DECEASED

Historians of the execution process in England suggest that the bodies of the hanged often betrayed the nature of their experience. Most evident was the swelling of the face, especially the ears and lips. The eyes were usually red and were on occasion partially forced out of their cavities. A bloody froth sometimes flowed from the lips and nostrils, and the fingers often were clenched firmly. Urine and feces were sometimes involuntarily expelled.

The newspaper reports of Canadian executions rarely contained descriptions of the physical changes to a killer's body following a hanging. John Traviss and the duo of John Hendershott and William Welter were exceptions, though their bodies evidenced little of the trauma detailed in accounts of English executions.

Traviss was hanged in Toronto in 1872. After remaining suspended for an hour, his body was cut down, revealing a slightly discoloured face and blue hands. Twenty-three years later, Hendershott and Welter were hanged in St. Thomas, Ontario. When the pair was placed on the trap of their gallows, they could stand, but barely. A look of abject terror was pasted on the face of each man, whose arms were fastened to his sides by straps that passed around his body and arms, just above the elbows. While Hendershott moaned over and over, "Lord have mercy on us," Welter looked into the crowd standing below and recognized a friend. All he managed was "Goodbye" before he, too, began sobbing.

The area into which the bodies fell was enclosed by boards, and when a door under the scaffold was opened, both men were hanging partly in a pit dug under the trap to ensure the drop was long enough to cause their death. Welter was suspended closest to the door, his mouth open and his teeth exposed by drawn lips. His neck was livid and slightly swollen. The head of each man was tilted sharply to one side, suggesting the fall had dislocated their necks.

More common in accounts of Canadian executions were stories of how peaceful and unchanged were the faces of the hanged. In June 1872, Phoebe Campbell was executed in London, Ontario. When her body was cut down, officials saw scarcely a change in her appearance, with the exception of redness around her neck. Campbell's face was pale but displayed no indication she suffered any pain. Four years after that execution, Angus McIvor was hanged in Winnipeg. His face, too, was calm and placid.

An examination of James Kane's body following his 1891 execution in Belleville, Ontario, indicated that, like most condemned prisoners, he died of strangulation rather than as a result of a broken neck. Still, the rope left few marks on his body, apart from faint red lines and a slight abrasion on his neck. The face of the wife killer wore almost a peaceful expression. His eyes were partially open, and except for the whiteness of his face, Kane appeared to be at rest. But he could have been hanged better, according to his executioner. The hangman gave Kane a drop of almost two metres. He admitted, however, that if he had to do it over, he would have given him seven.

The remains of killers whose executions were bungled appeared little different from those whose death came more easily. An example is the hanging of Charles Luckey.

The Luckeys farmed about 10 kilometres from Smiths Falls, Ontario. If ever the family had a bad sheep, it was Charles. After spending most of his young life in trouble, Luckey ended up in jail, sentenced to two years imprisonment for stealing a cap and coat. His fed-up father finally reached the breaking point and vowed never again to come to his son's aid. Charles, in turn, promised to get even with his father.

When Luckey was released from jail in 1892, he went home. The next day, the family residence was in flames. In the ruins of the house, investigators located the charred remains of Luckey's sister, his father and his stepmother. When Charles was arrested, he was wearing his father's boots and his clothing was spotted with blood.

His executioner did not place the noose around Luckey's neck in the proper manner, and the force of the drop caused the rope to slip under the killer's chin. For almost three minutes, Luckey struggled, clutching at his bindings. Yet when his body was cut down, he appeared as calm and unaffected as he had while standing on the gallows.

About the only thing peaceful in the life and death of Charles (Sonny Jones) Matthews was the way he looked after his execution. The former fighter was sentenced to hang for the 1953 hammer murder of a British Columbia woman. Matthews spent a difficult time on death row, five times attempting suicide. To make sure he was around long enough to hang, officials kept the killer sedated. In death, he looked peaceful, though apparently unloved.

As Matthews' body lay on the floor of the gallows, a black hearse waited outside. Its driver was instructed to take his customer either to a local funeral home, where the body would be prepared for a family service, or if unclaimed, to drive the corpse straight to a New Westminster cemetery for interment in the section reserved for paupers, which is where Matthews was buried.

EUGENICS

In the late 1800s and early 1900s, many of the world's most respected scientists believed in eugenics. Proponents of the theory argued that the human race could be improved through a close examination of those presumed to possess genetic defects. Eugenicists found a huge pool of subjects in Canadian prisons, and none were more valued than those sentenced to death.

When news reports of murder trials and executions referred to prisoners, they often described characteristics allegedly associated with the criminal element in society. John Young was an example. Before he was hanged in Cayuga, Ontario, in 1876, reporters expressed surprise that he possessed so few of the physical characteristics they suggested were normally evident on the faces of run-of-the-mill wrongdoers. "His features were even and regular, the low receding brow, pug nose and thick lips of the street rough were all wanting."

A year after Young was executed, a Toronto man was hanged for beating his wife to death. Witnesses at John Williams' execution noted that he bore none of the characteristics attributed to the lower classes, which they suggested most often spawned killers. According to the *Toronto Globe*, "His bend is not of an animal bend; his eyes deep set, blue, by no means restless. There is not much character in the mouth, which is large, nor is there that strength in the jaw which is usually found in men of strong animal natures."

Williams had sufficient of the animal in him to abuse his wife, the mother of his 14 children. Shortly before he murdered her, she complained to a friend about her treatment, though her blackened eyes and bruised flesh made her sufferings all too evident. Instead of apologizing for what he did, Williams swore that the next time he would kill her, and he did.

When Rémi Lamontagne was hanged in Sherbrooke, Québec, he was described as a magnificent-looking specimen of a man, not at all the type to murder. Those who attended his December 1890 execution were right; Lamontagne was indeed handsome. But they were wrong about his character. Not only did he cut the throat of his brother-in-law, but he also placed the still living man on a bed, covered him with a mattress and set his room on fire.

Although mortally wounded, the victim managed to escape the flames and crawl to the home of a neighbour. Before he died, he gave a statement implicating Lamontagne. He also implied that the fight that resulted in his injuries had to do with the intimate nature of the relationship between his wife and her brother.

Shortly before John Sullivan was executed in Dorchester, New Brunswick, he allowed the police chief of St. John to examine his head. From his observation, the police officer concluded that Sullivan was not a criminal. His head, according to the chief, was not wedge-shaped, like the heads of true criminals. Just as spectators at the execution of Lamontagne may have misjudged his character by focusing on his looks, so too was Sullivan misjudged.

The crime that earned the Moncton mill hand a trip to the gallows was as callous as any committed in New Brunswick. The home of his victim sat near a lonely crossroad about halfway between Moncton and Dorchester. The woman, a bootlegger, lived with her two young children and was known to keep a large amount of money in her home. Six months before Sullivan was hanged, the victim's neighbours were awakened by shouts and the sight of a fire engulfing the home of the young family.

Although the eight-year-old daughter of Sullivan's victim escaped, the girl's older brother did not. He and his mother perished in the blaze. The first indication that the fire was not an accident came when the young girl was examined to see if she was injured in the conflagration. Concerned neighbours were shocked to discover that she had suffered a terrible head wound. Sullivan was soon suspected of causing both the injury and the fire, largely because he was seen around the home shortly before it burned and he could not explain where he obtained the large quantity of money he was spending so freely.

BURIAL

Early in the era when the government controlled what happened to the bodies of executed criminals, most murderers were buried in the jails where they died. In England's Newgate prison, for example, killers were interred under the flagstones of the corridor through which they walked on their way to the gallows. The only reminders of their passage are marks cut on the wall opposite spots where each prisoner is entombed.

Even though the law mandated that prisoners executed in Canada had to be buried in the yard of the jail where they were hanged, occasionally exceptions were made. That was why in 1870, the sheriff of Kingston asked the lieutenant-governor of Ontario if the bodies of Daniel Mann and James Deacon could be given to their friends for burial in a public cemetery. The answer was no. Since there was room in the jail yard, they must be buried there.

Well into the 20th century, it was still common for con-demned prisoners to be buried where they were hanged, though few were buried quite so near their gallows as Elizabeth Work-man. In the early 1870s, Workman and her much older husband lived in poverty near Sarnia, Ontario. Although the two had many differences, they shared a passion for liquor.

The Workmans' cycle of drink followed by abuse may have continued indefinitely had not Samuel Butler arrived in the area to open a barbershop. Whether the black man started his affair with Elizabeth before or after he hired her to clean his shop is not known, but James Workman quickly realized something was not right.

Three weeks after she started working for Butler, Elizabeth's husband followed her to the barbershop and insisted that she return home with him. An argument ensued, and Butler threw the drunk husband into the street. Back at home, the argument between the Workmans became physical when Elizabeth started beating her husband with a mop handle. The next day, things were no better. Although now bedridden, James continued berating his wife, but this time she'd had enough. Elizabeth tied up her husband and beat him to death.

Probably because she had the audacity to take up with a man of colour, Elizabeth is the only woman in Canadian history executed after a jury recommended mercy. When the rope by which she was suspended in June 1873 was cut, Workman was lowered into a pit dug under the scaffold. The flowers clutched in her hands were gently taken from her and placed over her heart, her body was appropriately aligned and she was covered with earth.

On rare occasions, the bodies of condemned prisoners did not get where their previous owners wanted them to go. Reginald Birchall was executed in 1890 and his remains were placed in an airtight metallic coffin. His wife, family and friends all wanted the con artist returned to England, but they realized for that to happen, they needed the approval of Ontario's Attorney General. To put a little pressure on him, someone came up with the idea of encasing Birchall's embalmed remains in a metal coffin, all ready for shipment. In the end, lacking the approval needed to alter the traditional way things were done, Woodstock officials buried the expensive coffin, and Birchall, in their jail yard.

The family of gang member and convicted killer Fred Rice fared better with the office of Ontario's Attorney General. After Rice was hanged in Toronto in 1902, his remains were handed over to a city funeral director to prepare the corpse for its last journey. After Rice was embalmed and his body placed in one of the most expensive caskets manufactured in Canada, the killer was sent home to Champaign, Illinois, with his mother.

Just as Phoebe Campbell did not want her body dissected, George O'Brien did not want his buried in a Dawson, Yukon, urinal. In his last days, O'Brien was convinced that following his execution, his remains would be buried in the area of the

North West Mounted Police barracks reserved for storage of body waste. On the way to the gallows, he reminded the town's sheriff of his concern.

"That was all concluded yesterday. I don't propose to repeat it a dozen times," replied the sheriff.

Unhappy with the response, O'Brien turned to the two constables walking beside him. "You'll stand by me, Jack, and you, Bourke. I want to be buried in clean dirt. Not in the urinal."

Arguably the most unusual funeral of a killer took place in Vancouver following the execution of Mewa Singh. In late 1914, the Sikh pulled out two revolvers and shot an immigration inspector to death in the corridor of the Vancouver courthouse. The man was waiting to begin his second day of testimony about a shooting in a city Sikh temple, and Singh was unhappy about what he believed the official was going to say. Two and a half months later, the killer died on a New Westminster gallows.

More than 500 Sikhs walked for blocks behind Singh's hearse, their chanting occasionally drowned out by the sound of beating drums and smashing cymbals. In the driving rain, and five abreast, Sikhs marched to the place where the murderer's body was put on a funeral pyre and burned.

Marvin McKee did not want his body burned, but he did want it used as a warning for others not to follow his path. The Ontario killer was hanged in February 1960. Just before his execution, the 20-year-old asked to be buried in the yard of the Parry Sound jail, as a visible lesson to others of what the future may hold. His request was granted.

CLAIMED BY FAMILY

By the 1920s, it was customary for provincial governments to allow families of executed killers to bury their loved ones on the understanding that such burials would be without fanfare. Officials had ample reason to be cautious. The 1869 burial of Nicholas Melady offers an appropriate illustration.

As soon as the corpse of the man who murdered his father and stepmother was cut down, his friends placed it in a pine coffin and carried it out of the Goderich, Ontario, jail yard to a waiting sleigh. Thirty minutes later, Melady arrived at the local train station. Faithful even in death, Melady's friends rode with him in a baggage car to the nearby town of Seaforth. There they were met by two sleighs that took the body back to the very house in which the murders were committed.

Although some area residents were surprised that Melady's wake was being held in his dead father's home, by the time Nicholas arrived for his final visit, the house belonged to his sister, and she would not let her brother be taken anywhere else. His coffin was carried into the parlour at the front of the house and gently placed on two sawhorses.

As soon as the men who brought their friend home paid their respects, they departed. Other people came and left, all expressing their condolences. By the end of the evening, almost everyone in the community turned up. The next day, Nicholas was buried with family.

BURIED BESIDE VICTIM

In what seems like a cruel twist of fate, some killers were buried beside the very people they murdered. After Thomas Nulty was hanged for slaughtering three sisters and a brother on his family's farm near Joliette, Québec, his father was given his son's remains. In the spring of 1898, they were interred beside the bodies of his four victims.

James McGrath wanted to be buried beside his victim, and for a brief time he was. McGrath was 23 when he murdered his wife. After a brief marriage that produced one child and dozens of incidents of abuse, he seemed to snap. He later said that he killed his wife because he loved her. To prove it, he beat her with a shovel and stabbed her 28 times.

Freda May Bloomfield was a teenager when she met McGrath and had just celebrated her 20th birthday when she died. In the days before her murder, Freda was determined to break out of the cycle of violence in which she found herself. Finally, she left a note for her husband, telling him that she was leaving for good. James did not take the news well.

According to a witness who saw him after he read the note, McGrath was sobbing incoherently as he made his way to the Souris, Manitoba, home of his mother-in-law. There he broke down completely. After crying for hours, McGrath lost any semblance of self-control and rolled off his chair onto the floor.

So complete was his collapse that his in-laws called a doctor. Ironically, he was the same physician who would perform an autopsy on Freda three weeks later. The doctor arrived to find McGrath in what he diagnosed as a state of extreme mental anguish. Although he initially was inclined to have the distraught husband admitted to the Brandon mental hospital, as the evening wore on, the doctor was able to calm McGrath, and he eventually felt the young man no longer posed a danger to himself or others.

Over the next three weeks, McGrath regularly visited his wife and their infant son. Even after moving to Winnipeg, he made the journey to Souris by stealing rides on freight cars.

On June 2, 1931, something went awry. McGrath arrived at the home of his mother-in-law in the middle of the afternoon, but because it was raining, his wife refused to let him take their son outside so McGrath left. He came back when the rain stopped and this time took the infant with him. When the two returned, McGrath said that he wanted to spend more time with his child, since he was returning to Winnipeg.

About suppertime he returned again, holding the baby in one hand and something behind his back with the other. He announced that he would no longer be visiting his son because he was going away. He asked his wife if she would change her mind and come back to him. Her answer sealed her fate.

She said no, there was no chance. McGrath responded by dropping the baby on the floor and rushing at the horrified woman, striking her over the head with a small shovel he was concealing. Freda's sister heard the racket. She hurried into the kitchen and attempted to grab her brother-in-law. In the ensuing struggle, both women ended up on the floor, screaming for help.

Their mother arrived just as Freda ran through the kitchen and out of the house. When Mrs. Bloomfield attempted to prevent her son-in-law from going after her daughter, he hit her in the face, knocking out her front teeth.

McGrath caught up with his wife outside. He pushed her down and began stabbing her with the two butcher knives he had grabbed off the kitchen counter. As blow after blow struck home, the panicked woman pleaded with her husband, repeating over and over, "I will live with you. I will live with you."

While this was going on, Freda's mother and sister ran to a nearby railway office. They told the yardmaster about the attack, and he immediately rushed to the Bloomfield residence. He saw McGrath standing over Freda, stabbing her. As soon as the railroader yelled at him, McGrath ran off.

He eventually arrived at the home of a married couple he knew. The woman noticed that he was covered in blood and asked what happened. When the out-of-breath McGrath gasped that he just killed his wife, the husband told him to "beat it."

Within hours, the killer was arrested and confessed to the murder. He did not attend the inquest that followed because he was on the brink of a complete nervous breakdown. Five months later, McGrath was still an emotional wreck, but when his hearing began in Brandon, his attendance was not optional.

McGrath went to trial in November 1931. He did not testify, and no one was called on his behalf. The jury returned its verdict in just over two hours. After being in a state of near hysteria throughout the proceeding, McGrath became calm and

James McGrath stood on the trapdoors behind the sign suspended between the iron railings. On the right, a sign is draped over the base of the lever that opened the doors.

appeared almost relieved when he was sentenced to hang. Asked if he had anything to say, he replied that it was his hope "that my body shall be laid beside that of my wife as close as it can be."

Two months after his trial, McGrath walked unassisted to the gallows at Headingley Jail. His final request was granted, albeit briefly. McGrath's body was indeed returned to Souris and buried next to his wife. Shortly thereafter, however, her body was disinterred and reburied 200 kilometres away from the man who loved her too much to let her live. James McGrath remains buried in the Souris cemetery.

THE GIFT OF SIGHT

In May 1956, Robert Graham was hanged for kicking an acquaintance to death in a Vancouver parking lot. The 24-year-old killer died calmly, determined to make something of himself in death, even if he was unable to do so in life.

An hour after Graham dropped through an Oakalla scaffold, a doctor removed the corneas from his eyes. Before the day was out, they were grafted onto the eyes of a blind eight-year-old boy. According to Graham's father, "Bob found Christ at the end. He wanted to do something for somebody. Really, he wanted to do something for children. That's why he decided to leave his eyes to blind children. He got the proper form for it and we signed our approval." He said his son was not a bad boy. "He just got in with the wrong crowd. He became a Christian three weeks ago. That was something we could never get him to do."

Two years after Graham was executed, another Canadian killer also gifted his eyes. In the summer of 1957, Thomas Laplante robbed a Hamilton, Ontario, drugstore. Before he got away, a male customer walked in. The next day, the man's stabbed and beaten body was found on a deserted side road. A short time later, Laplante was arrested while hitchhiking in the United States. After confessing to the murder, he was extradited to Welland, Ontario. In mid-January 1958, he was executed.

Seventeen minutes after the trap was sprung, Laplante was pronounced dead, and his body was taken to the laundry room of the Welland jail. A doctor removed his corneas and placed them in dry ice. A waiting police cruiser rushed the package to a hospital in an undisclosed Ontario city, where they were used in a corneal transplant.

The last condemned prisoner to make a gift of his eyes was Marvin McKee. He was executed in 1960 for the robbery-murder of two men. Almost immediately after being told his application for a commutation was turned down, the 20-year-old killer willed his eyes to the Eye Bank of Canada.

Chapter Eleven

The Unusual

~

D espite the efforts of federal officials to make sure executions followed some kind of pattern, the proceedings often went off the rails. Sometimes mistakes were made, but on other occasions the unexpected just happened. In some cases, the unusual occurred before anyone even set foot on a gallows.

CONFESSING TO REPORTERS

In 1947, 23-year-old Frederick Bussey raped and murdered an 11-year-old Ontario girl. Four days later, he surrendered. Not to the police, but to a newspaper reporter.

Just after 9:00 PM, a few days after the Owen Sound murder, a *Montréal Herald* reporter was working alone transcribing his notes when a young man slipped unnoticed into the news room. The stranger spoke briefly with an office boy before being directed to the reporter's desk. When he arrived, the man said he had a story to tell.

Within minutes, the men were sitting in a private office. Bussey asked the reporter if he knew about the "Owen Sound affair." When the reporter replied that he did, Bussey said that if he was interested, he could take the reporter to the guy who committed the murder. The as yet unidentified killer said the man wanted to confess, but he also wanted the $1000 reward posted for his capture. The money would provide the unnamed murderer with some creature comforts in jail, and Bussey wanted the *Herald* to guarantee that the money would be paid.

The reporter decided to hide Bussey from prying eyes and took him to a hotel with the idea of renting a room. When told none was available, the two talked in a bar. Bussey admitted that he was the girl's killer, and he wanted to tell his side of the story before the police became involved.

At Bussey's trial, the reporter recalled what happened next:

He told me he arrived in Owen Sound. It was raining heavily. He lost the road. Suddenly, a girl appeared in front of his car. He stopped and asked directions. She gave them to him. Then, because it was raining, he offered her a ride home, and she got in the car. He started off and missed the turn. The girl began to yell: "Let me out, you're not taking me home."

Bussey told me he slammed on the brakes and put both arms around the girl. The car slowed toward the ditch. The girl slumped down in the seat and he unbuttoned her coat and felt her heart. It was beating. He turned the car around to take her home and she started to scream and tried to get out of the car. Fred told me he seemed to lose his mind. He grabbed the first

thing he saw, which was a hammer, and struck her. Then he
pushed her out of the car and drove off.

After his car stalled, Bussey told the reporter he hitch-hiked to Barrie, then Toronto and finally to Montréal.

Continuing his trial testimony, the reporter said he and Bussey returned to the *Herald* office, where he typed out the killer's statement. As he was doing so, Bussey told him to add a reference stating that he did not rape or attempt to sexually assault the girl. Asked if he had been drinking prior to picking up the girl, Bussey said he consumed a quart and a half of wine.

An Owen Sound jury tried and convicted Bussey in November 1947, and he was hanged less than three months later.

Six years after Bussey was executed, a Montréal labourer was hanged after he, too, confessed his crime to a newspaper reporter. In the case of 27-year-old Peter Mentenko, the victim was his half-brother, whose battered body was found by children exploring a sunken shaft in a city field.

One of the highlights of the first of Mentenko's two trials was the testimony of two Montréal journalists who interviewed the accused while he was in police custody. The murderer told the reporters he was drinking beer with his stepbrother in a Montréal tavern before they got into a fight and he struck his sibling over the head with a piece of metal.

Mentenko appealed his conviction, and Québec's Court of Appeal ordered a new trial after ruling that Mentenko's confession was obtained illegally. The killer went through three trials before he was finally found guilty and executed in March 1953.

Murders and Exhumations

In August 1875, Henry and Susannah White attended a flax bee near Guelph, Ontario. They walked home with Susannah's brother, and if the couple was not exactly devoted to each other, they were at least friendly. That was the problem. Henry suspected his wife was altogether too friendly with a neighbour.

Just before midnight, Henry knocked on his landlord's door. He told him that Susannah accidentally stumbled into a well and he needed help getting her out. A few days later, an inquest held that she had drowned. Before long, however, rumours began to spread that the death was anything but accidental, and Susannah's body was exhumed. A post-mortem revealed that she suffered a terrible beating, and that the drowning came later. Henry was promptly arrested and charged with his wife's murder.

Before the trial began, the police discovered two important facts. The first was that White was convinced his wife was having an affair. The second was more damning. They learned that on the day of the flax bee, Henry had left a heavy stick near the well where his wife's body was found and told his son not to touch it—he would be needing it later.

Shortly before his execution date, Henry confessed his guilt. He sought spiritual guidance from two local ministers who were unremitting in their attention to his needs. About 9:00 PM the night before he was executed, the exhausted men left White's cell. They were soon replaced by members of Henry's church, who held a prayer service in the corridor outside his cell. At midnight they departed.

The next morning, White awoke prepared to die. After spending some time with his spiritual advisers, he ate sparingly of the breakfast provided. While he dined, area residents provided with passes by Guelph's sheriff began gathering in the jail yard. Those without the proper credentials were forced to climb poplar trees outside the prison or sit on the roofs of neighbouring buildings.

What they saw was an incredibly crude structure made up of four posts, a small platform suspended well above the ground, a beam just over two metres above the platform and a narrow pit less than a metre deep dug directly under the scaffold. It was designed to ensure that White died when he dropped and to collect the body waste associated with most executions. Wrapped around the beam was a rope, its noose already prepared, and a little farther away, an open grave, mute testimony to what was to come.

The bell of the Wellington county jail began tolling a little before 8:00 AM, signalling that all was in readiness. A few minutes later, the executioner entered White's cell. He pinioned White's arms, and as White walked down the corridor past other prisoners, he exhorted them to beware of following a life of crime: "Goodbye. Trust in the Lord, and be good boys."

On the scaffold, White made a few comments to the spectators assembled below the gallows, and then his executioner pulled a black hood over his face and guided the wife killer to the trap. The hangman slipped the noose around White's neck and retreated to the lever that controlled the drop.

No sooner had White's spiritual adviser started reciting the Lord's Prayer than the trap opened and White descended. The suddenness startled spectators, yet when his body was cut down, his face showed no evidence of surprise or fear.

Two years before his 1927 execution, railway brakeman Ulric Germain poisoned his wife in what for a time seemed a much more sophisticated murder than the one carried out by Henry White. While Marie-Louise Germain was recovering from an illness, her husband several times dropped an unknown substance into her prescribed medicine. Witnesses who saw this did not connect the woman's passing to her husband's actions until the grieving widower remarried a couple of weeks after Marie-Louise's death.

Relatives of Marie-Louise immediately became suspicious and began gathering evidence of foul play. They passed along what they discovered to the Attorney General of Québec, and Marie-Louise's body was exhumed. When an autopsy revealed the presence of poison, Ulric was arrested, tried and convicted of murder.

Although Ulric said he was ready to die, for a time he seemed determined to put it off as long as he could. While standing on the gallows, he asked witnesses to pray with him three times. Finally, without waiting for a fourth prayer, the executioner sprung the trap. Six and a half minutes later, the mastermind behind a near flawless crime was declared dead.

Like Ulric Germain, Roland Asselin very nearly got away with a perfect murder. The 37-year-old bus-taxi service operator shot Ulric Gauthier to death in what the police ruled was a suicide. Things may have stayed that way if six months later the victim's widow had not killed herself. The chance of a husband and wife both dying by their own hands in less than a year was thought slight, and it prompted the police to exhume the body of Gauthier and re-open their inquiry into the suicide of the well-to-do garage owner. Their investigation soon resulted in the arrest and, after 145 witnesses finished testifying, the murder conviction and hanging of Asselin.

CANNIBALISM

Few killers executed on a Canadian gallows were as vile as Ka Ki Si Kutchin, better known as Swift Runner. The Aboriginal lived with his family in the northern portion of what is now Alberta. Or at least he did, until he killed, cooked and ate them. All nine of them.

The first clue anyone had of the terrible crime perpetrated by Swift Runner was late in 1879, when he showed up at the Roman Catholic mission of St. Albert and told shocked priests that in the preceding months, hunting was bad and his family had perished from starvation.

From the beginning, few believed the story, partly because it was widely known that hunting was exceptionally good that fall, and partly because the six-foot-three-inch giant who claimed to have lost his mother, wife and seven children to starvation was anything but skinny.

Swift Runner's reputation was well known in the mission. He was addicted to drink and was extraordinarily strong. The combination made him a formidable antagonist, and Aboriginals and non-Aboriginals alike feared him. When his fellow Cree packed up their summer camps and prepared to leave for their winter lodges, they refused to let Swift Runner travel with them. For a time, the troublemaker's family remained with the band, but after he promised to behave better in the future, they agreed to live with him. At the same time, a Cree chief advised members of the North West Mounted Police that the huge man had become a cannibal. Lacking evidence, the police did nothing.

When Swift Runner turned up in St. Albert alone, the circumstances were different. A small group of officers persuaded the suspect to take them to his winter campsite. According to contemporary accounts of what happened next, Swift Runner was living in a cave at the foot of a hill, and the bones of all his victims were scattered about. The exception was the remains of a young son, who was apparently killed and consumed elsewhere.

Swift Runner allegedly killed his victims in a single evening and buried their bodies in the snow, cooking them as required.

In August 1879, the cannibal was convicted of eight of the nine murders. Because officials could not find what remained of the missing son, they decided not to proceed with that charge. Five days before Christmas, carpenters finished Swift Runner's scaffold and officials informed the killer his wait was over. The gallows was erected just outside the main gate of the Fort Saskatchewan jail, and the execution was well attended, despite the darkness and a snowstorm that engulfed the area.

While they waited to watch the first hanging carried out in the Canadian northwest, a group of Aboriginals built fires to keep warm. Swift Runner stopped in front of one as he walked toward the gallows. He stayed longer than he should have. The execution was scheduled for 7:30 AM, but the group had used the wooden trapdoor of the scaffold for fuel and officials were forced to scrounge more wood for a replacement. During the hour it took to do so, the convicted killer sat down and ate breakfast, a noose dangling from his neck.

A local army pensioner was hired to hang Swift Runner, in part because he volunteered and also because he claimed to have seen several executions while serving with the British in India. The hangman may have agreed to execute his victim, but he did not come equipped to do so. When everything else was in readiness, it was discovered he did not have leather straps to pinion Swift Runner's arms and legs, and another delay ensued until some were found.

About 50 Aboriginals were camped around the gallows, either curious to see what a hanging entailed or just wanting to ensure that Swift Runner was going to be well and truly dead. The cannibal was anxious to do what he could to accommodate them, volunteering to do himself in with a tomahawk if that would save time. His offer was refused, but based on what happened next, perhaps it should not have been.

When the hangman returned with pinioning straps, he was trembling so much that the witnesses to the execution had to bind Swift Runner themselves. That done, spectators began a death dance, much to the amusement of Swift Runner, who seemed to regard the entire execution process as a joke. Watching the dancing seemed to make the cannibal hungry, and he demanded something more to eat before he was hanged. Thirty minutes later, the executioner regained control of the situation. After Swift Runner publicly confessed his guilt, amid the jeers and shouts of the spectators, he dropped to his death.

Estate Problems

The day John Worobec, a tailor from Alberta, and Walter Prestyko, an unemployed machine operator from Ontario, broke into the Vancouver home of Michael and Mary Geluch, they started two separate legal processes. In February 1950, one process ended with their deaths on an Oakalla prison farm gallows; the other lasted longer.

After they were convicted of strangling the Geluchs, Prestyko and Worobec refused to say which victim died first. That left unsettled the question of who inherited the couple's $11,000 estate. Michael Geluch's children claimed it on the basis that they, and they alone, were his surviving kin. Mary Geluch married her husband a year before they were murdered, and her relatives also filed a claim. According to law, if Mary was killed after her husband, even if just minutes later, she would be his legal heir and entitled to everything. Then when she died, her estate would devolve to members of her own family. The Geluch children would receive nothing.

The lawyer acting on behalf of Michael's daughter met with Worobec at Oakalla. He asked the murderer who he killed first, but got little response. "I am not going to say any more whether you like it or not; I don't care who takes the estate."

According to Worobec's spiritual adviser, both murderers slept well the night before they were executed. The prison chaplain arrived at Worobec's cell around 9:00 PM, and while the prisoner made a confession of faith, he said nothing regarding the Geluchs. He did, however, talk about his own family until about 2:00 AM, when he lay down for awhile. Prestyko's priest joined the killer late in the evening, and the two played cards and talked. Shortly before the murderers were called to the gallows, each was given a glass of Scotch whiskey.

They died with no last statements, no tears and little waste of time. Worobec entered the death chamber between two guards, ahead of his partner. Both men were dressed in their prison uniforms and seemed calm. It took their hangman two tries before he was satisfied Worobec was properly noosed, and then he moved to the lever. The pair dropped face-to-back into the middle of a small circle made by three guards posted under the scaffold.

It took 11 minutes for Worobec and Prestyko to die. Following a brief inquiry, members of the coroner's jury quickly left the prison as the sun was just starting to peak over mountains on the north shore. Seemingly unaware of the events of the morning, a prisoner just out of bed stood in his underwear behind a barred window, watching something more free than himself.

HANGING THE UNCONSCIOUS

When a Canadian Pacific Railway (CPR) ironworker was brutally murdered near Toronto in 1918, he was either the victim of a serial killer or his death the result of a labour dispute. Or perhaps it was both.

George Tucker was employed as scab labour, hired to carry out repairs to a rail bridge while regular CPR employees were on strike. His partially clad body was found in the railway car he used as a place to sleep, stabbed 14 times. Although initially the police had no idea who committed the murder, they surmised that it was in some way connected to the ongoing labour problems that soured relations between the rail company and its southern Ontario workers.

Two weeks after the killing, investigators arrested Has-san Neby at a Toronto rooming house. He denied any knowl-edge of the murder and said he had nothing to do with the CPR, but both claims were lies. He not only matched the description of a man observed near the murder scene shortly before the bridge worker's body was found, but he also regularly cashed wage cheques—all issued by the Canadian Pacific.

Neby went to trial in late October and, two days later, was sentenced to hang. During his two-month stay on the Don Jail's death row, he maintained a stoic silence, perhaps because everything officials learned about his background made him look bad, such as his murder conviction in the state of Connecticut and his subsequent prison escape.

It was only in the hours immediately preceding his execution that Neby seemed finally to realize that he was about to die. The 38-year-old Albanian rejected the spiritual services offered by the prison chaplain and began for the first time to pray, always looking toward Mecca.

Just minutes before 8:00 AM on the day Neby was hanged, his executioner and a Toronto deputy sheriff entered his cell and bound his arms together behind his back. A few moments later, the killer was standing on the scaffold, though not for long. Before his hangman could release the trapdoor, Neby collapsed. The semi-conscious man was quickly grabbed and held upright, and in the blink of an eye he dropped to his death.

But the story of Neby does not end there. Although a post-mortem revealed that the man's spinal cord was severed by the fall, his heart continued to beat for almost 20 minutes. City newspapers heralded it as a new Toronto record.

BAD LUCK CAT

Even before he strangled his mother in late November 1925, Eugène Bigaouette was regarded as more than just eccentric. He lived in a Québec City house occupied by family members and was referred to by neighbours as "Bigaouette the Fool." The 42-year-old posted notices in the backyard, in both official languages, warning cats to stay away from the house after 9:00 PM. He also spread pieces of broken glass and nails on the street in front of his residence to flatten the tires of cars.

While Bigaouette was not violent, he was someone people feared. Even his own mother said she felt uncomfortable when she was alone with her son. Despite his eccentricities, however, Eugène could understand the significance of being named the only beneficiary in his mother's will. When she died, he would inherit her house, $5000 in cash and all her possessions.

So perhaps it should not have come as a total surprise when the body of Marie-Anne Boivin was found lying across her bed. Shortly before the discovery was made, Eugène showed up at the office of his family's doctor and told the startled practitioner that he just found his mother's body. The men hurried to the woman's residence, where she was indeed dead.

An autopsy revealed that the 76-year-old Boivin was strangled after being beaten with a blunt instrument. When he was arrested, Eugene asked one of the detectives investigating his mother's murder a legal question. "If I pleaded guilty, I would get 10 years, 15 years. Would I get my money afterwards?"

Bigaouette's first trial took place in early 1926. He was found guilty of murder and sentenced to death. His lawyer launched a successful appeal, and the Supreme Court of Canada ordered a new trial. When it concluded, he was again sentenced to hang.

Until the evening before his scheduled execution, the condemned man did not know whether his application for a reprieve would be allowed. When he was told he must die, Bigaouette appeared to take the news in stride. He went to bed early and slept well. The next morning he and two members of his death watch made their way to the prison chapel, where he celebrated Mass.

On August 19, 1927, Bigaouette ate breakfast for the final time and appeared at last to realize what was to come. When a jail official arrived to inform him that it was time to go, he was overcome by emotion and cried bitterly. He was still distraught as the death procession began to make its way to the gallows, and guards held him by each shoulder as he crossed the jail compound to the scaffold.

There, waiting on a step, was a cat. By the time Bigaouette arrived, the animal was chased away, though it did not stray far.

On the scaffold, the condemned man was placed under the noose. His priest was worried about a scene and cautioned the killer, "Remember what I told you. Ask God to forgive you all your sins." In response Bigaouette merely shrugged his shoulders, saying nothing. When a crucifix was held to his lips he instinctively kissed it, although to everyone present it seemed he had no idea where he was or what he was doing.

Bigaouette's hangman quickly brought everything to a halt. He pulled a black hood over the prisoner's face while his assistant strapped the man's feet. The executioner then pulled the lever, opening the trapdoor. Bigaouette was suspended for about seven minutes before he was pronounced dead. But before that happened, the cat returned.

No one saw it crawl into the space beneath the gallows until it was there. The animal seemed fascinated by the body hanging just above it and refused to leave when the jail surgeon arrived. Only with considerable effort were officials able to force the cat away from Bigaouette's dangling corpse.

When the cat disappeared, so, too, did Bigaouette. While two guards held onto the body, the rope suspending the dead man's remains was cut, and the body was placed in a coffin lying beside the gallows.

TRIALS AND STAYS

The two years that elapsed between Bigaouette's crime and his punishment was an unusually long time in a country where most killers were executed just months after they committed their crime. Although federal officials could come up with an answer, it's difficult to determine with certainty who was tried the most times and whose sentence was most often stayed before that person was finally put to death. There is little doubt, however, that Ovila Boucher's record would be right up there.

In June 1951, the 32-year-old blacksmith hacked to death his elderly next-door neighbour in the small Québec village of Saint-Henri-de-Lévis. The merchant's body was found in the room he occupied above his store. The police said someone ransacked the little apartment as if in search of something and speculated that the something was likely $4000 in cash they found hidden in a box.

Boucher was tried four times for the murder of his neighbour, his appeal was heard three times by the Québec Court of Appeals and it went to the Supreme Court of Canada twice. Throughout his series of trials and appeals, he received 13 stays of execution. More than five years elapsed between the murder and Boucher's execution. The axe killer went to the gallows less than 15 hours after he was advised that his latest application for a reprieve was turned down.

Hanged in an Armchair

In the late 19th century, Pah-Cah-Pah-Ne-Cappy lived on a Blood Indian reserve in the southwest corner of what is now the province of Alberta. The warrior was also known as Bad

Young Man, an appellation that seemed perfectly to sum up his character. By the time he was executed in a Fort McLeod police barracks, the killer was referred to simply as Charcoal.

In October 1896, Charcoal shot a man who was having an affair with his wife. He knew he was bound to hang for what he did and grew determined to kill someone important before he died, thereby ensuring he would enter the great beyond as a warrior. His first choice was Red Crow, a Blood chief and the brother-in-law of the man he murdered. When that opportunity was denied him, he headed for the home of the local Indian agent. That too came to naught.

Charcoal's next target was an instructor the federal government hired to turn buffalo hunters into farmers. He shot the man but did not kill him. Soon a posse was on his trail, and Charcoal was cornered in the Porcupine Hills. A member of the Pincher Creek detachment of the North West Mounted Police attempted to sneak up on the killer, but in the gunfight that ensued, he was slain.

Two days later, the exhausted and hungry fugitive sought shelter at his brother's home. Instead of helping, his brother sent for the police and held Charcoal until they arrived. When he went on trial for murder, the verdict was a foregone conclusion. The Blood warrior was sentenced to hang on a gallows in the Fort Macleod police barracks.

In the days before his execution, Charcoal became so ill that he had to be carried to the scaffold in a chair. He was hooded and noosed, and still sitting his chair, dropped to his death.

Another execution-in-a-chair occurred in 1914, again in Alberta. Before Jasper Collins was hanged at the Royal North West Mounted Police barracks in Calgary (in 1904, "Royal" was added to the name of the NWMP), he attempted to delay his execution by going on a hunger strike, hoping the government would not hang someone in his condition. His plan didn't work. Although weakened after days without food, Collins managed to walk to the gallows. Once there, however, he showed signs of collapsing, and officials quickly brought out an armchair. In no time at all, both plummeted through the scaffold floor.

Shortly after Collins died sitting down, a British Columbia railroader was dispatched the same way. Rocco Ferranto was working as a section hand with an electric railway company when he became embroiled in an argument with a fellow worker. During the heated exchange of words, the Italian immigrant pulled out a knife and stabbed the man in the throat. He then cut off and threw his victim's head down a well, hoping to make it difficult for the authorities to identify the body.

By the time Ferranto's trial opened in 1916, he had captured the imagination of people all across Canada. A few months before his trial got underway, the killer was tried for an earlier murder, and before that he was accused of killing yet another fellow worker. Ferranto's association with his first two victims, and the fact that both bodies were discovered naked, was not enough to convince the authorities that the crimes were connected, nor sufficient to show that Ferranto was the killer. On both occasions the Italian went free. But not this time.

Ferranto was hanged in New Westminster. Until a few hours before his execution, the doomed man was convinced he was going to win a second trial. When told that there would be no reprieve, he became hysterical, demanding he be returned to court. To ensure that his execution went off without a hitch, jail officials tied the killer to a chair and placed it and its occupant where an "X" marked the spot. After that, all the executioner was required to do was pull the lever.

FIRST LIVE REPORTING OF A CANADIAN EXECUTION

In November 1890, Reginald Birchall was hanged for murdering a man he lured from England to buy non-existent Ontario farmland. The killer was the son of a prominent Anglican churchman, handsome, married to a beautiful young woman and an alumnus of Oxford University. Newspaper readers in England and throughout North America were captivated by the person, his crime and especially his pending execution.

When Birchall's trial got underway, Woodstock, Ontario, lacked a courthouse. The old building was torn down before a new one went up, so the trial was held in the town hall. The Great North Western Telegraph Company ran wires to the tables at which reporters sat, so its operators could send out instant reports of the proceedings. Local entrepreneurs went one step further. They suspended telephone transmitters from the ceiling of the hall and broadcast testimony to the homes of some of the town's wealthiest citizens and to a local bar. The owner of the Thompson House rented out his "telephone tubes" for 25 cents an hour.

After Birchall's conviction, the Canadian Pacific Railway sought permission to run their own wires inside the jail yard so that it could notify customers of the precise moment the trap opened.

As it turned out, the two cable operators with ringside seats to the execution worked on behalf of the Dunlap & Dalziel Cable News Association and an affiliate of Reuter's Cable Agency. Each company placed its cables within metres of the scaffold, and when the execution took place at 8:27 AM, the news was almost immediately posted on bulletin boards in Europe and elsewhere.

Chapter Twelve

The Dance of Death

~

It is sweet to dance to violins
When Love and Life are fair:
To dance to flutes, to dance to lutes
Is delicate and rare:
But it is not sweet with nimble feet
To dance upon the air!

–Oscar Wilde,
"The Ballad of Reading Gaol Prison," verse 9, stanza II

To state the obvious, murder is all about cruelty. Whether we are talking about the slaughter of innocents or the execution of killers, the taking of life offends us. Yet it also fascinates. The media constantly bombard us with tales of murder and mayhem, and it seems we can't get enough. But the stories described in this book suggest there is much we can learn from examining our past, and in particular the 95 years when we hanged those who killed.

For instance, through examining the lives and deaths of those who died on a Canadian gallows, we learn that we are a much more violent nation than previously thought. That is primarily because of the tendency by officials to under-report murders. This was done for a variety of good reasons, but over time, the effect was to distort our understanding of just how violent some citizens of this country are.

The killing spree of a 38-year-old Québec man is an apt illustration. In the fall of 1934, Joseph Bilodeau drove two male cousins into the woods near Québec City. For a reason never explained, he killed them. Bilodeau then returned home, picked up his two elderly sisters and a young female cousin and took them to a different section of the same woods.

After he shot the three women to death, the former mailman showed up at the post office where he once worked. Bilodeau was well known in the building, and when he asked to see his former boss, no one suspected anything was wrong. The postmaster was talking to his divisional superintendent and a senior mail clerk when Bilodeau walked in and started shooting. By the time he was overpowered, the ex-employee had killed the superintendent and wounded the clerk.

Although he murdered six people, Bilodeau was tried on only one charge, and the records of the federal government refer to a single victim.

A similar result occurred when the Crown tried Thomas Young for one murder after a shooting rampage that claimed five lives. The 27-year-old killer lived in a cabin near Ear Falls in western Ontario when a group of friends and relatives showed up on Christmas Day 1958. Among them was a former love interest, now the teenage wife of one of his friends. The visitors were just metres from the cabin when Young started shooting them with a rifle.

The first person killed was the husband of the young woman. As two other members of the party ran from the carnage, they heard more shots. Within hours a police constable arrived at the home of Young's uncle, and the men made their way to the murder scene. The police officer was wounded as he neared the cabin, and the uncle was shot as he charged toward his nephew.

The constable was badly injured, but while Young was killing his uncle, the police officer managed to drag himself along a path away from the cabin. Young quickly caught up with him, and using the service revolver of the downed officer, shot the helpless man through the mouth.

When reinforcements showed up, they trailed the killer to the cabin of his grandparents and used tear gas to flush him out. A little less than three months later, a Kenora jury convicted Young of the murder of the constable. The multiple murderer who technically killed only one person was hanged in June 1959.

Two other ways statistics tend to distort the tendency of Canadians to kill are occasions where a mass murderer is never convicted of a capital offence and where a murder is followed by the suicide of the killer before she or he can be charged.

In August 1968, a family of nine living in a four-room cabin near Shell Lake, Saskatchewan, were slaughtered by a man released from a mental hospital three weeks earlier. At the time, authorities said he posed no danger to the community.

When 21-year-old Victor Ernest Hoffman arrived at their farm, the Petersons were already in bed. His first victim was James. According to the father's four-year-old daughter, who survived the carnage by hiding under the covers between the bodies of two of her sisters, Peterson confronted Hoffman in the kitchen. He was shot several times in the abdomen. The young killer then went from room to room, shooting the rest of the family as they lay in their beds. Everyone except Evelyn Peterson and Larry. Mrs. Peterson grabbed her youngest child and tried to escape by jumping through a bedroom window. Their bodies were found in the front yard, where Hoffman had caught the pair and shot them at point blank range.

Less than a week after he massacred the Petersons, Hoffman was arrested, charged and sentenced to hang for the murders of James and Evelyn. The following January, a North Battleford jury found him not guilty by reason of insanity.

In 2007, two Saskatchewan historians referred to John Morrison as the greatest mass murderer in the province's history. He killed eight members of the same family, one fewer than Hoffman's toll of victims. Yet the claim of the historians is technically correct. According to law, Hoffman was not guilty of the crimes for which he was charged, since he was judged insane.

In much the same way, a member of the Alberta legislature was not responsible for causing the deaths of seven people in early June 1956. John Etter Clark was born and raised on the farm where the bodies of his wife, four children, his hired man and a mortally wounded guest were discovered. Clark was found the following day, wearing his pajamas and lying face down in a muddy slough about 550 metres from his house. He killed himself with the same single-shot, .22-calibre rifle used to murder his victims.

The 41-year-old politician was a Social Credit member of the legislature and suffered a series of nervous breakdowns in the years preceding his murder spree. His most recent episode had occurred just a few months before he killed himself. Clark's name does not appear on federal murder records.

THE PACE OF JUSTICE

Media reports of American killers spending decades on death row have influenced the way Canadians think about the time between crime and punishment. Some of us perhaps have forgotten that Canada's legal system, like that of England, is much less multi-tiered than that of the United States, and our courts and politicians have always been committed to the notion that justice must be both swift and sure. Even with that in mind, it is surprising how speedy justice was when killers in this country were hanged.

An example is the crime and execution of a Saskatchewan man in 1911. Hungarian immigrants James Alak and his wife Theresa should never have married. The newlyweds were better known around Vanscoy, Saskatchewan, for their disagreements than their ability to farm. The Alaks' relationship deteriorated so quickly three weeks after the couple's wedding that Theresa was back living with her parents.

In early fall she, her father and a neighbour arrived at the Alak homestead to pick up her remaining possessions. When Theresa would not agree to return home, and her father refused to try to persuade her to do so, Alak shot them both. The neighbour escaped, but before long, Alak showed up at his homestead. Instead of shooting him, the distraught killer confessed that after murdering his wife and his father-in-law, he went to the home of his mother-in-law and killed her as well.

Three weeks later, it took a Saskatoon jury just 10 minutes to find Alak guilty of murder. Two and a half months after slaughtering his family, the young farmer was hanged in Prince Albert.

The case of Emmett Sloane, better known in the Sydney area of Nova Scotia as Ingvald Anderson, is another example of how justice was carried out swiftly. The champion ski jumper turned electrician killed a hotel night clerk in early February 1930, and less than a month later was sentenced to hang. Three months after committing his crime, the American killer was executed, despite his lawyer's claim that repeated falls on the ski slope so weakened his mind that the native of New Hampshire was not legally responsible for his actions.

Speedy justice in Canada was not always about how long it took to send an accused to trial. Often, it referred to the length of jury deliberations. Joseph Currie did not go to trial until a year after he murdered a Good Samaritan in northern Ontario, but from that point on, the criminal justice process sped up considerably.

For most of his young life, Currie was a migrant. After being drafted into the Canadian army during World War I, he deserted, changed his name and made his way north. Between his arrival in the Capreol area of Ontario and the day he committed murder, the Hamilton man drifted from job to job.

Currie was working with a gang repairing railway tracks when he met a 65-year-old trapper living near Crerar. The man recently received a small fortune from the sale of furs, and Currie was determined to get his hands on it. Sometime during the evening of January 19, 1920, a very drunk Currie took a train to Crerar, and with the thermometer hovering well below freezing, walked seven kilometres through bush to the trapper's cabin.

He was quickly invited in and offered food and drink. He took both, along with the life of his host. A Sudbury jury deliberated for only 12 minutes before finding Currie guilty, albeit their decision was made easy since he admitted to committing the murder. A little less than two months later he was hanged.

In 1932, a Joliette, Québec, jury was out a little longer before it convicted Albert Préville of murder, but unlike the trial of Currie, his was hotly contested. The 31-year-old was deeply enamoured with a local woman, and when he arrived at her home to find his brother keeping her company, he flew into a jealous rage. Préville shot the object of his affection three times, cut her throat from ear to ear and repeatedly stabbed her. Jurors deliberated for 40 minutes before finding him guilty.

The killer mounted the scaffold in the bitter cold of an early January morning. Despite the loss of control evident when he slaughtered his victim, Préville met his death calmly. He climbed the steps of his red-painted scaffold, borrowed specially for his execution, without hesitation, and within seconds dropped to his death.

Although it's impossible to prove, there is little doubt the length of time it took a jury to decide the guilt of an accused was related to the circumstances surrounding the crime and the attitude of the presiding judge. Both factors worked to the disadvantage of a young Ontario man in March 1925.

Thomas Collison was infatuated with a Matilda-area woman but grew increasingly frustrated when she did not return his affections. He ended any chance the two would have a relationship after he went to the home of the teenager and spied on her through a kitchen window. As Matilda was sweeping her floor, Collison fired shots her into side and abdomen, killing her.

The judge who presided over Collison's trial was clearly horrified at the cowardliness of the murder and made his feelings clear. In his closing address to the jurors, the justice said there could be little doubt that the accused knew that the weapon he used was going to bring about the death of his intended target. He also said it was his opinion that Collison understood that taking the life of the 18-year-old was wrong both in the sight of the law and in the eyes of God.

Members of Collison's jury deliberated only 53 minutes before finding him guilty of murder. Two and a half months later he was executed.

DYING WITH PROTEST

To even casual observers, the stories of the crimes and punishments of Canadian killers reveal a surprising fact. Almost without exception, the women and men who were hanged died without protest. There was rarely any shouting, pushing or shoving, nor indeed anything that would slow the process—with one exception. Lawrence (Corky) Vincent did not go quietly.

The 28-year-old operated a shooting gallery in a travelling circus, which in the fall of 1953 was set up in Quesnel, British Columbia. It was there he met the young girl he sexually assaulted and strangled. Four months after his third trial ended, Vincent's executioner arrived to bind his arms and lead him to Oakalla's death chamber.

A very difficult situation immediately became much worse. As soon as the hangman tried to tie the prisoner's arms,

Vincent hit him. The executioner swung back, striking the killer with a leader strap and managing to tie Vincent's arms together. The bound man was not pleased. Told it was time to head for the gallows, he said, "Just whenever you're ready, pig. Just whenever you're ready. Dirty, rotten pig! Dirty, rotten pig!"

In the death chamber, Vincent became even more troublesome. Surrounded by six guards, the hangman stooped to bind Vincent's feet. Without warning, the condemned man kneed the executioner in the groin, and for a second time the hangman fought back. A guard tried to grab Vincent, but he jumped to one side and kicked at the hangman again. The executioner and his victim squared off a few feet apart on the gallows, glaring at each other.

Like a schoolyard bully taunting his victim, the killer started shouting, "Hit me! Hit me! You big fat pig! You yellow, rotten pig." Finally the prison warden leaned over and put his hand on the prisoner's shoulder. "A prayer would be more appropriate than this," he said without raising his voice.

"I've already said my prayers," Vincent replied. "I've the greatest respect for you, warden. I will go when I've made up my mind." Then the killer turned to his spiritual adviser. "I'm sorry I can't shake your hand. You've been awfully kind to me."

For a few seconds he remained silent, then Vincent spit in the executioner's face and sneered, "Just whenever you're ready, pig." With that, the hangman finished strapping the murderer's legs, and in what seemed like a single motion, noosed, hooded and dropped him.

Delaying the Inevitable

In September 1885, Benjamin Simmons was found guilty of murdering his common-law wife.

The crime was both senseless and impulsive. His wife was his sole means of support, and because she was a reformed drinker herself, could no doubt empathize with the difficulty he had dealing with alcohol. On the day of the murder, Simmons drank all afternoon, and when he came home, he demanded more drinking money from his wife. When she refused to give him any, he stabbed her to death.

He was found guilty of her murder and sentenced to hang. Asked if he had anything to say before his sentence was imposed, he replied, "I have nothing to say, my Lord; I've only one request to make, that is to give me as long a time as you can before my execution, that I may be prepared to meet my Maker." He was allowed a little less than three months.

Edward Cook's request for more time came well after his 1914 conviction for murdering a Syrian peddler near his uncle's Sheet Harbour, Nova Scotia, farm. A few minutes before he was led to a Halifax gallows, Cook was visited by the jail doctor. He asked if it might be possible to hang a little later in the day, preferably in the afternoon. As politely as possible, the killer was advised that was not an option.

A surprising number of death row prisoners attempted to commit suicide, preferring to take their own lives rather than be subjected to the helplessness associated with dying on a gallows. That was certainly the case for a pair of Montréal bank robbers.

In September 1948, Donald Perreault and Noel Cloutier were leaving the bank they had just held up when they were confronted by two Montréal police officers. In the ensuing gunfight, both constables were killed.

The 24-year-old Cloutier twice tried to cheat the gallows. The first time he slashed his wrists while awaiting trial. On the second occasion, he made an ill-fated attempt to escape from his death cell at Montréal's infamous Bordeaux Jail. Donald Perreault's suicide attempt came just hours before he was hanged. He slashed both wrists with a razor blade he managed to hide from guards, but he was well enough to make it to the scaffold under his own power.

Henri Séguin succeeded where Cloutier and Perreault failed, and apparently without really trying. The young Québecer killed the taxi driver he robbed near Cornwall, Ontario. An hour before his 1954 execution, the prisoner burst into tears and, for reasons unknown, began convulsing. Before jail officials could get him medical assistance, Séguin died. In the yard outside the jail, a grave was already waiting.

KILLING WITH FAMILY

Canadian statistics suggest that when husbands and wives teamed up to commit murder, as often as not, only the husband went to the gallows. That is what occurred in 1919, after Paul Kowalski and his wife killed a friend in their Hamilton home.

When Ignace Trembluk arrived at the Kowalski residence for a night of drinking, he was known to have about $800 with him. The next morning, his badly beaten and nearly nude body was found lying on a manure pile behind the home, without the money. The police quickly learned that he spent his last evening alive with the Kowalskis, and in no time they appeared on the Kowalski doorstep. The house was in a shambles, with blood everywhere, and a search soon turned up the murder weapon—a bloody axe. The couple was arrested, and in late October tried for Trembluk's murder.

When she was taken into custody, Kowalski's wife had in her possession almost the exact amount of money Trembluk was missing when his body was found. Despite being unable to explain where the money came from, she was acquitted, and her husband was found guilty of the murder. In a bit of irony, Kowalski was on his way to a death cell when the police returned to his wife the money the couple took from Trembluk.

But the story does not end there. While awaiting his execution, Kowalski attempted to break out of the Hamilton jail, killing two guards in the process. With his execution just a couple of days away, the authorities decided not to try him for the murders. So it was that two months after being convicted of killing Trembluk, a shackled and sobbing Paul Kowalski walked

to the gallows, still protesting his innocence. His wife was not
seen among the 200 people gathered around the jail when he
was hanged.

Fathers and sons committed far fewer murders together
than did husbands and wives, but in a way, the result was the
same—as a rule, only one of two hanged. That was the case with
Fred and Rodney Montgomery.

On October 9, 1957, a clerk working at the Blind River,
Ontario, branch of the Royal Bank of Canada was returning
with mail an hour before the bank was to open. The manager
was in his office, and several tellers were already at work. Before
the clerk could enter the building, he was accosted by two men,
one of whom carried a rifle and the other a revolver. As the three
walked through the bank toward the area where the money was
kept, one of the robbers shouted "Everyone down on the floor—
this is a holdup!"

The manager heard the commotion and started out of
his office to see what was going on. One of the holdup men saw
him and fired a bullet into his chest from point blank range.

Were it not for the tragic death of the bank manager, the
robbery was more farce than crime. The Montgomerys were frequent customers of the bank, and when they ran from the building, the mask tied around the face of young Rodney slipped
down, and he was immediately recognized by customers waiting
for the bank to open. Then, when the men tried to drive away,

their car stalled. Father and son were forced to leave it behind and make their escape in a stolen vehicle.

The pair managed to make a clean getaway. After ditching the car they commandeered, they started hitchhiking west, despite police forces across the country looking for them. A week after the robbery, a Good Samaritan picked up the Montgomerys between Kenora and what is now Thunder Bay. He dropped the robbers off in Saskatoon, Saskatchewan, where they were hired to work on a nearby farm.

A short while later, the Montgomerys were arrested and returned to Ontario, and early in 1958, they stood trial in Sault St. Marie. At the end of a weeklong hearing, their jury deliberated for three hours before finding the 42-year-old father and his 17-year-old son guilty of murder. Four days before they were to hang, the federal government commuted the sentence of the younger Montgomery to life imprisonment. The father was hanged on July 15, 1958.

A young Alberta killer was not as fortunate as Rodney Montgomery. In September 1932, a father and son from Tennessee were farming in Alberta when they killed a man during a robbery. Although Kenneth and William McLean successfully made their way back to their hometown in Tennessee after the murder, their life of crime continued. William was in jail on a charge unrelated to the Canadian murder when American authorities tied him and his father to the Alberta shooting. Before long, the pair was back in Canada.

In July 1933, a Vegreville jury tried and convicted the McLeans. Before the year was out, both died on a Fort Saskatchewan gallows. William was hanged first, followed 20 minutes later by his father.

Effect on Others

The effect executions had on prison workers was a source of concern to jail officials, and no doubt was one reason Canadian executions were carried out so quickly. Still, participating in a state-sponsored murder was a traumatic experience, even for prison doctors. An example is the 1915 execution of John Ziolko. His hanging was proceeding uneventfully, but while waiting to declare the killer dead, the doctor for Toronto's Don Jail was overcome with emotion and collapsed. Although assisted from the gallows, he soon revived and returned to carry out his duties.

Among others affected by executions were the men charged with imposing sentences of death. When Ontario Chief Justice Sir William Mulock pronounced the death sentence of five men in 1919, he almost broke down. His voice barely audible, he told the prisoners that sentencing them was the most painful thing he had ever done.

Seven years later, Mr. Justice Herbert Mowat was similarly affected. In early October, the Ontario judge presided over the trial of John Barty, who was accused of the hammer slaying of a Hamilton woman. It was Mowat's first death sentence, and he was deeply affected by what he was forced to do.

He paused several times, and on two occasions appeared unable to continue.

Sometimes members of a victim's family never recovered from the shock of a relative's murder. That was especially the case when the crime was committed by someone close. In 1869, a married but very young Mary Melady had the misfortune to discover the bodies of her father and stepmother in a residence later described as a slaughterhouse. Six weeks after her brother was hanged for their murder, she died, still suffering from the emotional impact of the double tragedy.

Family members of a prisoner on death row felt especially helpless when distance prevented them from visiting their doomed loved one. The family of Sion Azuhally were living in the Middle East when the Syrian was convicted of murdering a fellow peddler. Shortly before his 1903 execution, the killer received a letter from his father. Its simple statement of continued love moved the condemned man to tears.

> *My Dear Son. I have a letter telling me that you have been convicted of murder, and that the death sentence has been passed upon you. All the family are heart-broken. Your mother, sister, wife and brother join with me in this message of love and farewell to you. We all pray for you to Mohamet and God. We keenly feel your position. All of us are thinking of you. We send our love and offer our prayers. We tried to clear you and endeavoured to pay money to the Turkish government for the relatives of the dead boy, so that you might come home to us again. But we found that the law in Turkey and the British law are not the same, and that the crime cannot be condoned with anything but*

your life. It was sad and sorrowful news for us. If fate ordains
that you must die we send to you our blessing and last farewell,
and hope that, if you are guilty, our God will forgive you. We
hope this will reach you before it is too late. Good-bye, from your
stricken home. FATHER

Charles Bullock was the son of loving parents, and shortly after they established a homestead in the Battle River area of what is now Alberta, he and Leon Stainton returned home from the United States for a visit. Only Bullock arrived. The young man stayed with his parents for a few days before abruptly announcing that he was leaving for British Columbia. In late spring 1901, the body of Stainton, shot twice in the back of the head, was discovered two months after his murder, near the farm of Bullock's parents.

In time the police learned that Bullock travelled with the dead man, and that when he left Battle River he journeyed south, not west. In late 1901, the fugitive was arrested in Montana and returned to Canada to face trial. Early the following February he was sentenced to hang.

Bullock's father arrived in Fort Saskatchewan the day before his son was executed. Everyone with whom he came into contact could see that he was much affected by his son's predicament. His son's mother, he said, was completely devastated. As for himself, it was a question whether he would stay at home to see his wife die or come to Fort Saskatchewan to see his son die.

They Deserved to Die

It's probably not unfair to suggest that some prisoners deserved to die, but in the case of a few Canadian killers, that was especially true. A surprising number of condemned prisoners confessed to murders with which they got away.

John Barty neither denied nor admitted he killed several times. In 1926, the Hungarian immigrant used a hammer to murder a Hamilton woman. Less than a year earlier, two men and another woman were also beaten to death by someone wielding a hammer. Not long before the three were killed, one of the men obtained a civil judgment against Barty for money owed.

Although the triple murder was never officially solved, the police were convinced they knew who the killer was. All four victims were not only killed by a similar-type weapon, but they also were very likely killed by the same weapon.

Some may not be satisfied that Barty was a serial killer, but there is no doubt about the guilt of Owen Feener. In his case, however, it was a little hard to keep track of who was killed when. Ironically, the 23-year-old Halifax miner might have gotten away with all of his murders if he hadn't been so enamoured with flashy sports cars and had kept his mouth shut.

According to what police know for sure, a 17-year-old waitress from Kirkland Lake went missing in mid-April 1959. Two years later, just hours from being executed, Feener confessed to murdering her. He said that he picked up the young woman while his wife was convalescing in the hospital then drove her to a spot about 80 kilometres southeast of town. When the two began to argue, he choked her to death and threw her body into a bush. Berry pickers found her skeletal remains a year later.

After that, the facts surrounding his other murders are a little unclear. What is known is that sometime before October 1960, the body of a 34-year-old model and dress designer from Nova Scotia was discovered along a highway near Fredericton. Her red sports car was missing.

On October 4, 1960, Feener's girlfriend disappeared from Timmins, Ontario. The following day he was seen driving the car belonging to the murdered woman and was arrested. As soon as the police began questioning him about how he got the car, Feener asked investigating officers if they thought he murdered his girlfriend. When they admitted that they did, he confessed to stabbing her to death.

According to Feener, his girlfriend became upset after he told her about the Nova Scotia woman, and she insisted he go to the police. When he refused, she tried to get out of the car. Feener hit her several times with a large flashlight before stabbing her to death.

After Feener was charged with the murder of his girlfriend, officers asked him about the missing waitress. Feener denied knowing anything about her disappearance, and that is where things stood until two hours before he went to the gallows. Only then did he admit that he killed the young woman, and he told investigators where he left her body. Even though there is little doubt he killed her, Feener refused to say anything about the murder of his first victim.

The case of Roland Genest and Marie-Paule Langlais was a departure from the norm in that a woman committed murder on behalf of her lover, rather than the other way around. Things returned to normal two years later, when Genest killed the woman who killed for him.

The saga started in 1950, when Genest and Langlais began to date. Sometime early in their relationship he told his lover that they could no longer see each other, since he was a married man. Soon the two were discussing the possibility of killing Genest's wife. Langlais said she was willing to make her boyfriend a widower if that would keep them together. Genest bought an iron bar from a Montréal junk dealer and suggested it be used as a murder weapon.

The night of the killing, Genest provided himself with an alibi by spending the evening at the home of his brother-in-law. Langlais bludgeoned her rival to death and then set fire to the Genest apartment to destroy whatever evidence was left behind.

For almost two years, it seemed like the perfect crime. By 1953, however, the murderous pair was no longer in love, and in mid-February the nude, badly battered body of Langlais was found near Montréal. Genest was arrested soon after, and he admitted clubbing his lover over the head with a baseball bat, then repeatedly stabbing her. Six months later he was executed.

Worse than killers who get away with a murder are those who kill after being given a second chance at life. Manitoba's Albert Victor Westgate was one such person.

Westgate was born to money, but his English parents were embarrassed by his troublemaking, and in his mid-teens he was shipped to Canada. Like other remittance men of the early 20th century, his family sent him enough money to ensure his survival, but not enough to return home.

Westgate arrived in Winnipeg in time to enlist in the Canadian Expeditionary Force. He was immediately sent to France, eventually leaving the army with an honourable discharge after suffering wounds to his head, arms and stomach. When he returned to Winnipeg, he got a job driving a taxi. He was a hard worker and seldom spoke, earning the nickname "Wordless Westgate."

Early in 1924, Westgate met Lottie Adams, the wife of a store detective. He was infatuated with her and paid messengers to deliver gifts and letters to the Adams residence. His overtures were unwelcome; Lottie soon asked him to leave her alone. In mid-February 1928, Westgate begged for one last meeting. She agreed, and two days later he picked her up.

While they drove around the city, Westgate pleaded with Lottie to run away with him. When she refused, he stopped the car near a golf course, pulled out a .32 calibre revolver and fired at her. Lottie realized the trouble she was in and fought Westgate off, badly bruising herself in the process. Westgate's second shot hit the woman in the left side of her head, splattering blood over her killer and the inside of his car.

For some reason, Westgate stabbed an obviously dead Lottie in the face, dragged her into a ditch and struck her four times over the head with an axe. He then covered her body with snow and drove away. He was so preoccupied with throwing his weapons and his victim's clothes out of the window that he drove into a snowbank. Six people, all later to testify against him, asked if he needed help before a tow truck finally arrived to pull him out.

Although Lottie's husband reported his wife missing, her body was not discovered for almost two weeks, and then it was found by chance. An unusual mild weather spell melted the snow that fell two weeks earlier, and a man walking his dog noticed a human hand sticking out of a drift. Before the day was out, Westgate was arrested.

His trial lasted four days and ended in his conviction. Although Westgate was sentenced to hang, his lawyer appealed the verdict, arguing that because a juror had suffered from dementia 12 years earlier, he should have been disqualified from serving. The Court of Appeal agreed and ordered a new hearing. It, too, ended in a conviction, and for a second time, Westgate was sentenced to hang.

Two days before his scheduled execution, his sentence was commuted to life in prison. During his 14 years in Stony Mountain Penitentiary, the diminutive killer was a model prisoner. When Westgate was paroled in June 1943, he rented a room in a Winnipeg boarding house and got a job as a mechanic. Two months later, a 16-year-old girl moved into an adjoining apartment.

Grace Edith Cook left home after her parents became concerned about her fascination with older men, and she quickly became enamoured with her 42-year-old fellow boarder. Edith was working as a waitress at a local restaurant, but she agreed to move to Vancouver with Westgate when he promised to pay her way and get her a job. The two made plans to leave on December 5, but Westgate had no connections in British Columbia, and he could not leave Winnipeg because of his parole conditions. Worse, he could not even afford the price of Edith's train ticket.

Notwithstanding his economic circumstances, Westgate suggested that Edith rent a room at the Marlborough Hotel until they left Winnipeg. Sometime over the next two days, Westgate squeezed Edith by the throat until she stopped breathing.

When Edith's parents did not hear from her, they became frantic. The Cooks went to Westgate's rooming house and asked if he knew where their daughter was. He said he did not, but suggested they inquire at the Marlborough. Although Mr. and Mrs. Cook received no answer to their knock when they arrived at Edith's room, they noticed a strong odour and insisted that a chambermaid open the door. Inside they found their daughter.

Headstone of the second of the two women murdered by Albert Westgate.
The 16-year-old was killed six months after Westgate was released
on parole for murdering another Winnipeg woman.

• ◆ •

Westgate was held on a coroner's warrant until the cause
of death was established, and then formally arrested. Four
months later, he was tried for his second murder. His hearing

lasted six days, and like his previous trials, it ended with a verdict of guilty.

Albert Victor Westgate was executed on July 24, 1944. Because he was a veteran, he was buried in the military section of a Winnipeg cemetery. Later, officials reconsidered their decision, and although Westgate's remains were left undisturbed, his headstone was removed.

Whether out of anger at their daughter's killer or frustration with a legal system that gave a murderer a second chance to kill, the Cooks filed a $100,000 lawsuit against Westgate. Although the Manitoba Court of Appeal dismissed the claim, it is believed to be the only time someone on a Canadian death row was sued.

In the opening paragraph of this chapter I said murder was cruel, and that is certainly the case. Whether state-sponsored killing is as contemptible as acts of violence that occur outside the confines of Canada's jails and prisons is an open question. But the stories described in this book suggest that binding the arms and legs of condemned criminals and dropping them through a hole in the floor does nothing to prevent future violence. Few of those hanged planned what they did, and except for a small group of the most violent among us, like Albert Westgate, it is likely none would have repeated their horrible deed had they been given a second chance.

Notes on Sources

Newspaper Sources

Globe & Mail: Allison (4 December 1897) 20, (5 February 1898) 25; Auger
(29 December 1873) 1; Barty (8 October 1926) 3; Bilodeau (26 April 1934)
1; Bilton (10 December 1946) 3; Boyeff (27 February 1920) 3; Brown
(18 May 1899) 7; burial (3 August 1921) 1; Bussey (14 November 1947) 9;
Campbell, P. (21 June 1872) 4; Carrier (12 June 1880) 6; Clark (4 June
1956) 1, (5 June 1956) 3; Collison (13 March 1925) 3, (30 May 1935) 5;
Chatelle (1 June 1895) 5; Currie (13 October 1920) 4, (11 January 1921) 7;
Davis (21 June 1890) 13; Deacon (15 December 1870) 1; Feener (7, 8,
9 March 1961) 9, 4, 1, (16 May; 13, 14, 15 June 1961) 1, 1, 12, 37; Gagné
(14 January 1948) 2; gallows (5 February 1898) 25; Giovanzzo (23 August
1919) 7; Gordon (21 June 1902) 5; Goyette (29 April 1904) 7; Hammond
(16 September 1898) 7; Hendershott (18 June 1895) 1; Hoffman (16, 17, 21,
23 August 1967) (12 January 1968) 1; Humphrey (23 May 1877) 1; Ivanchuk (19 July 1929) 2; Jackson (16, 17 December 1952) 1, 9; Jones
(16 October 1868) 2; Kane (22 May 1891) 6; Kolesar (6 June 1942) 5;
Konuch (26 September 1914) 15; Kowalski (20 December 1919) 12;
Laplaine (14 December 1901) 13; Lindsley (8 February 1902) 8; Lucas
(11 December 1962) 2, (24 February 1973) 4; Luciano (11 May 1894) 1;
Luckey (15 December 1893) 5; Mann (15 December 1870) 1; Martin
(12 November 1904) 18, (11 March 1905) 7; McConnell (15 March 1876)
4; McKee (4, 9 November 1959) 2, 1, (16 January 1960) 5, (9 February
1960) 1; Morrison (18 January 1901) 2; Mowat (8 October 1926) 3; Mulock
(10 October 1919) 1; Neby (4 January 1919) 9; Neil (29 February 1888) 8;
Nesbitt (23 December 1873) 1; Newgate (16 November 1892) 2; Olsen
(2 December 1892) 1; O'Rourke (6 January 1883) 2; Parrott (24 June 1899)
23; Pearson (6, 8 December 1900) 8, 27; Pertella (19 December 1908) 2;
Philippines (1 October 1955) 6; Pickard (29 December 1871) 1; Popovitch
(11, 12, 13 September 1946) 8, 8, 1, (5 December 1946) 1; Potter (14 January 1946) 2; Ramesbottom (26 April 1932) 2; reprieve (26 October 1968)

50; Rice (19 July 1902) 9; Robinson (12 September 1904) 1; Shelley
(20 December 1915) 5; Shortis (3 January 1886) 5; Simmons
(28 November 1885) 3; Smith (16 June 1890) 3; Sokoloff (26 September
1914) 15; Steinberg (14, 15 July 1931) 1; Stevenson (5 April 1937) 9; Suchan
(16 December 1952) 1; Sweden (8 December 1868) 4; Thain (29 October
1940) 8, (14 January 1941) 7; Tilford (17, 18 December 1935) 1; Traviss
(23 February 1872) 4; Truskey (15 December 1894) 31; Tryon (31 December 1873) 1; Turpin (11 December 1962) 2, (24 February 1973) 4; Van
Koughnet (29 June 1882) 3; Voltaire (30 September 1882) 2; Welter
(18 June 1895) 1; White (24 December 1875) 1; Williams (1 December
1877) 1; Young: (23 September 1876) 5; Young (27 December 1958) 1,
(30 June 1959) 12; Yuzik (15 July 1920) 14; Ziolko (14 April 1915) 8.

Halifax Herald: Anderson (20 May 1930) 1; Azuhally (18 March 1903) 1; Cook
(1 July 1914) 4; Olsen (2 December 1892) 5; Roberts (24 November 1922)
3; Robinson (12 September 1904) 1; Sparks (27 July 1917) 2; Stanley
(1 August 1906) 1; Sullivan (12 March 1897) 1.

Montréal Gazette: Asselin (10 June 1949) 3; Bannister (23 September 1936) 10;
Beaulne (23, 24 August 1929) 13, 3; Bélanger (11 June 1904) 3; Bigaouette
(20 August 1927) 11; Bilodeau (15 June 1935) 6; Boucher (26 October
1956) 19; Candy (18, 19 November 1910) 16, 8; Cloutier, M. (23, 24 February 1940) 10, 13; Cloutier, N. (11 March 1949) 1; Cortland (18 October
1930) 5; Donafrio (30 March 1935) 5; Dubé (7 July 1900) 16; Dubois
(21 June 1890) 8; Farrell (11 January 1879) 3; Gagliardi (30 March 1935) 5;
Genest (28 August 1953) 1; Germain (11 June 1927) 19; Grondin (23,
24 February 1940) 10, 13; Hanson (14 June 1902) 3; Hayvern (10 December 1881) 3; Lacroix (22 March 1902) 16; Lamontagne (20 December 1890)
8; Laplaine (14 December 1901) 1; Lavallée (13 August 1927) 3; Lefebrve
(23, 24 August 1929) 13, 3; Lebel (22 July 1949) 3; Mauro (20 February 1926)
4; McDonald (23 March 1928) 1; Mentenko (6 March 1953) 19; Merle
(6 August 1927) 4; Mooney (7 July 1900) 16; Nantel (23 May 1931) 5;
Nulty (21 May 1898) 1; Parslow (10, 11 March 1899) 1, 2; Préville (14 January 1933) 10; Simoneau (23 January 1942) 15; Teolis (30 March 1935) 5;
Thomas (23 May 1931) 5; Viau (10, 11 March 1899) 1, 2; Wilkinson
(19 February 1932) 5.

New York Times: Battista (29 December 1912) 10; Mailman
(31 December 1873) 1.

StarPhoenix: Pfeifer and Leyton-Brown (1 December 2007).

Toronto News: Birchall (14, 15 November 1890) 1; bodies (9 March 1910) 1;
Bussey (4 February 1948) 10; Campbell (16 January 1932) 1; Davis
(20 June 1890) 1; Dlugos (3 July 1940) 24; Emory (20 June 1890) 1; gallows
(14 November, 18 December 1890) 1; Harvey (29 November 1889) 1;
Hotrum (2 August 1921) 2; Jardine (16 June 1911) 15; Kane (12 February
1890) 1; Laplante (17 January 1958) 29; Mann, F. (12 October 1883) 4;
McCoskey (21 April 1927) 26; McFadden (3 August 1921) 1; Murrell
(10 April 1924) 21; Nulty (3 February 1898) 6; Petrekowich (4 October
1939) 3; Phipps (17 June 1884) 4; Topping (10 April 1924) 21.

Toronto Star: Barty (12 January 1927) 9; Bilton (10 December 1946) 9; Campbell, W. (16 January 1932) 1; Laplante (17 January 1958) 29; McCoskey
(21 April 1927) 26; McCullough (13 June 1919) 1; McLean (24 November
1933) 23; Murrell (10 April 1924) 21; Petrekowich (4 October 1939) 3;
Popovitch (5 December 1946) 15; Schmidt (1 March 1945) 3; Skrypnyk
(1 March 1945) 3; Topping (10 April 1924) 21; White (25 April 1940) 25.

Vancouver Sun: Bordeniuk (29 March 1955) 9; Chong Sam Bow (15 January 1925)
1; Cunningham (5 August 1952) 2; Debortoli (14 July 1926) 1; Ducharme
(14 July 1950) 1; Eaton (16 July 1957) 1; George (6 November 1936) 1;
Gordon (2 April 1957) 15; Graham (22 May 1956) 1; Hoodley (17 May
1955) 2; Houston (1 October 1947) 1; Macchione (26 October 1938) 6;
Mantha (28 April 1959) 18; Matthews (10 November 1953) 2; Medos
(1 October 1947) 1; Nassa (23 July 1929) 1; Ouelette (29 May 1951) 1;
Pasquale (14 July 1926) 1; Prestyko (27, 28 February 1950) 2, 1; Prince
(28 November 1945) 1; Russell (6 November 1936) 1; Singh (12 January
1915) 7; Sylvestre (4 January 1941) 4; Viakin (20 January 1953) 7; Vincent
(14 June 1955) 3; Wagner (28 August 1913) 1; Worobec (27, 28 February
1950) 2, 1; Wright (16 June 1939) 5.

Winnipeg Free Press: Alak (29 November 1911) 8; Arosha (5 May 1909) 11;
Bernardi (23 May 1914) 14; Bullock (26 March 1902) 10; Carmel (18 October 1919) 1; Collins (18 February 1914) 17; De Lena (22 May 1915); Dougal

(29 July 1903) 9; Fletcher (27 February 1918) 8; Frith (28 November 1903) 19; Gaddy (14 June 1888) 1; Gervais (18 October 1919) 1; Hack (17 January 1929) 2; Heipel (26 April 1939) 4; Huss (23 February 1924) 1; Knudson (7 February 1931) 1; Leek (11 April 1916) 2; Member of Parliament (13 July 1923) 1; Morrison (18 January 1901) 2; O'Brien (11 September 1901) 6; Potter (15 January 1946) 5; Racette (14 June 1888) 1; Sepepil (5 May 1909) 11; St. Germain (18 October 1919) 1; Stroebel (31 January 1894) 2; Swift Runner (16 January 1880) 1; Wagner (29 August 1913) 2; Wysochan (21 June 1930) 5; Zbyhley (22 December 1909) 2.

Other Sources

Abbott, G. *Lords of the Scaffold: A History of the Executioner.* London: Robert Hale, 1991.

Abbott, G. *The Executioner Always Chops Twice: Ghastly Blunders on the Scaffold.* New York: St. Martin's, 2004.

Ayre, J.D. *Felons of Hamilton, Haldimand and Brant, 1828–1953.* Simcoe, ON: J.D. Ayre, 2000.

Boyd, N. *Last Dance: Murder in Canada.* Scarborough, ON: Prentice-Hall, 1988.

Boyle, T. *Fit to be Tied: Ontario's Murderous Past.* Toronto: Polar Bear Press, 2001.

Clark, C. *B.C. Provincial Police Stories, V. 1 & 2.* Surrey, BC: Heritage House, 1986.

Coates, K., and W.R. Morrison. *Strange Things Done: Murder in Yukon History.* Montréal: McGill-Queen's University Press, 2004.

Duff, L.B. *The County Kerchief.* Toronto: Ryerson, 1949.

Grant, B.J. *Six for the Hangman.* Fredericton: Fiddlehead, 1983.

Hustak, A. *They Were Hanged.* Toronto: Lorimer, 1987.

Jobb, D. *Shades of Justice.* Halifax: Nimbus Publishing, 1988.

Laurence, J. *A History of Capital Punishment*. New York: Citadel, 1963.

MacKay, M. *The End of the Line in The Guardian*, "The Hanging of George Dowie." www.dowie.org/Hanging_of_George_Dowie.htm.

Melady, J. *Double Trap: The Last Public Execution in Canada*. Toronto: Dundurn, 2005.

Morriss, W.E. *Watch the Rope*. Winnipeg: Watson & Dyer, 1996.

Newton, D. *Tainted Justice 1914*. Sydney, NS: University College of Cape Breton Press, 1995.

Paterson, T.W. *Outlaws of Western Canada*. Langley, BC: Mr. Paperback, 1977.

Pfeifer, J., and K. Leyton-Brown. *Death By Rope, Volume One: 1867–1923*. Regina: Centax Books, 2007.

Saunders, K. *The Rectory Murder: The Mysterious Crime That Shocked Turn-of-the-Century New Brunswick*. Toronto: Lorimer, 1989.

Silverman, R., and L. Kennedy. *Deadly Deeds: Murder in Canada*. Scarborough, ON: Nelson, 1933.

Thurston, A. *Poor Annie Kempton: She's in Heaven Above*. Yarmouth, NS: A. Thurston, 1987.

About the Author

DALE BRAWN

Dale Brawn was born in Saskatchewan and raised in Manitoba, where he received his Master of Arts degree and Master of Laws degree, both from the University of Manitoba. He entered grad school, finishing with his doctorate in law and teaches in the Department of Law and Justice at Laurentian University. He has published three books on law and history and has written articles for various newspapers. Brawn shares a house with a demanding dog and a belligerent parrot, and spends equal time working and playing tennis.